T0207427

Lecture Notes in Computer Science 14410

Founding Editors

Gerhard Goos
Juris Hartmanis

Editorial Board Members

The series Lecture Notes in Computer Science (LNCS), including its subseries Lecture Notes in Artificial Intelligence (LNAI) and Lecture Notes in Bioinformatics (LNBI), has established itself as a medium for the publication of new developments in computer science and information technology research, teaching, and education.

LNCS enjoys close cooperation with the computer science R & D community, the series counts many renowned academics among its volume editors and paper authors, and collaborates with prestigious societies. Its mission is to serve this international community by providing an invaluable service, mainly focused on the publication of conference and workshop proceedings and postproceedings. LNCS commenced publication in 1973.

Gabriel Zachmann · Krzysztof Walczak ·
Omar A. Niamut · Kyle Johnsen ·
Wolfgang Stuerzlinger · Mariano Alcañiz-Raya ·
Greg Welch · Patrick Bourdot
Editors

Virtual Reality and Mixed Reality

20th EuroXR International Conference, EuroXR 2023
Rotterdam, The Netherlands, November 29 – December 1, 2023
Proceedings

Springer

Editors
Gabriel Zachmann (iD)
University of Bremen
Bremen, Germany

Omar A. Niamut (iD)
TNO
The Hague, The Netherlands

Wolfgang Stuerzlinger (iD)
Simon Fraser University
Surrey, BC, Canada

Greg Welch
University of Central Florida
Orlando, FL, USA

Krzysztof Walczak (iD)
Poznań University of Economics
and Business
Poznań, Poland

Kyle Johnsen
University of Georgia
Athens, GA, USA

Mariano Alcañiz-Raya
LabLENI, Universitat Politècnica de Valencia
Valencia, Spain

Patrick Bourdot (iD)
Université Paris-Saclay, CNRS
Orsay, France

ISSN 0302-9743   ISSN 1611-3349 (electronic)
Lecture Notes in Computer Science
ISBN 978-3-031-48494-0   ISBN 978-3-031-48495-7 (eBook)
https://doi.org/10.1007/978-3-031-48495-7

This Springer imprint is published by the registered company Springer Nature Switzerland AG
The registered company address is: Gewerbestrasse 11, 6330 Cham, Switzerland

Paper in this product is recyclable.

Preface

We are pleased to present in this LNCS volume the scientific proceedings of the 20th EuroXR International Conference (EuroXR 2023), organized in colocation with the Immersive Tech Week, Rotterdam, the Netherlands, and held during November 29 – December 1, 2023.

This conference follows a series of successful international conferences initiated in 2004 by the INTUITION Network of Excellence on Virtual and Augmented Reality, which was supported by the European Commission until 2008. From 2009 through 2013, it was embedded in the Joint Virtual Reality Conferences (JVRC). Since then, it was known as EuroVR, then EuroXR International Conference, in line with the renaming of the umbrella association.

The focus and aim of the EuroXR conferences is to present, each year, novel results and insights in Virtual Reality (VR), Augmented Reality (AR), and Mixed Reality (MR), commonly referred to under the umbrella of Extended Reality (XR), including software systems, immersive rendering technologies, 3D user interfaces, and applications. EuroXR also aims to foster engagement between European industries, academia, and the public sector, to promote the development and deployment of XR techniques in new and emerging, but also in existing fields. To this end, all EuroXR conferences include not only a scientific track, but also an application-oriented track, with its own proceedings.

Since 2017, the EuroXR Association has collaborated with Springer to publish the proceedings of the scientific track of its annual conference. In order to maintain the scientific standards to be expected from such a conference, we established a number of committees overseeing the process of creating a scientific program: the scientific program chairs, leading an International Program Committee (IPC) made up of international experts in the field, and the EuroXR academic task force.

For the 2023 issue, a total of 42 papers were submitted, out of which 14 papers were accepted (4 long, 8 medium, and 2 short papers). This amounts to an acceptance ratio of 33%. The selection process involved a double-blind peer-review process (each and every paper was reviewed by at least 3 members of the IPC, in many cases even 4), followed by a rebuttal phase, and a final discussion and scoring phase amongst the revewiers. Based on the review reports, the scores, and the reviewers' discussions, the scientific program chairs took the final decision and wrote a meta-review for each paper.

This year, the scientific program of EuroXR and, hence, this LNCS volume, is organized into three sections: Interaction in Virtual Reality, Designing XR Experiences, and Human Factors in VR: Performance, Acceptance, and Design.

In addition to the regular scientific papers track, EuroXR invited three keynote speakers: Tabitha C. Peck (Davidson College, Davidson, NC, USA), Ferran Argelaguet (Research Scientist, Hybrid team, IRISA/Inria, Rennes, France), and Zerrin Yumak (Assistant Professor of Utrecht University, The Netherlands). Furthermore, the conference hosted an application track, demos and posters sessions, and lab tours. Finally, there were dedicated sessions, for instance, by Greg Welch on VERA, and a workshop on "Vocational Training".

We would like to thank all the IPC members and external reviewers for their insightful reviews, which helped ensure the high quality of papers selected for the scientific track. Furthermore, we would like to thank the application chairs, demos and posters chairs, and the local organizers of EuroXR 2023.

We are also grateful to the staff of Springer for their support and advice during the preparation of this LNCS volume.

September 2023

Gabriel Zachmann
Krzysztof Walczak
Omar A. Niamut
Kyle Johnsen
Wolfgang Stuerzlinger
Mariano Alcañiz-Raya
Greg Welch
Patrick Bourdot

Organization

General Chairs

Greg Welch   University of Central Florida, USA
Patrick Bourdot   Université Paris-Saclay, CNRS, France
Benjamin de Witt   Immersive Tech Week, The Netherlands

Scientific Program Chairs

Krzysztof Walczak   Poznań University of Economics and Business, Poland
Gabriel Zachmann   University of Bremen
Omar A. Niamut   TNO, The Netherlands
Mariano Alcañiz   Universitat Politècnica de València, Spain
Kyle Johnsen   University of Georgia, USA
Wolfgang Stuerzlinger   Simon Fraser University, Canada

Application Program Chairs

Frédéric Noël   Grenoble-INP, Université Grenoble Alpes, France
Kaj Helin   VTT, Finland
Armin Grasnick   IU Internationale Hochschule, Germany
Mario Lorenz   Chemnitz University of Technology, Germany
Despina Michael-Grigoriou   Cyprus University of Technology, Cyprus

Posters and Demos Chairs

Wolfgang Schäfer   ZHAW Zurich University of Applied Sciences, Switzerland
Arcadio Reyes Lecuona   Universidad de Málaga, Spain
Hugo Falgarone   SkyReal, France
Matthieu Poyade   Glasgow School of Art, UK

Organization Team

Mariano Alcañiz-Raya	EuroXR
Patrick Bourdot	EuroXR
Frédéric Noël	EuroXR
Jérôme Perret	EuroXR
Arcadio Reyes-Lecuona	EuroXR
Krzysztof Walczak	EuroXR
Gabriel Zachmann	EuroXR
Rayyan Farrukh	Immersive Tech Week
Pierre-Stuart Rostain	Immersive Tech Week
Manuel Toledo	Immersive Tech Week
Regina van Tongeren	Immersive Tech Week
Benjamin de Wit	Immersive Tech Week

International Program Committee

Mariano Alcañiz	Universidad Politécnica Valencia, Spain
Toshiyuki Amano	Wakayama University, Japan
Sara Arlati	Consiglio Nazionale delle Ricerche, Italy
Pauline Bimberg	Universität Trier, Germany
Josep Blat	Universitat Pompeu Fabra Barcelona, Spain
Andrea Bönsch	RWTH Aachen University, Germany
Pierre Boulanger	University of Alberta, Canada
Antonio Capobianco	Université de Strasbourg, France
Julien Castet	Immersion, France
Weiya Chen	Huazhong University of Sciences and Technology, China
Fabrizio Cumo	Sapienza University of Rome, Italy
Angelica De Antonio	Universidad Politécnica de Madrid, Spain
Thierry Duval	IMT Atlantique, France
Mariella Farella	National Research Council of Italy, Italy
Jakub Flotyński	Poznań Univ. of Economics and Business, Poland
Arnulph Fuhrmann	TH Köln, Germany
Akemi Galvez	Universidad de Cantabria, Spain
Michele Gattullo	Polytechnic University of Bari, Italy
Pascual Gonzalez	Universidad Castilla-La Mancha, Spain
Andrey Gorbunov	Aviareal, Russia
Filip Górski	Poznań University of Technology, Poland
Polina Häfner	KIT Karlsruhe, Germany
Kaj Helin	VTT, Finland
Krista Hoek	LUMC, The Netherlands
Chris Hughes	Salford University, UK

Andres Iglesias — Universidad de Cantabria, Spain
Victoria Interrante — University of Minnesota, USA
Daisuke Iwai — University of Osaka, Japan
Yvonne Jung — Hochschule Darmstadt, Germany
Alina Kadlubsky — Open AR Cloud Association, USA
Ioannis Karaseitanidis — ICCS, Greece
Tina Katika — Institute of Communication and Computer Systems, Greece
Hirokazu Kato — Nara Institute of Science and Technology, Japan
Uwe Kloos — Reutlingen University of Applied Sciences, Germany
Torsten Kuhlen — RWTH Aachen University, Germany
Vladimir Kuts — Tallinn University of Technology, Estonia
Nicolas Ladeveze — Université Paris-Saclay, CNRS, LISN, France
Fabrizio Lamberti — Politecnico di Milano, Italy
Guillaume Lavoue — École Centrale de Lyon, France
Paolo Leoncini — Centro Italiano Ricerche Aerospaziali, Italy
Roberto Llorens — Universidad Politécnica Valencia, Spain
Mario Lorenz — TU Chemnitz, Germany
Mitsunori Makino — Chuo University, Japan
Anjela Mayer — Karlsruhe Institute of Technology, Germany
Daniel Mestre — Aix-Marseille University / CNRS, France
José Pascual Molina Massó — Universidad Castilla-La Mancha, Spain
Omar Niamut — TNO, The Netherlands
Peter Nickel — Deutsche Gesetzliche Unfallversicherung, Germany
Frédéric Noël — Grenoble Institute of Technology, France
Jérôme Perret — Haption, Germany
Matthieu Poyade — Glasgow School of Art, UK
Dirk Reiners — University of Central Florida, USA
Arcadio Reyes-Lecuona — Universidad de Malaga, Spain
James Ritchie — Heriot-Watt University, UK
Wolfgang Schäfer — ZHAW School of Management and Law, Switzerland
Hakim Si-Mohammed — University of Lille, France
Agata Marta Soccini — University of Torino, Italy
Lorenzo Sommaruga — University of Applied Sciences and Arts of Southern Switzerland (SUPSI), Switzerland
Oliver Staadt — Universität Rostock, Germany
Toni Tan — University of Bremen, Germany
Madis Vasser — University of Tartu, Estonia
Yi Xu — Oppo, China

Contents

Human Factors in VR: Performance, Acceptance, and Design

Interaction in Virtual Reality

A Model for Assessing and Sorting Virtual Locomotion Techniques According to Their Fidelity to Real Walking

José P. Molina(✉) ⓘ, Pascual González ⓘ, Arturo S. García ⓘ,
and Jorge Juan González ⓘ

LoUISE Research Group, I3A, University of Castilla-La Mancha, 02071 Albacete, Spain
{JosePascual.Molina,Pascual.Gonzalez,ArturoSimon.Garcia,
Jorge.JGonzalez}@uclm.es

Abstract. Travel is a challenging task in virtual reality applications due to space constraints of the setup or limited range of the tracking systems. This prevents the user from moving away from the installation and requires developers to implement smart solutions that overcome these limitations. Some of these solutions, known as virtual locomotion techniques, try to mimic real walking movements, while others introduce some kind of magic. We developed a model that is meant to classify and sort these techniques as regards to their fidelity to real walking. This can be useful both for research, to find opportunities for new techniques, and for development, to find the technique that best fits a target application. Whereas previous works typically divide techniques into real and virtual classes, we propose a 12-point scale where all techniques fit into and therefore makes easier to compare and select techniques. Besides, we perform a retrospective analysis of a previous travel technique evaluation using this tool. Comparing the results of the experiment with the proposed fidelity scale allows us to both evaluate the proposal and find ways of improving it in future revisions.

Keywords: Virtual reality · travel techniques · classification model

1 Introduction

Travel is one of the most challenging interaction tasks in virtual reality (VR), as there is no solution that fits all cases, no silver bullet, and this way it has attracted the attention of the research community for many years [1]. From a theoretical point of view, there are several and different taxonomies [2] that try to address and explain the design space of this task. From the practical side, there are many different implementations, called interaction techniques or, in this particular task, virtual locomotion techniques (VLTs), each one with its own pros and cons. In the last decades, different researchers have proposed new

G. Zachmann et al. (Eds.): EuroXR 2023, LNCS 14410, pp. 3–20, 2023.
https://doi.org/10.1007/978-3-031-48495-7_1

techniques or variants of existing ones, have evaluated them against others, and have shared their findings in conference and journal papers.

In this work, we propose a way of comparing different travel techniques according to their fidelity to real walking, then we perform a restrospective analysis of a previous evaluation that examined usability and comfort of five travel techniques for a urban rehabilitation environment. The five techniques are described as they were implemented, and they are now classified based on the proposed fidelity model. Finally, the results of that evaluation are re-examined and compared with rank of each technique in the fidelity scale. The main contributions of this paper are two-fold: firstly, a new approach to classify travel techniques based on several dimensions that are turned into a single-numeric scale that makes easier sorting and comparing techniques; secondly, a comparison of that level of fidelity with the results from practical tests.

This paper is structured as follows. First, in the next section, a review of previous works on travel technique classification is given, which is the starting point for our proposal of a real-walking fidelity-scale, described in detail and illustrated with examples in Sect. 3. Section 4 presents an application example of this work, which consist of five travel techniques that were implemented for a virtual rehabilitation environment, and that are now classified based on the proposed fidelity score. The evaluation of these VLTs is summarized in Sect. 5, followed by a complete discussion in Sect. 6. Finally, conclusions and future works are given in the last section of the paper.

2 Travel Technique Classification

Different researchers have addressed the problem of navigation in virtual environments proposing taxonomies and classifications that shape the design space of travel techniques. The most-simple ones differentiate between physical/real/natural and virtual/artificial/magical techniques [2, 3]. For instance, after a systematic literature review, [1] derived a topology of VR locomotion techniques that starts by dividing them based on interaction type (physical, artificial), next on VR motion type (continuous, non-continuous), then on VR interaction space (open, limited) and, finally, on VR locomotion types (motion-based, room-scale-based, controller-based, teleportation-based), resulting in a tree-shaped classifier that ultimately leads up to the three prevalent techniques identified by the author: walking-in-place, controller/joystick, and teleportation. However, as in the well-known Reality-Virtuality continuum of Milgram and Kishino [4], we state that there is a mixed space between the two ends (physical, artificial) where techniques are not completely natural neither fully virtual. Thus, at one end we find real walking, where travel translation and rotation is physical, that is, the user physically turns in the direction of travel and physically moves in that direction; at the other end, on the contrary, we can find desktop 3D interfaces where both translation and rotation are virtual, that is, the user controls travel using keyboard and mouse, but they neither physically turn nor move, it is purely virtual. In the middle space between these two ends, many techniques allow users to virtually travel in a virtual environment without physically moving from the place where they are standing on. The difference with desktop interfaces is that, even though translation is virtual, these techniques allow users to physically rotate in the direction they want to travel. For instance, in walking-in-place (WIP) techniques [5] the user physically turns their body in the desired direction, then they move their feet up and down as they were walking, but they do not physically move forward. This way, these techniques mix virtual translation with physical rotation.

In this work, we are especially interested in knowing the level of fidelity of a technique as compared to real walking, that is, how far or close is the technique to the way we use our body to travel in real world, which also relates to its ecological validity and physical exertion. Then, focusing on walking, another known taxonomy [3] classifies techniques into three categories: full-gait, partial-gait and gait-negation. This taxonomy accounts for the phases of gait cycle that are involved in the travel technique: stance phase and swing phase. For instance, walking in place is a partial-gait technique because users move their feet up and down (stance phase of gait), but they remain in the same location (no swing phase). This partial-gait class also includes, according to the authors, techniques that recreates the motions of the gait cycle using anatomical substitutions, such as finger walking. However, as fidelity regards, to move fingers like walking cannot be taken the same as to stamp feet on the ground.

Other taxonomies are not aimed at classifying techniques but rather decomposing them into different elements and then identify the values that these elements can take. However, these taxonomies are also interesting for the interaction aspects that they point out and that can lead to other ways of classifying techniques. For instance, Nabiyouni and Bowman [6] identified six main components of walking-based travel techniques: movement range, walking surface, transfer function, user support, walking movement style, and input properties sensed. From them, it is interesting that in the walking movement style they considered not only natural walking but also marching and sliding, but we find more important to highlight that the transfer function refers to the way physical translation and rotation are mapped to virtual travel. In relation to this, Nguyen-Vo et al. [7] focused on body-based motion cues and control, which for the purpose of their study were divided into translational cues and control, on one hand, and rotational cues and control, on the other hand. Each of these components were also categorised into three levels: none (almost no motion cues and control), full (one-to-one mapping between physical motion and simulated motion), and partial (involves distorted or transformed information). Finally, [8] investigated how body-based information helped users to perform a navigational search task, and for this purpose authors considered that a distinction needed to be made between the rotational and translational components of movement. In any case, it is relevant that in these works both translation and rotation are considered separately, and that authors find important to highlight how physical movements link to virtual ones.

3 Proposal for Comparing Techniques: Fidelity Score

Our proposal builds upon those previous ideas but extending them to make a more practical model. Firstly, as in [6, 7, 8], we split walking into two components: translation (move forward/backward) and rotation (turning left or right). Then, we classify each component of walking based on two dimensions: body motion and physicality (see Table 1). The first dimension -body motion- accounts for the body parts and motions involved in real walking during translation or rotation that are included in the technique, and it can take one of the following values: full body –walking-motion (3), partial body motion –e.g. alternately lifting each foot, swinging the arms or nodding the head- (2), anatomical substitution –e.g. letting the fingers do the walking- (1), and any other case –e.g. automatic or not present- (0). The second dimension –physicality- accounts for the amount of magic that is added to the technique, and it can take one of the following values: fully physical (3), mixed (2), fully virtual (1), and any other case (0). As it can be seen, for each dimension there are four qualifiers and, in parenthesis, four numbers. The numbers represent a 0–3 scale that provides a way of numerically sorting techniques in each dimension. With two dimensions (body motion and physicality) for each walking component (translation and rotation), any technique can then be described using a 4-dimensional vector: translation-body motion (TBM), translation-physicality (TP), rotation-body motion (RBM), rotation-physicality (RP).

Table 1. Dimensions of travel techniques and scores for the proposed fidelity scale.

Translation		Rotation	
Body motion	Physicality	Body motion	Physicality
Full body motion (3)	Physical (3)	Full body motion (3)	Physical (3)
Partial body motion (2)	Mixed (2)	Partial body motion (2)	Mixed (2)
Anatomical substitution (1)	Virtual (1)	Anatomical substitution (1)	Virtual (1)
Any other case (0)	Any other case (0)	Any other case (0)	Any other case (0)

For example, in the seven-league boots technique [9], translation involves full body motion (TBM = 3, full) but this physical translation is artificially scaled (TP = 2, mixed), rotation also involves full body motion (RBM = 3, full) and is purely physical (RP = 3, physical). As another example, in an omnidirectional treadmill (such as, for instance, VRKAT (https://www.kat-vr.com/products/kat-walk-c), translation involves all phases of gait cycle (TBM = 3, full body motion) but the user does not move forward except in the virtual world -they walk in place- (TP = 1, virtual), rotation also takes full body motion (RBM = 3, full) and is completely physical as the user has to turn her body to the desired direction (RP = 3, physical). In the teleport technique [10, 11], translation does not involve any body motion but pressing a button (TBM = 0, any other case) and is purely virtual (TP = 1, virtual), rotation is typically set by pointing with the hand which is an anatomical substitution for rotating the body (RBM = 1, anatomical substitution) but it is fully physical as the user actually points in the direction where they want to teleport (RP = 3, physical). As a last example, desktop games typically rely on the WASD keys and mouse to move the player character [12, 13], where translation is performed by pressing W/S keys to move forward/backward -usually with the middle finger- and A/D to strafe left/right -ring and index fingers- which is not part of walking motion nor can be considered as an anatomical substitution (TBM = 0, any other case), this translation is virtual (TP = 1, virtual), rotation is performed by moving the mouse left or right with the hand which is not considered an anatomical substitution neither (RBM = 0) and rotation is purely virtual too (RP = 1, virtual).

However, comparing techniques in this 4-dimensional space is not a straightforward task. A spider chart may help, but a more direct way is desirable. Having the same range in all dimensions (0–3), and assuming the same weight for all of them, we then propose to turn the four dimensions into just one by a simple addition. Thus, given a technique, we sum the values of the two components (translation and rotation) and their two respective dimensions (body motions and physicality) to get a final number that describes the level of fidelity of that technique in a 0–12 scale, where 12 corresponds to the higher level, that is, real walking. The resulting score makes it easier to compare fidelity to real walking among different techniques, and sort them according to this scale.

For example, in the seven-league boots technique, the resulting number in our scale is $3 + 2 + 3 + 3 = 11$, which accounts for its high level of fidelity, but it does not get the highest score (12) due to its added magic. The next technique, using an omnidirectional treadmill, obtains one point less ($3 + 1 + 3 + 3 = 10$) because the user does not move away from their place, but still is at the top end of the scale. In the teleport technique, the final score is $0 + 1 + 1 + 3 = 5$, which places it in the lower half of our scale. Finally, the WASD + Mouse technique gets just 2 points ($0 + 1 + 0 + 1$), highlighting how different this technique is from real walking.

4 Application Example: Travel Techniques for an Urban Rehabilitation Environment

To put the fidelity scale into practice, we decided to perform a retrospective analysis of a previous evaluation of different VLTs for an urban rehabilitation environment, named UrbanRehab [14]. The aim of UrbanRehab is helping people to recover cognitive abilities that were lost due to illness or accident, practicing daily activities in a controlled, supervised environment. More specifically, this system is focused on virtual urban scenarios (VUEs) and daily tasks that involve travel from one place to another in a tailored environment. To this end, the system consists of two main parts: one of them is the urban editor, where the therapist can easily design the city layout for the different tasks; the other one is the immersive simulation, where the patient carries out the tasks. The editor was developed in order to aid the therapists in the design of the urban scenarios adapted to each patient's needs without the need of knowing how to use 3D design programs.

As for the inmmersive simulation, UrbanRehab required a travel technique that could resemble as much as possible real walking, for its ecological validity, but at the same time it should be based on affordable devices, so that it could not only be used in rehabilitation centers but also at home. With this aim in mind, five travel techniques were selected, implemented and evaluated. In this work, we revisit that evaluation and try to analyse and compare the results with the proposed fidelity scale. All these techniques have in common the use of an HTC Vive helmet as the VR visor and the Valve lighthouse as the tracking system. Two of them also use the Vive controllers, whereas the other three are based on different input devices, namely a gamepad, a 3D mouse and a Nintendo Wii balance board. As said before, they are all based on consumer gaming and VR hardware. Besides, these techniques were selected because they are not limited by the tracking space, that is, they allow the user to travel beyond the range of the tracking system. They differ, however, in their level of fidelity but, because translation is virtual in all of them, they all get just 1 point out of 3 for that dimension in our fidelity scale (TP = 1, virtual), and so the maximum total score they could get is 10 points out of 12. The highest score is actually lower because, in addition, none of them involve full walking motions in translation nor rotation, only partial ones.

4.1 Arm-Swinging

As we walk, we do not only move our legs but also the whole body with them, including our arms, which swing partly due to inertia but to balance the body too. Thus, even though arms are not directly involved in walking as the legs are, arm swinging can also be considered part of this body motion. The idea of this technique [15, 16] is to let the user travel simply by swinging their arms as it would happen in real walking, but remaining in the same physical place, that is, is a kind of walk-in-place technique. In our implementation, the user holds one Vive controller in each hand and presses the grip buttons in each controller while they swing their arms to travel (see Fig. 1). The direction of travel is based on the arms, not the head, so that travel is decoupled from gaze, and then the user can freely look around while walking, as they could do in reality. As for the fidelity score, the translation only involves partial body motions -arms- (TBM = 2, partial) and translation is virtual (TP = 1, virtual), rotation also involves partial body motions -again, arms- (RBM = 2, partial) but is fully physical (RP = 3, physical), which gives a total score of 8 points in our scale (2 + 1 + 2 + 3). This is the highest score among the selected techniques.

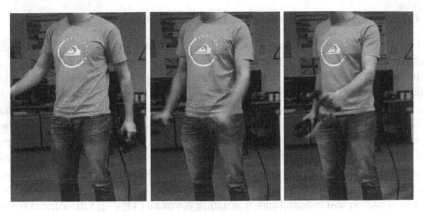

Fig. 1. Arm-swinging travel technique.

4.2 Gaze-Directed Steering with Gamepad (GDS-Gamepad)

A gamepad is a well-known device for playing games in PC and consoles. Held in one or two hands, it typically consists of several single buttons, a special 4-way button for moving the game character or the camera and even a mini-joystick for the same purpose. In our implementation, the user can move in the virtual environment using four single buttons, but placed in the gamepad in a cross layout, so they work together like the 4-way button and can also be controlled by a single finger (thumb) -see Fig. 2-. In any case, these buttons are only meant for translation (forward, backward and strafe), as rotation is controlled by the gaze (actually, the helmet put on the head). This way, travel and gaze direction are coupled, which happens most of the time when walking as we normally look in the direction we walk, but not all time. Regarding the fidelity score, translation involves one finger (the thumb) that moves in four directions to press the buttons (in contrast to WASD + Mouse technique, where the keys are typically pressed by different fingers) and can then be considered as an anatomical substitution for moving the body (TBM = 1, anatomical substitution), translation is virtual (TP = 1, virtual), and rotation involves partial body motions -head orientation- RBM = 2, partial) but is fully physical (RP = 3, physical), so the total score for this technique is 7 (1 + 1 + 2 + 3).

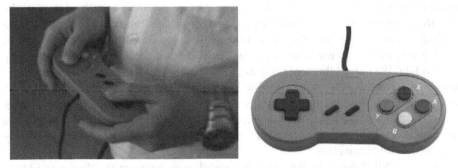

Fig. 2. Gamepad used in one of the GDS travel techniques.

4.3 Gaze-Directed Steering with 3D-Mouse (GDS-3DMouse)

A 3D mouse is a 6DOF device mainly used in 3D design applications for manipulating objects or the camera. We use a light and compact-design 3D mouse that the user can hold in their hands (see Fig. 3). Similarly to the gamepad travel technique, the user uses this device for translation, while rotation is controlled by gaze. Thus, we do not use the full 6 degrees of freedom of this device for implementing a kind of camera-in-hand technique, but instead we couple travel direction with gaze again. The difference with the gamepad technique is that the user does not press any button, but instead they push or pull the device for moving forward, backward and to strafe. As regards the fidelity to real walking, translation involves one hand that moves in four directions to pull/push the device and can then be considered as an anatomical substitution for moving the body (TBM = 1, anatomical substitution), translation is virtual (TP = 1, virtual), and rotation involves partial body motions -head- (RBM = 2, partial) but still is physical (RP = 3, physical), so the final score is 7 points $(1 + 1 + 2 + 3)$, same as the gamepad technique but with a different device and implementation.

Fig. 3. Our GDS-3DMouse technique is based on a compact 3DConnexion device.

4.4 Segwii

The Wii balance board has been previously used to implement travel techniques, such as the Pointman [17], where the user acts as a human joystick, or a simulation of the real-life metaphors such as skiing/Segway and snowboarding/skateboarding [18]. In our implementation, we use this board to recreate a popular urban mobility solution, the Segway, where the user moves forward or backward and make turns by shifting their weight. We named this technique as "Segwii" (see Fig. 4). In contrast to the other implemented techniques, travel direction is not set in a direct way (i.e. pointing with head or hand) but instead the user shifts their weight to left or right to start rotating (steering), then re-centre their weight when the desired direction is reached, as in a real Segway vehicle. The gaze is decoupled from travel direction, so that the user can freely look around while traveling.

We used Wii Balance Walker v0.4 as a middleware between the device and Unity input system. This software was the responsible of the calibration of the device for each user and triggering keyboard keys for each of the following actions: move forward, move backward, turn left, turn right. This way, the Wii balance board was used like a gamepad with four buttons that were triggered according to the position of the centre of mass of the user standing on top of the device.

In order to prevent motion sickness, translation and rotation were performed at constant linear/angular speeds, without accelerations [19, 20]. For the same reason, it was not possible to perform translation and rotation at the same time. The Wii board was complemented with a physical support which users could hold on to avoid losing their balance while leaning, as well as to have a tangible reference of their real position during traveling in VR.

As for the level of fidelity, translation involves partial body motion -body weight shifting- (TBM = 2, partial), and is virtual (TP = 1, virtual), rotation involves the same partial body motion (RBM = 2, partial) and is virtual too as the user does not physically point in the direction of travel (RP = 1, virtual), which results in a final score of 6 points (2 + 1 + 2 + 1) out of 12.

Fig. 4. Wii balance board used in our Segwii travel technique.

4.5 Hand-Directed Steering (HDS)

In this technique, travel simply follows the direction of the user's hand. In our implementation, the user holds a Vive controller and presses its trigger button to start moving, and travel follows the controller orientation in the horizontal plane (see Fig. 5). Gaze is decoupled from travel direction. This implementation differs from teleport in the sense that travel is not instantaneous but continuous, as it is in the real world. This allows observing the environment while traveling and also allows direct comparison of performance metrics between VLTs, since traveling speed is the same in all of them. Regarding fidelity, translation does not involve any body motions except for pressing the trigger, which cannot even be considered an anatomical substitution (TBM = 0, any other case), translation is virtual (TP = 1, virtual), rotation follows the hand which can indeed be taken as an anatomical substitution (RBM = 1, anatomical substitution), and rotation is fully physical because the user directly points with her hand in the direction of travel (RP = 3, physical), which gives a total of 5 points (0 + 1 + 1 + 3), the lowest score among the implemented techniques in this work.

Fig. 5. Pointing and steering with Vive controller.

4.6 Graphical Comparison of VLTs with the Fidelity Score

Table 2, Fig. 7 and Fig. 8 show different ways to present the scores of the above VLTs. Thus, Table 2 list the scores in each dimension and the final sum. In Fig. 6, a radial chart is used to represent the same 4 dimensions but in a graphical way. Then, in Fig. 7, at the top, two charts show the partial sums of the scores in translation (TBM + TP) and rotation (RBM + RP), separately. Finally, at the bottom of that figure, the final fidelity score is represented in one single scale that allows for an easy comparison of the VLTs with respect to real walking and among them. Apart from the VLTs implemented, which are in bold in Fig. 7, this figure also includes the VLTs discussed in Sect. 3 for comparison.

Table 2. Summary of scores of different VLTs in each dimension and their final score.

VLT	Translation		Rotation		Fidelity score
	TBM	TP	RBM	RP	
Arm-swinging	2	1	2	3	8
GDS-Gamepad	1	1	2	3	7
GDS-3DMouse	1	1	2	3	7
Segwii	2	1	2	1	6
HDS	0	1	1	3	5
Seven-league boots	3	2	3	3	11
Omni Treadmill	3	1	3	3	10
Instant teleport	0	1	1	3	5
WASD + Mouse	0	1	0	1	2
Real walking	3	3	3	3	12

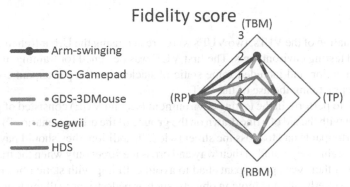

Fig. 6. A radial chart shows the 4 dimensions of the fidelity score of the VLTs evaluated in this experiment.

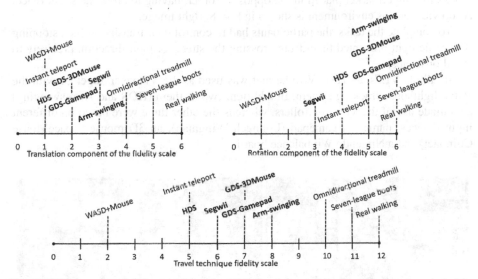

Fig. 7. Fidelity score of different VLTs. The VLTs implemented for the experiment are in bold.

5 VLT Evaluation

The previous evaluation of the VLT techniques that is revisited in this paper was carried out to find out which one was more suitable for the objectives of the UrbanRehab application. In this work, we are only interested in those parts of the evaluation that are more related to the fidelity scale, that is, how users felt the techniques and compared them to real walking. This way, the following sections do not fully describe that evaluation, but rather summarize the parts that are of interest for this work.

5.1 Setup

For the evaluation of the VLTs, two VUEs were created using the UrbanRehab editor: the training and testing environments. The first VUE was designed for training, it consisted of a street junction and included some static obstacles that the participant could try to reach while practicing the use of the VLT.

The task to perform in the testing environment (second VUE) consisted of going to a supermarket with the aid of a line drawn on the ground of the urban scenario. To reach this goal, the participants had to cross the street twice. In addition, they should pay attention to the traffic lights they found in their way and cross the street only when the traffic lights allowed it. On their way, participants had to avoid colliding with static objects, such as benches and streetlights, and moving objects, such as pedestrians walking towards them. This second VUE is shown in Fig. 8, left image. This environment consisted of two city blocks bounded by street junctions. The user had to go from one corner of one of these blocks to a supermarket placed in the opposite corner, having to cross the street twice. A top view of this environment is shown in Fig. 8, right image.

To complete the tasks, the participants had to control their translation (i.e., stopping if a traffic light prevented them from crossing the street) or their direction precisely to avoid obstacles.

In all the VLTs, an HTC Vive helmet was used as the VR visor, together with the Valve lighthouse tracking system. In addition, two of them (HDS and Arm-swinging) also made use of the Vive controllers, whereas the other three were based on different input devices, namely a gamepad (Logitech Wingman), an 3D mouse (SpaceMouse Compact) and a Nintendo Wii balance board.

Fig. 8. Screenshot of the testing VUE (left), and top view of the same VUE (right).

5.2 Participants

Twenty participants took part in the experiment, with gender parity, 50% women (24,5 years old average) and 50% men (26 years old average), in an age range of between 20 and 34 years old. An equal representation of male and female users is remarkable, as the latter are often overlooked in technology tests.

5.3 Procedure

The evaluation was designed as a within-subject experiment, in which each participant explored all the different VLT proposals, because it enables comparing the performance of the same participant under all the conditions. To avoid some problems, such as the impact of the learning effect, a Latin Square Design was used to organise the different VLTs for each experiment. Moreover, another potential problem of the within-subject design is fatigue. In order to avoid it, the task to be carried out was simplified, and after each condition participants could take the helmet off, fill out a questionnaire and rest for a moment between trials.

Participants took approximately 2–3 min to learn how to manage the VLT selected in each step of the experiment by using a different VUE conceived for training. Following that, they carried out the experiment, and as all the VLTs were stationary, the participants had to be at a specific location to start the evaluation. The task consisted of getting from one point to another while avoiding collisions with fixed and mobile objects and respecting the traffic lights that were on their way. To simplify the task and avoid the influence of disorientation, all participants were asked to follow a line drawn on the ground of the VUE that indicated the desired path they had to follow to reach the destination. Moreover, participants never received indications about how to avoid obstacles or how to use the devices once the test started, and never received any comments from the evaluator that could condition their answers to the questionnaires. Finally, after testing each VLT, they had to fill out the standard USE questionnaire for analysing usability issues (Table 3).

5.4 Gathered Data

The USE questionnaire was used to analyse the usability of the VLTs. This questionnaire, proposed by Arnold M. Lund [21], analyses four main aspects related to usability: Usefulness; Ease of Use; Ease of Learning; and Satisfaction. Several questions are used to analyse each of these components. The original questions were rephrased to fit the specific needs of the evaluation (see Table 3). For example, the question written as "It helps me be more effective" was rewritten as "This technique helps me to move effectively, without colliding with objects and following the path marked". A 7-point Likert scale was used for the USE questionnaire, ranging from strongly disagree (1) to strongly agree (7).

5.5 Results

All the participants were able to successfully finish the tasks using the different VLTs. The results for the USE questionnaire for each of the VLTs implemented are summarised in Fig. 9. The responses given by the participants to each item that compose a dimension in the USE questionnaire were used to analyse each dimension.

Table 3. Questions included in the USE questionnaire used in the experiment.

USE questionnaire

Usefulness

US1: This technique helps me to move in an effective way, avoiding collisions with objects and following the path set
US2: It helps me to move quickly
US3: It is useful
US4: It helps me to make controlled movements similar to the real ones
US5: It makes the things I want to accomplish easier to get done
US6: It covers my needs to move around in the virtual environment
US7: It does everything I would expect it to do to get around

Ease of use

EU1: It is easy to use
EU2: I am comfortable with its use
EU3: It requires the fewest steps possible to accomplish what I want to do
EU4: It is flexible, can be adapted to my needs
EU5: Using it is effortless
EU6: I can use it without written instructions
EU7: I don't notice any inconsistencies as I use it. The way it is used and its behaviour has not changed while I was using it
EU8: Both occasional and regular users would like it
EU9: I can recover from mistakes quickly and easily
EU10: I can use it successfully every time

Ease of learning

EL1: I learned to use it quickly
EL2: I easily remember how to use it
EL3: It is easy to learn to use it
EL4: I quickly became skilful with it

Satisfaction

S1: I am satisfied with it
S2: I would recommend it to a friend
S3: It is fun to use
S4: I works the way I want it to work

6 Discussion

Based on the results gathered with the USE questionnaire, the technique that stands out -and in the four blocks of questions- is the HDS, which is the farthest technique to real walking from the ones that were tested according to our fidelity scale. Even though the experiment was not designed to assess the realism of the techniques but rather their use in a general way, there was -however- one particular item in the USE questionnaire that referred to realism: US4 "It helps me to make controlled movements similar to the real ones". The average scores for US4 (see Table 4), sorted in an incremental way, are: Segwii (1.95), GDS-Gamepad (4.05), GDS-3DMouse (5.20), HDS (5.35), and Arm-swinging

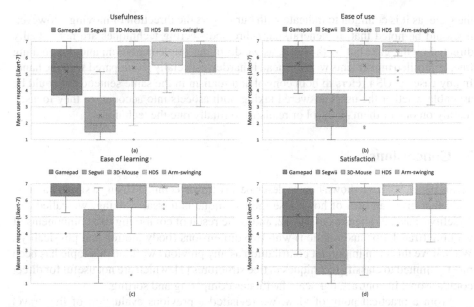

Fig. 9. Boxplots of the mean values of the user responses to the USE questionnaire (per block of questions).

(5.85). Then, comparing this with the same techniques sorted by their fidelity score -HDS (5), Segwii (6), GDS-Gamepad (7), GDS-3DMouse (7), and Arm-swinging (8)- we can spot two differences. The first difference is that both GDS techniques were given the same score in the fidelity scale but, in contrast, the average values of US4 set some distance between them. That is, the users considered that the GDS-3DMouse offered a better control, much like in real walking, than the GDS-Gamepad. The fact that one is based on a continuous-output device (3D mouse) and the other on a binary-output one (gamepad buttons) may explain this. The second difference is that the HDS technique jumps forward in the list, with higher scores than the GDS-based techniques, and right before the Arm-swinging one. This way, it could be interpreted that controlling direction with the hand is more similar to real walking than doing it with the gaze. In other words, this could be understood as if hands played a more important role in real walking than

Table 4. Results of US4 question.

VLTs	Mean	SD	Median	IQR
Arm-swinging	5.85	1.46	6.00	2.00
GDS-Gamepad	4.05	2.21	4.50	4.00
GDS-3DMouse	5.20	1.94	6.00	3.00
Segwii	1.95	1.54	1.00	1.00
HDS	5.35	2.21	6.00	3.00

the gaze, as it is common to indicate with our fingers the direction of moving. However, it should be noted that, in general, gaze-directed steering techniques are not actually directed by the gaze but by the head, as we do in our implementation, and that making fine, controlled movements with the head is harder, especially if compared with the hand. In any case, as US4 refers to both control and realism in the same sentence, it could be arguable whether the users answered taking both aspects into account, or they focused mainly on one of them –control or realism- to finally rate the technique.

7 Conclusions

In this paper, we have shown how to describe any travel technique using a single numeric scale that gives an idea of how close the technique is to real walking; we called this "fidelity scale", it ranges from 0 to 12, and is the result of combining two components of walking (translation and rotation) with two dimensions (body motion and physicality). We believe this is an important contribution as any previous work on this topic has been mostly limited to classify techniques in tree structures [1], which are not useful for direct comparisons. In contrast, our scale facilitates comparing and sorting.

From a practical point of view, we revisited a previous evaluation of five travel techniques and re-analysed the results to compare them with the scores that each VLT gets in our fidelity score. The main conclusion was that all the VLTs yielded good results but Segwii, which suffered from instability. However, if we analyse the results in more detail, we can see that the HDS and Arm-swinging are the ones that are best appreciated by the users, as they are the top-rated techniques in the block of questions "Satisfaction". This choice could also be related to the fact that both techniques have decoupled traveling and gaze direction, as opposed to the rest.

Finally, the fidelity scale introduced in this paper is a first version of a tool which we believe it can be useful for other researchers, and that similar scales could be produced for other families of techniques, such as selection and manipulation. As a first version, it can certainly be improved in future revisions. For instance, the scope of the current scale is limited to walking on a flat surface and does not consider going up and down stairs. Besides, even though it facilitates direct comparison, there are cases where techniques have the same score, yet they differ in some way that can play a significant difference. This is the case of the HDS and teleport techniques, both get 5 points in the score, but in the former the translation is performed in a continuous way, whereas in the latter is done instantly. In the case of the two GDS techniques implemented (GDS-3DMouse and GDS-Gamepad), both get 7 points but the results from the evaluation indicate that there can be a difference that users perceive but that the scale is not showing. Both GDS techniques were also given 1 point in the body motion dimension of the translation component (TBM) for considering that moving the finger in the four directions can be taken as an anatomical substitution for moving the body in such directions, a decision that can be argued by other researchers and then may be revised in future versions of this scale. As a last future work, we would also like to explore how to introduce into this scale the fact that in some techniques travel is coupled with gaze whereas in others it is not.

Acknowledgements. Grants PID2020-115220RB-C21, funded by MCIN/AEI/https://doi.org/10.13039/501100011033, and 2022-GRIN-34436, funded by UCLM, both also funded by "ERDF: A way to make Europe".

References

1. Boletsis, C.: The new era of virtual reality locomotion: a systematic literature review of techniques and a proposed typology. Multimodal Technol. Interact. **1**, 9 (2017)
2. Zayer, M.A., MacNeilage, P., Folmer, E.: Virtual locomotion: a survey. IEEE Trans. Visual. Comput. Graph. **26**, 6 (2020)
3. LaViola, J., Kruijff, E., McMahan, R., Bowman, D., Poupyrev, I.: 3D User Interfaces: Theory and Practice. Addison Wesley, Boston (2017)
4. Milgram, P., Takemura, H., Utsumi, A., Kishino, F.: Augmented reality: a class of displays on the reality-virtuality continuum. In: Telemanipulator and Telepresence Technologies, vol. 12 (1995)
5. Usoh, M., et al.: Walking > walking-in-place > flying, in virtual environments. In: Proceedings of the 26th Annual Conference on Computer Graphics and Interactive Techniques - SIGGRAPH '99 (1999)
6. Nabiyouni, M., Bowman, D.A.: A taxonomy for designing walking-based locomotion techniques for virtual reality. In: Proceedings of the 2016 ACM Companion on Interactive Surfaces and Spaces, vol. 11 (2016)
7. Nguyen-Vo, T., Riecke, B.E., Stuerzlinger, W., Pham, D.-M., Kruijff, E.: Naviboard and navichair: Limited translation combined with full rotation for efficient virtual locomotion. IEEE Trans. Visual. Comput. Graph. **27**(1), 165–177 (2019)
8. Ruddle, R.A., Lessels, S.: The benefits of using a walking interface to navigate virtual environments. ACM Trans. Comput.-Hum. Interact. **16**, 4 (2009)
9. Interrante, V., Ries, B., Anderson, L.: Seven league boots: a new metaphor for augmented locomotion through moderately large scale immersive virtual environments. In: 2007 IEEE Symposium on 3D User Interfaces (2007)
10. Bozgeyikli, E., Raij, A., Katkoori, A., Dubey, R.: Point & teleport locomotion technique for virtual reality. In: Proceedings of the 2016 Annual Symposium on Computer-Human Interaction in Play, vol. 10 (2016)
11. Buttussi, F., Chittaro, L.: Locomotion in place in virtual reality: a comparative evaluation of joystick, teleport, and leaning. IEEE Trans. Visual. Comput. Graph. **27**, 1 (2021)
12. Chertoff, D.B., Jerome, C., Martin, G.A., Knerr, B.W.: GamePAB: a game-based performance assessment battery application. Proc. Hum. Factors Ergon. Soc. Annu. Meet. **52**, 9 (2008)
13. Gerling, K.M., Klauser, M., Niesenhaus, J.: Measuring the impact of game controllers on player experience in fps games. In: Proceedings of the 15th International Academic MindTrek Conference on Envisioning Future Media Environments - MindTrek '11 (2011)
14. Juan-González, J., et al.: Urbanrehab: a virtual urban scenario design tool for rehabilitating instrumental activities of daily living. J. Ambient Intell. Human. Comput. **3** 2021
15. Ferracani, A., Pezzatini, D., Bianchini, J., Biscini, G., Bimbo, A.D.: Locomotion by natural gestures for immersive virtual environments. In: Proceedings of the 1st International Workshop on Multimedia Alternate Realities, vol. 10 (2016)
16. Wilson, P.T., Kalescky, W., MacLaughlin, A., Williams, B.: VR locomotion: walking > walking in place > arm swinging. In: Proceedings of the 15th ACM SIGGRAPH Conference on Virtual-Reality Continuum and Its Applications in Industry - Volume 1, vol. 12 (2016)
17. Templeman, J., Sibert, L., Page, R., Denbrook, P.: Pointman - a device-based control for realistic tactical movement. In: 2007 IEEE Symposium on 3D User Interfaces (2007)

18. Wang, J., Lindeman, R.: Leaning-based travel interfaces revisited. In: Proceedings of the 18th ACM Symposium on Virtual Reality Software and Technology - VRST '12 (2012)
19. Jerald, J.: The VR Book: Human-Centered Design for Virtual Reality. Morgan & Claypool, San Rafael (2015)
20. Kemeny, A., George, P., Merienne, F., Colombet, F.: New VR navigation techniques to reduce cybersickness. Electron Imag. **2017**, 48–53 (2017)
21. Lund, A.: Measuring usability with the use questionnaire. In: STC Usability SIG Newsletter, 8:2, vol. 8, pp. 3–6 (2001)

The WalkingSeat: A Leaning Interface for Locomotion in Virtual Environments

Leonardo Vezzani$^{(\boxtimes)}$, Francesco Strada , Filippo Gabriele Pratticò ,
and Andrea Bottino

Politecnico di Torino, Turin, Italy
{leonardo.vezzani,francesco.strada,filippogabriele.prattico,
andrea.bottino}@polito.it
http://www.polito.it

Abstract. When users experience immersive Virtual Reality (VR), the limited physical space available can become a significant problem when they use their real walk to navigate the virtual environment (VE). To address this limitation, various interfaces and metaphors have been proposed that combine different user inputs ranging from controllers, gestures, and body tracking. However, not all of these solutions are natural and intuitive, reducing the level of immersion and presence in VR. In this paper, we present Walking Seat (WS), a novel leaning interface (LI) for locomotion in VEs that the user can operate while seated. The main objective of this work is to design an interface that provides an intuitive and immersive locomotion experience. The WS interface uses pressure mapping and a gyroscope to track the user's upper body tilt and waist orientation. The WS interface has been thoroughly evaluated, using an articulated locomotion testbed and compared its performance with three non-leaning interfaces previously tested with the same reference protocol. The experimental results suggest that the WS interface could be a promising solution for navigation in immersive VR applications and open new directions for further research to refine and improve the WS interface for more complex tasks and scenarios.

Keywords: Virtual Reality · Locomotion · Leaning Interface · Human Computer Interaction

1 Introduction

Virtual Reality (VR) technology has opened up new possibilities for immersive experiences in various fields, including entertainment, education, and training. In all these fields, locomotion, or how users move within virtual environments (VEs), remains a fundamental activity. However, the limited physical space available to users while experiencing VEs often conflicts with the boundless nature of virtual spaces. As a result, this limitation can prevent users from freely exploring VEs by simply walking in the physical space, causing a mismatch between the user's body and virtual movements, leading to discomfort, disorientation,

G. Zachmann et al. (Eds.): EuroXR 2023, LNCS 14410, pp. 21–39, 2023.
https://doi.org/10.1007/978-3-031-48495-7_2

and even motion sickness [24,28]. To this end, finding a suitable interface and interaction metaphor for navigating in VR is still an open research topic [3]. To address these issues, researchers have explored several locomotion techniques that rely on a variety of tracking hardware and interaction metaphors.

These techniques include teleportation, joystick-based movement [2], walking in place [10], omnidirectional treadmills, and tools such as the Cyberith Virtualizer [6]. Despite their numerous advantages, each technique also has its own set of disadvantages. For instance, while teleportation is effective for enabling movement, it can also be disorienting and disrupt immersion [26]. On the other hand, omnidirectional treadmills and devices such as the Cyberith Virtualizer can provide a highly immersive experience, but they come with a significant cost and physical demand. Similarly, walking-in-place may offer a sense of plausibility [21], but it requires considerable physical effort. Lastly, although familiar to players, joystick-based movements have been reported to trigger motion sickness [28].

In addition to the aforementioned techniques, Leaning Interfaces (LI) represent a promising solution to the problem of limited space in VR locomotion [9]. This type of interface allows users to control their virtual movement by simply leaning their bodies in different directions. Research has demonstrated that LIs are intuitive and easy to learn, ultimately providing a natural and immersive locomotion experience [13,20]. Furthermore, requiring the user to tilt their upper body to simulate walking may elicit a vestibular response similar to that of actual walking [22].

Despite the positive outcomes observed in previous research on LIs [25], several limitations have been identified [11,18]. One issue is that peculiar hardware settings, such as pressure-sensitive boards or tiltable chairs, have made LIs uncomfortable and not user-friendly [11,25], at times compromising interaction with the VE [23]. Another limitation lies in the choice of how and which body parts to track. Several solutions relied on tracking only one body part (e.g., head, hands), restricting the degrees of freedom in navigating the VE [11]. Specifically, when relying on the head position and orientation to determine movement direction, users are prevented from moving in one direction while looking in another [12,23,29]. Furthermore, when designing LIs, combining multiple body parts tracking has been shown to be important in achieving complex locomotion features [1], and increasing the sense of self-location, agency, and body ownership in VR [17]. However, to the best of our knowledge, studies proposing LIs which rely on tracking multiple body parts are still limited.

To address the limitations of previous LIs and to achieve a more natural and immersive locomotion experience in the VE, this work introduces a novel methodology that focuses on a more extensive tracking of body posture. Specifically, we present the design and implementation of the Walking Seat (WS), a LI based on the combination of a weight-sensitive seat to determine upper body tilt and a gyroscope to assess waist rotation.

The proposed WS was evaluated against three relevant non-LIs locomotion techniques by leveraging a standard testbed proposed in the literature, i.e. the

Locomotion Evaluation Testbed (LET-VR) [7]. This testbed allowed us to measure the performances of the WS interface, collecting objective and subjective data to determine its strengths and weaknesses compared to other non-LIs, previously evaluated with LET-VR.

Overall, our experimental results suggest that WS is a promising technique for locomotion in VR applications and can match, and at times surpass (in specific dimensions), the performance of non-LIs in most of the tasks analyzed. The same experiments also allowed us to identify some limitations of the proposed WS that leaves room for future improvements of the interface in terms of efficiency, usability, and user experience.

2   Related Work

When examining the body of literature on LIs, two main categories can generally be identified: *standing LIs* and *sitting LIs*.

Standing LIs. Standing LIs allow users to control their movement in VEs by shifting their weight while standing on specially designed platforms. The *Joyman* LI, introduced in [23], uses a pivoting station to detect balance shifts, but despite providing satisfactory levels of immersion and presence, the interface was found to be unresponsive. As a result, users had to excessively lean, beyond the recommended limits, and were required to hold onto a handlebar, which prevented them from interacting with the VE. To address this limitation, several hands-free approaches have been proposed [12,25,29], which differ in the method of body stance detection. For instance, the *Surfboard* LI [29] exploits a pivoting table, similar to [23]. However, to provide a more stable control, it requires users to assume a skateboard-like stance making this interface best suited for a limited number of VR applications, such as board sports simulators. On the contrary, the works presented in [12,25] offer a more general-purpose stance but infer users' positioning through either a pressure-sensitive board composed of two Nintendo Wii Fit balance boards [12] or by calculating the displacement of the user's head (the headset position) from a fixed reference position (the board's center) [25]. However, all these board-based LIs suffer from the same problem of precarious user balance, resulting in stepping out of the platform when performing specific movements, like rapid weight shifts or swift direction changes. Due to this common issue, researchers have developed seated solutions to avoid the risk of falling.

Sitting LIs. The *Navichair* [19] is one of the earliest examples of sitting LIs, where a tiltable stool is used to control: (i) forward and backward movements through upper body leaning and (ii) direction by turning on the stool. However, the stool have been tested employing a single large projection screen. This prevented the user to rotate freely on the stool in order to maintain visual contact with the screen, restricting the angular rotation to only a few degrees from its original position. Consequently, users evaluated this approach negatively due to a mismatch between the physical movement and virtual rotation, resulting in cyber-sickness symptoms, navigation errors, and overall dissatisfaction with the user experience.

To overcome this limitation, a second version of the *Navichair* was proposed in [25]. Instead of projecting the VE onto a screen, users wore a head-mounted display (HMD), and the stool could rotate freely as the user movement direction was derived from the HMD orientation. Similarly, the LIs described in [11] orient movement along the HMD's facing direction but compute the upper body leaning from the device position and orientation, thus not requiring a tiltable stool. Although some slight implementation differences, both these works concluded that forcing movement along the same direction faced by the user limits usability and the exploration of complex multitasking VEs, where typically, the gaze and movement directions should be separated (i.e., users should be able to move in one direction while looking in another).

Comparison of LIs and non-LIs interfaces. In the previously mentioned studies, LIs have been mainly evaluated individually or compared with other LIs implementations. However, to gain a comprehensive understanding of the advantages and disadvantages of LIs, they should also be compared with other established locomotion techniques such as joystick, teleportation, or arm swing [5,18]. Nevertheless, to the best of our knowledge, research in this direction is limited and results were obtained from different experimental protocols. For instance, [14,18] compare different LIs with a Joystick interface. However, their results appear conflicting, as [18] reported that the joystick interface performed better than all the LIs assessed, while [14] found no significant difference. Moreover, their experimental approaches differed, as [18] only collected subjective metrics from interviews, whereas [14] also measured performance metrics (e.g., travel distance error, motion sickness, precise control) while users performed various navigation tasks. Despite these differences, both studies indicated that LIs are promising interfaces if specific characteristics such as comfort, usability, and precision can be improved. A more extensive study [5] compared a sitting LI with teleport and joystick interfaces. During the experiments, users were asked to reach several locations in a VE while objective (i.e., execution time) and subjective metrics (i.e., sickness, presence, usability and comfort) were collected. The subjective metrics were gathered administering several questionnaire to the subjects, such as the simulation sickness questionnaire [16], the Igroup presence questionnaire [27], system usability scale [4] and the device assessment questionnaire [8]. The results were similar to those in [14], showing that the teleport interface was more usable in terms of overall ease of use, fatigue, and smoothness of movement, while both the joystick and LI interfaces performed poorly with no significant difference between them.

In light of all these considerations, this work aims to contribute to the current state of the art by proposing a novel LI that combines tracking of multiple body movements (i.e., upper body leaning and hips rotation) to achieve a more comfortable and natural way of moving in VEs. Moreover, we comprehensively evaluate our LI solution with non-LIs relying on a standard testbed for locomotion techniques that includes a wide range of objective and subjective metrics collected in different scenarios involving complex tasks.

3   Walking Seat

This section provides a detailed description of the LI proposed in this work. As anticipated, the WS allows users to navigate a VE using only their body movements while seated on any swivel chair equipped with dedicated hardware.

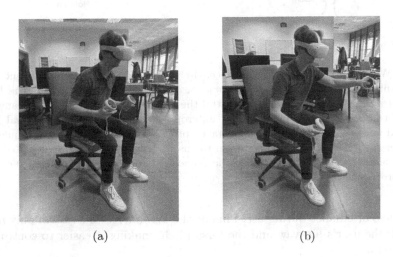

(a)   (b)

Fig. 1. Picture of the WS being used: (a) the user is leaning forward to navigate the VE; (b) the user extend his arm to reach for the virtual object

The WS hardware consists of two rigid surfaces containing four load cells and a gyroscope that are used to measure the users' center of mass position and infer the waist orientation, respectively. From these measures, the WS can infer the degree to which the user is leaning in different directions. Specifically, the weight measured by each load cell determines the projection of the user's body center of mass onto the rigid surface. The projection of the center of mass is the result of two components. The anteroposterior component (AP) is calculated by measuring the difference in weight between the front and the back cells, and the mediolateral component (ML) is calculated by measuring the difference between the right and left load cells. These two components are then combined with the orientation provided by the gyroscope to produce as output a two degrees of freedom motion vector (Fig. 2).

The WS enables the user to decouple the direction of her gaze from the one of her movement since the locomotion in the VE exploits only torso leaning and hip rotation. The swivel chair used in the implementation of the WS allows only yawing and restricts pitching and rolling movements, preventing potential falls

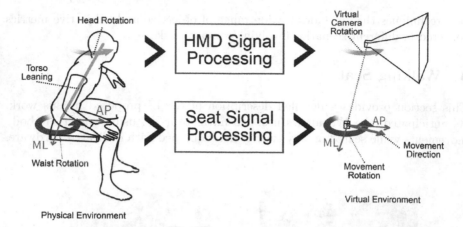

Fig. 2. While seated on the WS interface, the user can freely perform different body movements, such as *Head Rotation, Torso Leaning,* and *Waist Rotation.* The HMD tracks *Head Rotation* and uses it to control the *Virtual Camera Rotation.* Meanwhile, the WS tracks weight shifting along the anteroposterior (AP) and mediolateral (ML) axis, and waist rotation: the resulting data are processed and sent to the VE simulation. The *Movement Direction* is defined from the user's leaning direction (calculated from the AP and ML components), while the *Movement Rotation* results from the WS's signal processing of *Waist Rotation.*

due to loss of balance during use. Finally, the WS navigation system only needs to track the user's hip yaw and the torso pitch, making it easier to control the VR system.

3.1 Hardware and Data Capture

The WS is assembled from several commercial-off-the-shelf components enclosed between two wooden boards that are kept at a distance by four springs (Fig. 3a). The device includes a set of four load cells LC_{fl}, LC_{fr}, LC_{bl}, and LC_{br} (where the subscripts stand for f:front, b:back, l:left, and r:right) and a gyroscope connected to a circuit board containing an integrated WiFi antenna. These components are assembled as illustrated in the logical schematics of Fig. 3b. The process for computing the device output is illustrated in Fig. 4 and involves the following steps.

Calibration. The load cells are used to determine the position of the user's center of mass. However, different people's weight is distributed differently when sitting, which affects the measurement's accuracy. To address this issue, the device needs to be calibrated for each user (Fig. 4–1). To do so, the user must sit upright for a few seconds and during this time, the WS calculates the average output value for each load cell. In this way, we obtain a baseline measurement of the user's weight distribution on the seat, which is used to correct the output of the load cells as follows:

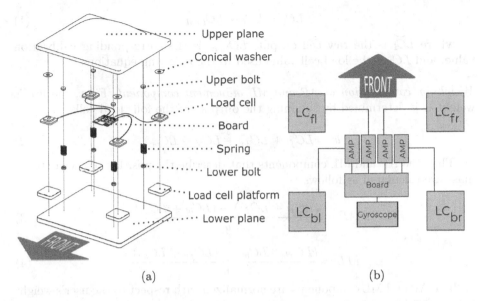

Fig. 3. The WS interface exploded-view (a) and logical schematics (b)

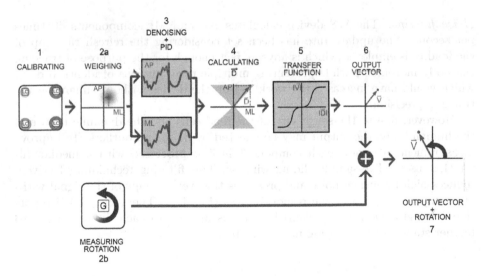

Fig. 4. Walking Seat signal processing: after the system is calibrated (1), both weight distribution and chair rotation are measured (2a, 2b). The components of the weight signal are denoised and the PID algorithm is applied (3). The vector D is calculated and it is then constrained to be mainly anteroposterior (4) and processed by a transfer function that further smooths the data (5). The resulting V (6) is combined with the measured chair rotation to determine the final output motion (7).

$$LC_l = \widetilde{LC}_l - LC_{l,cal} \tag{1}$$

where $\widetilde{LC}_l$ is the raw cell output, $LC_{l,cal}$ is the corresponding calibration value, and LC_l is the load cell value used in the following equations.

Weighing: computation of AP and ML movement component. First, the user's weight w is determined by summing the outputs of the four load cells.

$$w = LC_{fl} + LC_{fr} + LC_{bl} + LC_{br} \tag{2}$$

Then the AP and ML components that describe the position of the center of mass are calculated as follows:

$$AP = \frac{(LC_{fl} + LC_{fr}) - (LC_{bl} + LC_{br})}{w} \tag{3}$$

$$ML = \frac{(LC_{fl} + LC_{bl}) - (LC_{fr} + LC_{br})}{w} \tag{4}$$

The AP and ML components are normalized with respect to the user's weight (Fig. 4–2a). This ensures more accurate tracking since the weight variations measured by the load cells are only proportional to the user's movements and not also to the user's weight.

Noise filtering. The WS device calculates AP and ML components 40 times per second. The update rate has been set considering the refresh rate cap of the load cells employed,which is anyway fast enough for the purpose of tracking the body movements while preventing multiple transmissions of identical data, which would have increased the workload on the device without enhancing the tracking precision.

However, due to the sensitivity of the load cells and the dynamic nature of the human body, the output may be affected by noise and outliers. To improve measurement accuracy, each component is first processed with a median filter that uses a five-sample sliding window. This filtering technique effectively reduces high-frequency noise and preserves the overall shape of the signal without compromising the signal responsiveness (Fig. 4–3). Then, the PID (Proportional Integral Derivative) algorithm [15] is applied to each filtered signal to further stabilize the resulting motion vector.

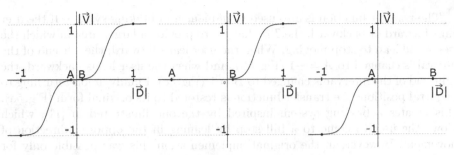

(a) TF-shape for a user in static position

(b) TF-shape when the user leans forward

(c) TF-shape when the user leans backward

Fig. 5. The shape of TF changes depending on the posture of the user. On the x-axis is the signed $|D|$ value (positive for leaning forward, negative for leaning backward); on the y-axis is the resulting $|V|$ value.

Calculation of D. The ML and AP components obtained from the previous step are used to determine the direction movement:

$$D = (ML, AP) \tag{5}$$

This vector can map any leaning direction of the user to the corresponding translational movement in the VE. This translational movement could be perceived as unnatural and uncomfortable when the mediolateral component (ML) of the direction vector is larger than the anteroposterior component (AP). Consequently, it has been decided that the mediolateral movement would be restricted.

Therefore, we consider the ML component only if it is at least as large as the AP component, otherwise D is set to zero. Figure 4–4 shows with the gray sectors the area in which the D vector is not zeroed. We have found that this behavior is useful (and quite natural) for making small lateral corrections during motion, and creates a more natural feeling of movement, similar to real walking.

Transfer function (TF) normalization. While users engage with the VE, they may need to interact with virtual objects while remaining stationary. However, even slight movements of the arms or head can alter weight distribution, resulting in the calculation of a non-zero vector D that would trigger unwanted movement within the VE. To avoid this issue, a transfer function (TF)(Fig. 4–5) is used to prevent unwanted movement. Based on the value of $|D|$, the TF produces a final motion vector V that has the same direction as D and a maximum magnitude of one.

If the user is in a rest position (i.e., sitting upright and not leaning), TF (Fig. 5a) defines an interval $[A, B]$ on the $|D|$ axis that provides a $|V| = 0$ as long as $|D|$ is small enough. When the user intentionally leans, $|D|$ becomes larger and the $|V|$ grows smoothly thanks to the TF's curve, resulting in a progressive acceleration.

The transfer function is also used to implement a braking system. If the user leans forward or backward, the TF changes to provide a larger area in which the user could lean to stop moving. When the user leans forward, the left end of the interval is changed to $A = -1$ (Fig. 5b), and when the user leans backward, the right end of the interval is changed to $B = 1$ (Fig. 5c). Finally, upon returning to a neutral position, the transfer function is restored to its original form (Fig. 5a). This creates a braking system inspired by the one illustrated in [11], which allows the user to come to a full stop by leaning in the opposite direction of movement. However, in the original implementation this was possible only for forward movements and the WS extends the original solution by allowing users to stop, regardless of their movement direction.

Integration of chair orientation. Up to this point, the motion vector is determined only by tracking the motion of the user's center of mass. However, since the user is sitting on a rotating swivel chair (Fig. 2), the rotation of the chair provides information about the orientation of the user's hip (Fig. 4-2b). Hence, the data acquired by the gyroscope are combined with the vector V (Fig. 4-6) obtained from the previous steps. The result is the final motion vector that represents the user's movements in the VE (Fig. 4-7). This motion vector is then transmitted to the host via the WiFi protocol, eliminating the need for a connection cable and ensuring a wider range of movement in the real environment.

4   Evaluation

To evaluate the effectiveness of the proposed navigation interface, we used the Locomotion Evaluation Testbed (LET-VR) proposed in [7]. This testbed was designed to compare different VR locomotion techniques with a common set of recurring tasks involving locomotion in VR. The goal of our assessment was threefold. First, to identify which kind of locomotion tasks proposed LI was more suitable for. Second, to identify potential areas in need of improvement for the next design iteration of the LI. Third, to compare the properties of our interface with other locomotion techniques previously evaluated using the same experimental protocol. To our knowledge, this is the first time a LI has been compared to multiple non-LIs in such a comprehensive manner.

The LET-VR testbed: LET-VR consists of five scenarios, each designed to stress and measure different capabilities of a given locomotion technique. The first scenario, "Straight Movements", examines walking in a straight line without changing direction. The second scenario, "Direction Control", evaluates walking with a change of direction. In the third scenario, "Decoupled Movement", participants walk in a direction that does not correspond to their line of sight. In the fourth scenario, "Agility", participants must avoid collisions with moving objects. Finally, the fifth scenario, "Interaction with Objects", examines the potential interference of the locomotion technique on object manipulation tasks. In addition to these scenarios, the testbed includes a training scenario to calibrate the system and allow participants to familiarize themselves with the locomotion technique to be tested.

In each scenario, the participant must complete several tasks. Each task is evaluated using objective metrics, some of which are common among different tasks (e.g., execution time) or are unique to specific tasks (e.g., number of collisions and projectiles avoided in the "Agility" scenario). These metrics are used to assign an objective score to each locomotion technique for the execution of the respective task.

Once each scenario is completed, the participant is asked to fill out a questionnaire to provide a subjective evaluation of the locomotion technique used, based on parameters such as input quality, ease of use, perceived errors, and satisfaction with the technology according to several subjective metrics. It also assesses the burden of use and the similarity of the technique to physical walking. These metrics are used to compute a subjective score, where the highest value corresponds to the most effortless locomotion technique.

A final score, which results by summing the objective and subjective ones, is used to determine a ranking between all the compared locomotion techniques. All scores are analyzed using the Weighted Sum Model (WSM) multi-criteria decision analysis. Hence, the scoring assignment is based on the statistical significance of the best technique within the comparison pool. Therefore, individual scores assigned in a particular group might differ numerically if the analyzed pool of techniques differs. However, the relative positioning of two techniques (i.e., technique A is better than technique B) is preserved regardless of the comparison pool. More details can be found in [7]. Overall, this scoring system allows both an overview evaluation of the analyzed locomotion techniques and their comparison by considering individual aspects.

Experimental protocol. The experiments were arranged as follows. At the beginning of the test, participants were asked to fill out the LET-VR pre-questionnaire. Then they were introduced to the WS and, in order to ensure the proper utilization of the interface, volunteers were given specific instructions to maintain a correct sitting posture and avoid engaging in behaviors that could interfere with weight distribution, such as lifting their feet or exerting pressure against the armrests of the chair. Afterward, they were requested to familiarize themselves with the WS via the training scenario. During this phase, the WS calibration step was run several times to help participants find their personal sweet spot on the swivel chair as they learned to use the device and become familiar with it. Participants then went through each of the five scenarios, which were organized as follows:

(i) while the participant is wearing the HMD, the heart rate is collected;
(ii) at the beginning of each scenario, locomotion is blocked, and the administrator explains the tasks the subject has to complete subsequently;
(iii) locomotion is unlocked, and the participant can now perform the given tasks;

(iv) after each scenario, the participant's heart rate is measured while still wearing the HMD and s/he is administered with the LET-VR post-scenario questionnaire.

Finally, at the end of all scenarios the LET-VR *post-test* questionnaire is administered as well.

In case of interruptions that prevent the experiment from resuming (e.g., extreme motion sickness), the LET-VR protocol prescribes that the gathered data could either be discarded or be completed with statistically significant values (e.g., mean of other values, worst scores, etc.) at the experimenter discretion. For the experimental evaluation of WS was selected the following strategy: in case a participant is unable to complete the experiments in Scenarios 1–4, their data are discarded; in case a participant could not complete Scenario 5, the collected data are padded with the mean of the scores collected for the finished tasks.

The HMD used for the experiments was an Oculus Quest 2 equipped with a Kiwi Strap for higher comfort. Although the original LET-VR experiments were conducted with an HTC Vive since the features of the two HMDs are comparable the impact of using a different HMD was deemed as negligible.

5 Results and Discussion

In this section we present and discuss the results of the experiment. We begin with a description of the overall experimental results in (5.1); then we discuss the results of the objective (5.2) and subjective (5.3) evaluations. Finally, we discuss the lessons learned from the experiments with the WS (5.4).

5.1 Experiment Overview

We recruited 12 volunteers (7 male, 5 female), matching the number of experimental subjects analyzed in [7] for each locomotion technique. The sample was made of individuals with ages ranging from 23 to 27 ($\overline{x} = 24.66$ y.o., $s.d. = 1.3$ y.o.). 58% of the users had little to no experience with VR (less than 1 h/week), and the remaining 42% had moderate to great experience with VR (more than 1 h/week).

The WS results were evaluated against the locomotion techniques considered in [7], whose data are publicly available. These techniques are: *(i) Walk-In-Place (WIP)*, selecting the variant adopted in [7] (formerly proposed in [10]), that prescribes to track the feet and hip orientation of the user, leading to an interesting comparison since WS also tracks the hip orientation of the user; *(ii) Cyberith Virtualizer (CV)* [6], as both WS and CV require high upper body movements and could lead to a similar vestibular response; *(iii) Joystick (JS)*, using the implementation presented in [2], which resulted the best technique in the previous ranking [7].

Table 1. Summary of the overall ranking of the LT's. Best values in bold, runner up values are underlined

Objective	WS (our)	WIP	CV	JS
Objective Scores	21.7	12.3	5.3	**32.2**
Subjective Score	16.4	14	21.6	**23.6**
Overall Scores	38.4	26.3	26.9	**55.8**

The comparison against the Arm Swing technique, originally included in [7], was neglected since it has no features in common with WS and was not the best-performing technique according to [7].

In the following sections, we present the results of the objective and subjective scores of the locomotion techniques, which are summarized in Table 1. Detailed scores will be discussed later in Table 2. The overall score obtained from the sum of objective and subjective components is reported as well. The scores indicate that the JS technique scored the highest, making it the best locomotion technique. The WS technique placed second, while CV and WIP placed third and fourth, respectively.

5.2 Objective Scores

The objective score assigned to WS, as seen in Table 2, indicates that the interface is overall reliable. To calculate this score, we summed the task scores and the perceived physical effort scores for each scenario.

In the *Straight Movements* scenario, WS performed well on the *straight line movement* and *sprinting* tasks (which requires the subject to move in a straight line while walking and running, respectively), but poorly on the *over/under shooting* and *chasing* tasks. The latter result can be attributed to the nonlinear transfer function (TF) used to control frontal movement. When the user starts to lean forward, there is no motion until the threshold B is reached. Then the initial movement speed is very low, causing the user to lean forward more and suddenly lurch forward due to the rapid increase in the curve. Therefore, many users have complained about this noticeable delay between the time they lean forward and the time they actually perceive the movement.

Similarly, WS performed well on anteroposterior motion in the *Direction Control* scenario (as in the *backward walking* and *fear* tasks, which require little turning) but poorly in the *Multi straight line walking* and *curved walking* tasks. We found that this problem was related to the constraint included in our design to avoid pure lateral motion. However, this constraint caused users to have difficulty navigating tight turns, likely due to their lack of experience with VR or with WS. Instead of moving by rotating the swivel chair, they ended up trying to move sideways. Future studies could investigate the possibility of reducing or eliminating this limitation.

In the *Decoupled Movement* scenario, WS proved to be the best performing technique, with good results in both the *Decoupled Gaze* task, which requires

Table 2. Objective scores of the compared LTs. For each scenario, the final objective score is the sum of the per-scenario physical effort and the per-task scores [7]. Best values in bold, runner up values are underlined

Objective	WS (our)	WIP	CV	JS
Straight movement				
Straight Line Walking	1	0	1	1
Over/Under-Shooting	0.67	1.33	0	1.67
Chasing	0	1	1	2
Sprinting	1	0	0	1
Physical Effort	2	0	0	2
Objective Score	4.7	2.3	2	7.7
Direction control				
Multi-Straight Line Walking	0	1	1.33	1
Backward Walking	3	0	0	4
Curved Walking	0	0	0	1
Stairs & Ramp	0	0	0	0
Fear	2	0	0	2
Physical Effort	0	0	0	0
Objective Score	5	1	1.3	8
Decoupled movement				
Decoupled Gaze	2	0	0	1
Stretched-out Hands	0	0	0	0
Decoupled Hands	3	4	1	0
Physical Effort	0	0	0	0
Objective Score	5	4	1	1
Agility				
Dynamic Agility	1	0	0	3
Stationary Agility	0	0	0	0
Evasion	2	0	0	2
Physical Effort	2	0	0	2
Objective Score	5	0	0	7
Interaction with objects				
Grabbing	0	0	0	1.5
Manipulation	0	3	1	1
Interaction in Motion	0	2	0	4
Physical Effort	2	0	0	2
Objective Score	2	5	1	8.5
Total Objective Score	21.7	12.3	5.3	32.2

the user to move while looking in a different direction, and the *Decouple hands* task, which requires the subject to collect objects with their hands while moving through a corridor. The LTs that used hip tracking to control the direction of movement performed better on these tasks, with WIP being the runner-up. Although hip tracking was helpful with both techniques, it was found that sitting provided more consistent results.

The combination of the swivel chair and hip tracking in WS provides high mobility, allowing the user to change direction quickly without losing balance, resulting in a high score on the *agility* task. In addition, WS performs well on the *Dynamic agility* and *Evasion* tasks, providing reasonable control when dodging objects while walking and when dodging incoming bullets. However, WS received a low score in *Interacting with objects*, placing it second to last and only outperforming CV. The problem arises when the user leans forward to grasp an object and thereby (accidentally) triggers a movement. To address this issue, a better riddance of weight shifting might be implemented to distinguish between leaning for moving and leaning for reaching an object.

In summary, WS offers advantages to complete some tasks but leaves room for improvement in other situations: decoupled movements could benefit from the gyroscope tracking of the user's hip orientation, whereas manipulation and interaction tasks in which the user is prescribed to lean in order to complete the task successfully conflict with the current implementation of the WS.

5.3 Subjective Scores

Table 3 shows the results of the subjective questionnaire highlighting the unique potential and areas for improvement of the WS interface. WS received the second lowest overall score from users, mainly due to the low score in the *decoupled movements* scenario compared to CV and the lowest rank in the *interaction with object* scenario.

Table 3. Subjective ranking per scenario. Best values in bold, runner up values are underlined

Subjective	WS (our)	WIP	CV	JS
Straight Movement	3.7	3	3.2	**7**
Direction Control	2	3	3.3	**3.6**
Decoupled Movement	1.5	1.6	**9.5**	0.3
Agility	**4.7**	2	2.3	4.2
Interaction with Objects	0	1.3	2.3	**5**
Overall Subjective	**4.5**	3	1	3.5
Subjective Score	16.4	14	21.6	**23.6**

Regarding decoupled movements, the results of CV are due to its very high appreciation from the users, which resulted in very low ranks for all other interfaces due to the design of the ranking system defined in LET-VR. Moreover, the high score of CV in this scenario contributes to 43% of its overall score, largely justifying its position as runner-up.

According to subjects' feedback, the main problem users faced when using WS while interacting with objects was that reaching objects that were moving or lying on the floor caused fluctuations in the user's posture, which in turn caused involuntary movements, leading to frustration, annoyance, and motion sickness among users.

If we restrict the analysis of the results to the remaining functional requirements, the perception of WS improves significantly. In this case, WS would rank second (with a score of 14.9) to the JS technique (score of 18.3), while the WIP technique would rank second to last (score of 11.0) ahead of the CV technique (score of 9.8). In this case, the ranking is the same as for the objective ratings (Table 2).

In addition, WS showed the best performance among all techniques in the following categories: (i) *Agility* tasks, where users appreciated the naturalness of WS and the low mental effort; (ii) *Subjective Overall Score*, where WS received the highest score due to its *intuitiveness, learnability, acclimatization*, and *overall system usability*.

Further analysis of the overall subjective results revealed that WS was perceived as more *natural, easy to use*, and *appropriate* for most tasks than other techniques. Moreover, the solicited *mental* and *perceived physical effort* were considered acceptable.

5.4   Limitations

Despite the positive results, some limitations should be noted. About the WS, two limitations are worth mentioning. Firstly, during the experiments, we found that after prolonged use of the WS, users adjusted their position on the chair to sit more comfortably, which invalidated the original calibration data. Nevertheless, in this case, new calibrations were immediately performed to ensure proper use of the interface. To address this issue, the implementation of adaptive adjustment techniques, such as the use of mean shift over time, will be considered.

Secondly, direct feedback from users indicated that the lack of lateral movement and the delay in input led to errors in task completion. Also, interaction with objects in the environment was sometimes complicated for users, especially when they bent down to reach for objects on the floor, as the WS sometimes detected a false-positive motion intention from the user.

There are also potential limitations of the study worth discussing. A larger sample size in the experiments would have allowed for greater statistical power in the analysis. However, the 12 subjects recruited were numerically equivalent to the sample size of the original LET-VR experiments, ensuring a balanced comparison between WS and the interfaces originally tested by LET-VR. In addition, the user sample recruited for the WS experiments included more participants familiar with VR applications than the LET-VR user sample. Although this difference may have affected the experimental results, this fact was not considered a possible reason for bias in the experiment because (i) the experimental protocol included a familiarization step that allowed users to become familiar with the devices and interaction metaphors, thus reducing the knowledge gap between the different groups of subjects, and (ii) none of the subjects had prior experience with the specific locomotion technique used in LET-VR or any other LI. Thus, the combination of these aspects reduced the potential influence of prior knowledge on the results of the study.

6 Conclusion

In this work, we proposed the Walking Seat (WS) as a novel seated and leaning interface for navigation in VR. WS uses pressure mapping and a gyroscope to track the user's upper body tilt and waist orientation. Our tests with the LET-VR [7] evaluation framework showed that WS performed better than two non-leaning interfaces, namely the Walk-in-Place and the Cyberith Virtualizer (an omnidirectional slippery shoe interface) in many situations such as straight movement, direction control, agility tasks, and decoupled movement tasks. Surprisingly, in decoupled motion tasks, WS also outperformed the joystick locomotion technique, which is commonly considered the best performing locomotion technique. Despite the limitations found, subjects considered WS to be a promising locomotion technique overall.

Future work should focus on analyzing alternative designs to obtain a more fine-grained and accurate weighing process, which would ultimately improve the users' experience. For example, this could be achieved by implementing specialized devices, such as the CONFORMat system[1]. Hence, the more detailed user's motion data could help distinguish between different actions (e.g., leaning to move forward and leaning to reach an object) and eliminate the need for the calibration step, thereby reducing the problems associated with the user's seating position. Based on these preliminary results, we believe that the WS interface has great potential for virtual reality applications and, with further development and improvement, could become a valuable tool for locomotion in VE.

References

1. Ashiri, M., Lithgow, B., Mansouri, B., Moussavi, Z.: Comparison between vestibular responses to a physical and virtual reality rotating chair. In: Proceedings of the 11th Augmented Human International Conference (AH 20). Association for Computing Machinery (2020). https://doi.org/10.1145/3396339.3396392
2. Boletsis, C., Cedergren, J.E.: VR locomotion in the new era of virtual reality: an empirical comparison of prevalent techniques. Adv. Human-Comput. Interact. (2019). https://doi.org/10.1155/2019/7420781
3. Boletsis, C., Chasanidou, D.: A typology of virtual reality locomotion techniques. Multimodal Technol. Interact. 6(9), 72 (2022). https://doi.org/10.3390/mti6090072

---

[1] Tekscan.com.

4. Brooke, J.: SUS: a quick and dirty usability scale. Usability Eval. Ind. 189 (1995)
5. Buttussi, F., Chittaro, L.: Locomotion in place in virtual reality: a comparative evaluation of joystick, teleport, and leaning. IEEE Trans. Visual Comput. Graphics **27**(1), 125–136 (2021). https://doi.org/10.1109/TVCG.2019.2928304
6. Cakmak, T., Hager, H.: Cyberith virtualizer: a locomotion device for virtual reality. In: Proceedings of the ACM SIGGRAPH Emerging Technologies. ACM (2014). https://doi.org/10.1145/2614066.2614105
7. Cannavò, A., Calandra, D., Pratticò, F.G., Gatteschi, V., Lamberti, F.: An evaluation testbed for locomotion in virtual reality. IEEE Trans. Visual Comput. Graphics **27**(3), 1871–1889 (2020). https://doi.org/10.1109/TVCG.2020.3032440
8. Douglas, S.A., Kirkpatrick, A.E., MacKenzie, I.S.: Testing pointing device performance and user assessment with the ISO 9241, part 9 standard. In: Proceedings of the SIGCHI Conference on Human Factors in Computing Systems. p. 215–222. CHI '99, Association for Computing Machinery, New York, NY, USA (1999). https://doi.org/10.1145/302979.303042
9. Farrow, R., Iacovides, I.: Gaming and the limits of digital embodiment. Philos. Technol. **27**(2), 221–233 (2014). https://doi.org/10.1007/s13347-013-0111-1
10. Feasel, J., Whitton, M.C., Wendt, J.D.: LLCM-WIP: low-latency, continuous-motion walking-in-place. In: Proceedings of the IEEE Symposium on 3D User Interfaces, pp. 97–104 (2008). https://doi.org/10.1109/3DUI.2008.4476598
11. Flemming, C., Weyers, B., Zielasko, D.: How to take a brake from embodied locomotion - seamless status control methods for seated leaning interfaces. In: Proceedings of the IEEE Conference on Virtual Reality and 3D User Interfaces (IEEE VR), pp. 728–736 (2022). https://doi.org/10.1109/VR51125.2022.00094
12. Harris, A., Nguyen, K., Wilson, P.T., Jackoski, M., Williams, B.: Human joystick: wii-leaning to translate in large virtual environments. In: Proceedings of the 13th ACM SIGGRAPH International Conference on Virtual-Reality Continuum and its Applications in Industry, pp. 231–234. ACM (2014). https://doi.org/10.1145/2670473.2670512
13. Hashemian, A.M., Lotfaliei, M., Adhikari, A., Kruijff, E., Riecke, B.E.: Head-joystick: improving flying in VR using a novel leaning-based interface. IEEE Trans. Visual Comput. Graphics **28**(4), 1792–1809 (2022). https://doi.org/10.1109/TVCG.2020.3025084
14. Hashemian, A.M., Riecke, B.E.: Leaning-based 360 interfaces: investigating virtual reality navigation interfaces with leaning-based-translation and full-rotation. In: Lackey, S., Chen, J. (eds.) VAMR 2017. LNCS, vol. 10280, pp. 15–32. Springer, Cham (2017). https://doi.org/10.1007/978-3-319-57987-0_2
15. Johnson, M.A., Moradi, M.H.: PID Control. Springer-Verlag (2005). https://doi.org/10.1007/1-84628-148-2
16. Kennedy, R.S., Lane, N.E., Berbaum, K.S., Lilienthal, M.G.: Simulator sickness questionnaire: an enhanced method for quantifying simulator sickness. Int. J. Aviat. Psychol. **3**(3), 203–220 (1993). https://doi.org/10.1207/s15327108ijap0303_3
17. Kilteni, K., Groten, R., Slater, M.: The sense of embodiment in virtual reality. Presence Teleoperators Virtual Environ.**21**(4), 373–387 (2012). https://doi.org/10.1162/PRES_a_00124
18. Kitson, A., Hashemian, A.M., Stepanova, E.R., Kruijff, E., Riecke, B.E.: Comparing leaning-based motion cueing interfaces for virtual reality locomotion. In: Proceedings of the IEEE Symposium on 3D User Interfaces (3DUI), pp. 73–82 (2017). https://doi.org/10.1109/3DUI.2017.7893320

19. Kitson, A., Riecke, B.E., Hashemian, A.M., Neustaedter, C.: NaviChair: Evaluating an embodied interface using a pointing task to navigate virtual reality. In: Proceedings of the 3rd ACM Symposium on Spatial User Interaction (SUI 2015), pp. 123–126 (2015). https://doi.org/10.1145/2788940.2788956
20. Kruijff, E., et al.: On your feet!: enhancing vection in leaning-based interfaces through multisensory stimuli. In: Proceedings of the 4th Symposium on Spatial User Interaction (SUI), pp. 149–158. ACM (2016). https://doi.org/10.1145/2983310.2985759
21. Lee, J., Hwang, J.I.: Walk-in-place navigation in VR. In: Proceedings of the ACM International Conference on Interactive Surfaces and Spaces, pp. 427–430 (2019). https://doi.org/10.1145/3343055.3361926
22. Levine, D., Richards, J., Whittle, M.W.: Whittle's Gait Analysis. Elsevier Health Sciences (2012), google-Books-ID: xZbQAQAAQBAJ
23. Marchal, M., Pettré, J., Lécuyer, A.: Joyman: a human-scale joystick for navigating in virtual worlds. In: 2011 IEEE Symposium on 3D User Interfaces (3DUI), pp. 19–26 (2011–03). https://doi.org/10.1109/3DUI.2011.5759212
24. Mayor, J., Raya, L., Sanchez, A.: A comparative study of virtual reality methods of interaction and locomotion based on presence, cybersickness, and usability. IEEE Trans. Emerg. Top. Comput. 9(3), 1542–1553 (2021). https://doi.org/10.1109/TETC.2019.2915287
25. Nguyen-Vo, T., Riecke, B.E., Stuerzlinger, W., Pham, D.M., Kruijff, E.: NaviBoard and NaviChair: limited translation combined with full rotation for efficient virtual locomotion. IEEE Trans. Visual. Comput. Graph. 27(1), 165–177 (2021). https://doi.org/10.1109/TVCG.2019.2935730, conference Name: IEEE Transactions on Visualization and Computer Graphics
26. Rahimi, K., Banigan, C., Ragan, E.D.: Scene transitions and teleportation in virtual reality and the implications for spatial awareness and sickness. IEEE Trans. Visual. Comput. Graph. 26(6), 2273–2287 (2020). https://doi.org/10.1109/TVCG.2018.2884468
27. Schubert, T., Friedmann, F., Regenbrecht, H.: The experience of presence: Factor analytic insights. Presence: Teleoper. Virtual Environ. 10(3), 266–281 (2001). https://doi.org/10.1162/105474601300343603
28. Sevinc, V., Berkman, M.I.: Psychometric evaluation of simulator sickness questionnaire and its variants as a measure of cybersickness in consumer virtual environments. Appl. Ergon. 82, 102958 (2020). https://doi.org/10.1016/j.apergo.2019.102958
29. Wang, J., Lindeman, R.W.: Comparing isometric and elastic surfboard interfaces for leaning-based travel in 3d virtual environments. In: 2012 IEEE Symposium on 3D User Interfaces (3DUI), pp. 31–38 (2012–03). https://doi.org/10.1109/3DUI.2012.6184181

Ubiquity of VR: Towards Investigating Ways of Interrupting VR Users to Obtain Their Attention in Public Spaces

Yu Wang[1]([✉]), Raphael Johannes Schimmerl[1], Martin Kocur[2], and Philipp Wintersberger[1,2]

[1] TU Wien, Vienna, Austria
yu.wang@tuwien.ac.at
[2] University of Applied Sciences Upper Austria, Hagenberg, Austria

Abstract. The portability of mobile virtual reality (VR) head-mounted displays (HMDs) allows users to immerse themselves in a virtual environment wherever they want at any physical place. While mobile VR has the potential to become ubiquitous as smartphones, it is still rarely used. Social acceptability is an important factor determining the usage of mobile technology. Previous work suggests that VR HMDs are considered not socially acceptable during social interaction. However, it is still unknown why the acceptance of mobile VR is reduced when being surrounded by other people. Therefore, we conducted two studies to investigate if and how interruptions by bystanders while wearing a mobile VR HMD contribute to reduced social acceptability. In the first study, we performed an observation in natural environments to find out how people interrupt VR users. In the second study, we used the same set of scenarios in an online survey to gather the opinions of a larger user group. Our results reveal still high skepticism towards VR use in public spaces, which can be mitigated partly by VR experience.

Keywords: Virtual Reality · Social Acceptance · Safety Concern · Field Experiments

1 Introduction

Whenever we enter public transportation or see people waiting in a queue, we see them using their smartphones. With the rapid development of mobile VR, users can also immersive themselves in virtual environments in any physical place. Hence, experts predict that mobile VR has the potential to become as ubiquitous as smartphones [28]. While smartphones are used in almost all situations in everyday life, such as sitting in a restaurant, commuting, or just waiting, mobile VR is, however, still not used in these situations today.

Schwind et al. [18] showed that one explanation for the lack of use of mobile VR in public situations is reduced social acceptance. Their results suggest that the general usage of VR HMDs in places like the bed, the metro, or the train

G. Zachmann et al. (Eds.): EuroXR 2023, LNCS 14410, pp. 40–52, 2023.
https://doi.org/10.1007/978-3-031-48495-7_3

is socially acceptable. However, being surrounded by other people where social interaction is expected significantly reduces social acceptance. While these findings indicate that wearing VR headsets in situations in which people are supposed to interact with surrounding people is considered to be less acceptable, the actual contributing factors to reduced social acceptance remain unclear.

In general, HMDs are more disposed to risks because of the lack of visibility to the outside world [20]. Wearable technologies, such as HMDs, face acceptability challenges that are affected by form factors, physical design, interaction, and privacy concerns [21]. As bystanders are entirely unaware of what users experience in VR while wearing headsets, privacy concerns also contribute to a reduced social acceptance [21]. Another important aspect of social interaction is the start of a conversation. Typically, people initiate conversations with others by non-verbal cues such as approaching a person or eye contact. However, when seeing a person wearing a mobile HMD, it is not possible to use non-verbal communication as the users cannot visually perceive the surrounding environment. In addition, wearing an HMD can be perceived as a sign for the surrounding environment that the user does not want to be interrupted or disturbed during the VR experience. This can be perceived as impolite by bystanders, as they cannot receive any attention as the user is mentally absent despite physical presence [29].

In this work, we, therefore, explore the underlying factors of reduced social acceptability by focusing on the interruption of users experiencing VR. Compared with smartphones, it is much harder to receive the attention of the users, as the visibility of the surrounding environment is occluded. Consequently, we aim to explore how bystanders interrupt the users' VR experience, e.g., by speech, touch, or any other possibilities. We present two studies on how bystanders may interrupt VR users in public spaces: In a field experiment, a potential user was wearing an HMD in a common public setting. To understand the bystanders' behavior, we recorded the bystanders' reactions and experiences of interrupting the user to solve a simple task. In addition, we conducted a subsequent online survey to assess different interruption strategies with a larger sample of participants. Results suggest that bystanders hesitated to interrupt VR users and that VR in public settings still faces safety and privacy concerns. This paper is of an exploratory nature and contributes to research on the social acceptability of mobile VR headsets.

2   Related Work

In the following, we present prior research on social acceptance and privacy concerns of mobile VR. We also summarize how people initiate conversations by obtaining the attention of others.

2.1   Social Acceptance and Privacy Concerns of VR

VR technology has gained increased attention in recent years and has been adopted in many areas ranging from research, e.g., psychology and psychotherapy [30, 31, 34], human-computer interaction [32,33] to commercially successful applications such as BeatSaber [35]. Hence, social acceptance and social acceptability are crucial factors that influence the usage of VR devices in public spaces. Social acceptance refers to the judgment of technology after being used while social acceptability refers to the phenomenon of future judgments [3]. If a technology does not follow social norms, it may disrupt the social flow [19]. Conversely, social acceptability pertains to the prospective evaluation of technological advancements in the future. Therefore, the level of social acceptance of mobile VR will dictate whether and how VR technology will be used in public. While George et al. [7] and O'Hagan et al. [13] have explored interruption strategies in a lab experiment, George [6] investigated how bystanders can be visualized to help VR users notice bystanders. Pohl et al. [15] noticed that one reason VR lacks social acceptance is that bystanders cannot see what the user is doing [15]. The broad adoption of a novel technical product depends on its capacity to deliver a fulfilling user experience, particularly in contexts where its application is not deemed mandatory [24]. Studies addressing mobile VR technology in public spaces are scarce [18,20,25,26].

Whether and how people use VR technology in social settings depends on the surrounding environment and the people being there, e.g., the number of people, their proximity, or their behavior [24]. Therefore, the presence of unaware observers in the surrounding environment might have an influence on many aspects, for instance, user's perceptions and responses that result from the use and/or anticipated use of a system, product, or service [27]. A study by Alallah et al. [25] presents guidelines regarding the subtleness of input modalities and concludes that the perspectives of both users and observers should be considered when exploring the social acceptability of emerging technologies. Wearing HMDs in public spaces may also lead to privacy concerns for bystanders due to the cameras on the devices. An online survey of the social acceptance of VR [18] investigated the social acceptance of VR usage in different scenarios: either in private spaces, for instance, in the living room, in bed, or in the car; or in public settings such as coffeehouses, the train, or on the subway. The findings indicate that the degree of social acceptance for VR is strongly contingent upon the situational context. Utilizing VR glasses within a vehicular setting was deemed unsuitable. Bystanders' discomfort and privacy concerns about the nearby HMD user in public spaces are noteworthy, particularly given the camera-equipped VR devices like Oculus Quest 2. Bystanders' privacy concerns may be further exacerbated by the potential for nearby HMD users to inadvertently record their actions or conversations without consent. Concerns may arise from the potential misuse of collected data, such as unauthorized sharing or distribution of personal information, which could lead to privacy infringements or identity theft. Consequently, the presence of HMD users in public spaces might instigate unease and affect social acceptance.

2.2   Bystanders of VR Users

Denning et al. [2] explored privacy concerns of Augmented Reality devices, which can record the surrounding environment without bystanders being aware of it.

Results show that the majority of the participants considered it as negative to be recorded by AR headsets without their explicit consent. Most privacy research is done from the user perspective rather than from the bystanders [16]. Research from Motti et al. [11] shows that privacy concerns increase when the devices are connected to a social media app. In addition, it is challenging for VR users to be aware of the physical environment when being immersed in virtual worlds. This situation can lead to a problem of communication and interaction with bystanders in a public space.

2.3 Interruption Possibilities

A study from George et al. [5] investigated the influence of presence, workload, and attention on interruptions. They concluded that an interruption method has to be designed as a trade-off between attention and presence instead of merely focusing on attention. Identifying whether a VR user is in-between tasks accurately can impact the modality of participants on how to interrupt the VR user [7]. Notifications with different modalities in VR, for instance, visual, auditory, or haptic feedback are possible to make the user aware of the bystanders' intention to interact.

Different designs of visual notifications can also affect the reaction time and the general behavior of a VR user [9], and disrupt the immersive experience [17]. Hence, for less significant messages, a notification shown on a wall inside the VR scenario is more appropriate, because the real-world message is part of the virtual environment and, therefore, does not break the sense of presence [17]. Previous studies represented that bystanders prefer to interrupt VR users by speech or a combination of touch and speech [5, 7–10, 13, 14, 17]. However, most of these experiments were conducted in laboratory settings and could not consider natural interactions as happening in reality.

3   Method

As receiving attention from persons who wear a mobile VR device appears challenging, we explored how bystanders intuitively interrupt the users' VR experience to communicate with them and obtain their attention. We, therefore, aimed to better understand bystanders' behavior while approaching mobile VR users to assess the different ways of interruption. Consequently, we conducted two studies.

The first study was a field experiment in which a user wore a mobile VR headset in two different scenarios. In the first scenario, bystanders approach the VR user who is blocking the way. In the second scenario, a VR user sits in a coffee house and needs to be interrupted by a waiter who aims to take an order. In line with Schwind et al. [18], we also conducted an online survey depicting the scenarios using photos to gain further insights with a larger sample of participants. The participants were selected randomly in the field experiment and the online survey. Using both studies, we wanted to assess (1) the acceptance of wearing VR glasses in public settings, and (2) how bystanders would interrupt VR users.

3.1   Field Experiment

The field experiment was conducted in two public environments, specifically a confined street and a coffeehouse. The investigation encompassed various aspects, including bystander-initiated interruption modalities, social acceptance, and the overall perception of VR devices by bystanders. In the first scenario (six randomly selected local coffeehouses), the examination focuses on the approach employed by the waiter to interrupt a customer who is wearing a mobile VR headset and is pretending to perform a task. In this scenario, interviews with the waiters at the coffeehouses were conducted after getting their consent.

In the second scenario, we aimed to discern the reactions of individuals encountering a person who is blocking the way while wearing an HMD. The interaction focuses on the chosen modality, time (duration from recognition to interruption), and behavior recorded by a camera in the chest pocket of the VR user (see Figure 1). During this outdoor observation, data and results were completely anonymized, and no identifiable information about the spectators was represented in the study, only reported their behavior descriptively. The spectators were briefly interviewed after the experiments about their impressions. To obtain representative results, both scenarios in the field experiment are common situations that can happen in everyday life.

Fig. 1. (a) The scenario of the coffeehouse (b) The scenario of blocking the way

3.2 Online Survey

To gain a better understanding of bystanders' reactions and experiences during both scenarios, we subsequently conducted an online survey (N=37). The questionnaire incorporated two images of both scenarios: one picture depicting a VR user blocking a pathway, and another one illustrating a VR user attempting to place an order at a coffeehouse while wearing an HMD. Initially, participants filled in their demographics and specified how often they use VR devices.

The first scenario presented involved an individual being late for a crucial appointment, with a VR user blocking their way. The participants were textually informed that they would have to find a way to proceed through the blocked entrance since an alternative route would be too time-consuming. For the coffee house scenario, we told participants to imagine being a waiter encountering a customer immersed in a VR experience. The questionnaire of the survey asked about whether participants would interrupt the VR user, and if so, how they would do it.

To obtain qualitative user feedback, we used open questions to learn about their potential interruption strategies and gain deeper insights into the bystanders' (i.e., study participants') experience. Additionally, we used the following 7-point Likert items for each scenario ranging from strongly disagree to strongly agree: *I feel uncomfortable in that situation; I am afraid for my own safety; I am afraid for the VR user's safety; I am concerned for my privacy (e.g. the person is recording me); I find the usage of VR in this setting disruptive for bystanders; I find the usage of VR in this setting unusual; The usage of VR in this context should not be allowed.*

3.3 Results

Field Experiment. In the obstruction scenario of the field experiment, we had a high variety of waiting times until the waiter interrupted the experimenter wearing the VR device. One waiter took the order promptly. However, during drink service, only one waiter interacts with the user, with others attempting to avoid disturbance. Besides, the VR user was asked to remove the headset in a coffeehouse once. In summary, verbal interruptions by waiting for staff occurred in three of six coffeehouses, while two showed no disruptions, and immediate order-taking was observed once. Upon serving beverages, only one server interacted with the VR user, while others avoided disturbance. Notably, a single request to remove the HMD occurred in a traditional coffeehouse, where customers were older on average. In two settings, there was no interruption at all (see Table 1).

In the obstruction setting, bystanders observed and photographed the VR user, sometimes assuming they were not visible to the user. This sparked discussions about VR technology among bystanders. The recordings showed that elderly people kept their attention and gaze more prolonged toward the VR user, while younger people (including children) were less interested.

Table 1. The results from the field experiment in the coffee houses. In two settings, the experimenter was not interrupted to give an order at all.

Location	Ambience of location	Time before interruption	Estimated age of waitress/waiter	Occupancy
1	modern	no interruption	30 - 35	high
2	modern/student	1 min	25 - 30	little
3	student	no interruption	20 - 25	little
4	modern/student	5 min	25 - 30	little
5	traditional	10 min	50 - 60	high
6	modern/bar	5 min	30 - 35	medium

Online Survey. The subsequent survey was conducted online and included 37 (15 female and 22 male) participants from the ages of 21 to 47. Participants were textually introduced to the scenarios. Hence, they were asked to imagine being in the respective scenario and complete the questionnaire based on their imagined reactions. In the first scenario of the obstruction case, the preferred interruption modality was speaking (15 participants). 7 participants would touch the participants, 6 participants would use a combination of speak and touch, 3 participants would walk around, and 2 participants would like to speak plus walk around if speaking is not successful. 4 participants gave no clear answer on how they were going to interrupt the VR user.

In the second scenario of the coffeehouse case, the preferred interruption modality was speaking again (19 participants), then touch method (7 participants), speaking plus touch (6 participants), no interruption at all (2 participants), waiting a certain amount of time, and then speak (2 participants), waving in front of the user (1 participant). Two participants stated that they would send the VR user away if other guests would feel disturbed. Participants' answers for both scenarios were similar. One distinction was that participants displayed marginally increased concern for the VR user's safety in the first scenario. Additionally, the results indicated that in the obstruction case, bystanders pose stronger disruption, and a higher number of participants expressed that VR usage should not be permitted in this context.

Table 2 represents the results from the online survey. Pearson's correlation analysis was conducted for the collected data. Results show that participants who are familiar with VR are more likely to use VR HMD in the future ($r=0.434$ and $p=0.007$). Furthermore, there is a correlation between using VR HMD in the next 10 years in general and using such devices in public with $r=0.464$ and $p=0.004$. Regarding privacy, one finding is that those who are familiar with VR are less likely to have privacy concerns (obstruction scenario: $r=-0.375$ and $p=0.022$, coffeehouse scenario: $r=-0.434$ and $p=0.007$). Additionally, there is a correlation (obstruction scenario: $r=0.437$ and $p=0.007$) between privacy concerns and the belief that situations such as the ones presented will happen more often in the future.

In the obstruction scenario, there is a correlation between being afraid of one's own safety and being afraid of the VR user's safety with r=0.419 and p=0.01. A strong correlation also exists for believing that a scenario (like the obstruction scenario) will occur more often when more people start adopting VR devices in the future (r=0.482 and p=0.03). On the other hand, participants who feel discomfort in such situations also think the usage of VR is disruptive in this setting with r=0.383 and p=0.19. These participants are also more likely to agree that VR devices should not be allowed in both situations (obstruction scenario: r=0.432 and p=0.008, coffeehouse scenario: r=-0.693 and p=0.000). Overall many of the equal statements for both scenarios also correlate with one another (e.g. afraid of VR user safety with r=0.379 and p=0.21).

Table 2. The results from the online survey. 37 participants in total, 15 females, and 22 males. Scenario 1: Obstruction Scenario; Scenario 2: Coffeehouse Scenario.

Scenario 1	Fully Disagree	Disagree	Neutral	Agree	Fully Agree	M	SD
I feel uncomfortable in that situation	4	8	6	16	3	2.84	1.19
I am afraid of my own safety	12	17	5	3	0	4.03	0.90
I am afraid of VR user's safety	7	9	7	12	2	3.19	1.24
I am concerned for my privacy	14	12	8	3	0	4.0	0.97
I find the usage of VR in this setting disruptive for bystanders	3	2	3	16	13	2.08	1.19
I find the usage of VR in this setting unusual	2	0	2	16	17	1.76	0.98
The usage of VR in this context should not be allowed	5	6	12	10	4	2.95	1.20
Scenario 2							
I feel uncomfortable in that situation	4	6	12	11	4	2.86	1.16
I am afraid of my own safety	16	14	5	2	0	4.19	0.88
I am afraid of VR user's safety	12	12	6	6	1	3.76	1.16
I am concerned for my privacy	12	12	10	3	0	3.89	0.97
I find the usage of VR in this setting disruptive for bystanders	5	3	8	14	7	2.59	1.28
I find the usage of VR in this setting unusual	3	0	4	12	18	1.86	1.16
The usage of VR in this context should not be allowed	7	9	13	6	2	3.35	1.14
General Questions							
I am familiar in general with VR	2	5	8	14	8	2.43	1.14
In 10 years situations like this will become more often	3	13	8	9	4	3.05	1.18
In the next 10 years I will use VR glasses	4	4	16	10	3	2.89	1.07
In the next 10 years, I will use VR glasses in public	7	19	9	2	0	3.84	0.80

4 Discussion

Bystanders often avoided interrupting VR users in public settings, e.g., waiters in the coffeehouse scenario of the field experiments. According to the results of the online survey, many participants preferred to avoid interruptions, with the reasons including discomfort and apprehension about the user's reaction. Speech is the main interruption method selected in both scenarios of the field experiment and the online survey, followed by touch or a combination of touch and speech. Participants proposed different ways of touching VR users, e.g., shoulder tapping. The customer-service relationship between the VR user and waiters may explain why the speech was the sole interruption method in the field experiments as it is the convention for waiters to ask customers how they're doing or how the meals or drinks taste orally in restaurants and coffee houses. Participants' qualitative feedback also indicated that their way of interrupting the users depends on whether they also experience audio in VR. When users experience sound as part of VR, bystanders would possibly change the method of interrupting, e.g., using touch instead of speech.

In the field experiment, the waiters expressed concerns regarding the VR user's reaction to interruptions as well as potential safety issues. One waitress cited her own epilepsy as a reason for caution. In the first survey scenario, 14 participants agreed they were concerned for the VR user, while the majority disagreed in the second scenario. This concern for safety could influence interruption avoidance. The correlation analysis revealed that fear for one's own safety correlated with concern for the VR user's safety. Familiarity with VR devices was associated with fewer privacy concerns. This contrasts with an interaction in a traditional coffeehouse, where a waiter expressed privacy concerns and unfamiliarity with the device.

The environment of VR usage influenced social acceptance, with younger customers showing less attention to the VR user than older bystanders. In one survey, a participant considered not removing the device as antisocial behavior, aligning with findings from Schwind et al. [18]. A participant suggested establishing new standards of politeness for VR usage in public. Most survey respondents found VR in public disruptive and unusual, as did those in the field experiment. Bystanders with less VR experience perceived wearing VR headsets in coffeehouses as inappropriate. People uncomfortable with VR in public were more likely to be against mobile VR. The majority still perceive public VR usage as disturbing, with bystanders taking pictures and staring. Most survey participants felt uncomfortable, indicating social acceptance for public VR usage has not yet been achieved.

In the correlation analysis of this study, the evaluation of the familiarity of participants with VR and the potential willingness of VR usage in future and public spaces, as well as their privacy concerns are conducted. Otherwise, whether their reaction is also related to their familiarity with the VR devices can also be measured in further research, and it can provide more hints of current social acceptance of VR usage in public scenarios. In this study, the interruption method is evaluated based on the bystanders' perspective, the preferred interruption methods from the VR user's perspective should also be noticed in the future and worth discussing.

5   Conclusion and Future Work

As mobile VR has gained popularity, VR users become more prevalent in public spaces. Numerous studies investigated how to interrupt VR users while wearing an HMD in relation to factors such as workload, immersion, and activities. However, most of these studies were conducted in laboratory settings. In this paper, we conducted a field experiment to evaluate how to interrupt mobile VR users and explore the social acceptance and safety concerns of bystanders in public spaces. The findings indicate that VR usage in public spaces is still considered unusual by the majority, and achieving social acceptance requires a shift in public understanding. From the data analysis of this study, participants with limited VR experience tend to disapprove of VR usage in public spaces. Interruptions present a challenge for bystanders, who may be hesitant to approach VR users due to safety concerns.

The predominant method of interrupting a VR user is through speech. Privacy concerns are generally less significant, especially for individuals familiar with VR technology. However, those unfamiliar with VR may feel intimidated by mobile VR devices and worry about potential privacy violations such as being recorded. It is also important for future research to delve into the ethical considerations, thereby enriching the understanding of the social acceptance of VR and its ethical implications. Overall, we could see a lot of skepticism among bystanders and participants regarding the use of VR devices in public. However, the results also show people familiar with VR felt more comfortable when being close to mobile VR users. To attain a more concrete and average understanding of bystanders' reactions and attitudes toward VR usage in public environments, it is important for future work to further investigate social acceptance and interruptions using in-the-wild experiments with larger sample sizes. Therefore, it is noteworthy to follow that will users integrate and utilize VR devices in public environments to the extent that smartphones are presently employed. The widespread adoption of VR devices in public spaces remains a topic of debate. While a notable portion of the population showcases skepticism, however, based on our correlation analyses reveal that experience with VR technology reduces doubts, potentially paving the way for the commonplace use of VR head-mounted displays in various settings.

References

1. Braun, V., Clarke, V.: Using thematic analysis in psychology. Qual. Res. Psychol. **3**(2), 77–101 (2006)
2. Denning, T., Dehlawi, Z., Kohno, T.: In situ with bystanders of augmented reality glasses: perspectives on recording and privacy-mediating technologies. In: Proceedings of the SIGCHI Conference on Human Factors in Computing Systems, CHI '14, pp. 2377–2386, New York, NY, USA, (2014). Association for Computing Machinery
3. Distler, V., Lallemand, C., Bellet, T.: Acceptability and acceptance of autonomous mobility on demand: the impact of an immersive experience. In: Proceedings of the 2018 CHI Conference on Human Factors in Computing Systems, CHI 18, pp. 1–10, New York, NY, USA, (2018), Association for Computing Machinery
4. Edwards, C.: Wearable computing struggles for social acceptance. IEE Rev. **49**(9), 24–25 (2003)
5. George, C., Demmler, M., Hussmann, H.: Intelligent interventions for IVR: Investigating the interplay between presence, workload and attention. In: Extended Abstracts of the 2018 CHI Conference on Human Factors in Computing Systems, CHI EA '18, pp. 1–6, New York, NY, USA, (2018). Association for Computing Machinery
6. George, C.: Virtual reality interfaces for seamless interaction with the physical reality. Ph.D. thesis, Ludwig-Maximilians-Universität (2020)
7. George, C., Janssen, P., Heuss, D., Alt, F.: Should I interrupt or not? understanding interruptions in head-mounted display settings. In: Proceedings of the 2019 on Designing Interactive Systems Conference, DIS '19, pp. 497–510, New York, NY, USA, (2019). Association for Computing Machinery
8. Ghosh, S., et al.: NotifiVR: exploring interruptions and notifications in virtual reality. IEEE Trans. Visual Comput. Graphics **24**(4), 1447–1456 (2018)
9. Hsieh, C.Y., Chiang, Y.S., Chiu, H.Y., Chang, Y.J.: Bridging the Virtual and Real Worlds: A Preliminary Study of Messaging Notifications in Virtual Reality, 1–14. Association for Computing Machinery, New York, NY, USA (2020)
10. Kudo, Y., Tang, A., Fujita, K., Endo, I., Takashima, K., Kitamura, Y.: Towards balancing VR immersion and bystander awareness. Proc. ACM on Human-Comput. Interact. **5**(ISS), 1–22, (2021)
11. Motti, V.G., Caine, K.: Users' Privacy Concerns About Wearables. In: Brenner, M., Christin, N., Johnson, B., Rohloff, K. (eds.) FC 2015. LNCS, vol. 8976, pp. 231–244. Springer, Heidelberg (2015). https://doi.org/10.1007/978-3-662-48051-9_17
12. Milgram, P., Kishino, F.: A taxonomy of mixed reality visual displays. IEICE Trans. Inf. Syst. **77**(12), 1321–1329 (1994)
13. O'Hagan, J., Williamson, J.R., Khamis, M.: Bystander interruption of VR users. In: Proceedings of the 9th ACM International Symposium on Pervasive Displays, PerDis '20, pp. 19–27, New York, NY, USA, (2020). Association for Computing Machinery
14. O'Hagan, J., Williamson, J.R., McGrill, M., Khamis, M.: Safety, power imbalances, ethics and proxy sex: surveying in-the-wild interactions between VR users and bystanders. In: 2021 IEEE International Symposium on Mixed and Augmented Reality (ISMAR), pp. 211–220 (2021)
15. Pohl, D., Tejada Quemada, de C.F.: See what I see: concepts to improve the social acceptance of HMDs. In: 2016 IEEE Virtual Reality (VR), pp. 267–268 (2016)

16. Pidcock, S., Smits, R., Hengartner, U., Goldberg, I.: NotiSense: an urban sensing notification system to improve bystander privacy. In: Proceedings of the 2nd International Workshop on Sensing Applications on Mobile Phones (PhoneSense), Seattle, WA, USA, pp. 12–15 (2011)
17. Rzayev, R., Mayer, S., Krauter, C.A., Henze, N.: Notification in VR: the effect of notification placement, task and environment. In: Proceedings of the Annual Symposium on Computer-Human Interaction in Play, CHI PLAY '19, pp. 199–211, New York, NY, USA (2019). Association for Computing Machinery
18. Schwind, V., Reinhardt, J., Rzayev, R., Henze, N., Wolf, K.: Virtual reality on the go? A study on social acceptance of VR glasses. In: Proceedings of the 20th International Conference on Human-Computer Interaction with Mobile Devices and Services Adjunct, MobileHCI '18, pp. 111–118, New York, NY, USA (2018). Association for Computing Machinery
19. Edwards, C.: Wearable computing struggles for social acceptance of technology: the ultimate fashion item? IEEE Rev. **49**(9), 24–25 (2003)
20. Eghbali, P., Väänänen-Vainio-Mattila, K., Jokela, T.: Social acceptability of virtual reality in public spaces: experiential factors and design recommendations. In: Proceedings of the 18th International Conference on Mobile and Ubiquitous Multimedia (MUM '19). Association for Computing Machinery, New York, NY, USA, Article 28, pp. 1–11 (2019). https://doi.org/10.1145/3365610.3365647
21. Profita, H.P., Albaghli, R., Findlater, L., Jaeger, P.T., Kane, S.K.: The AT Effect: How Disability Affects the Perceived Social Acceptability of Head-Mounted Display Use. In Proceedings of the 2016 CHI Conference on Human Factors in Computing Systems (CHI '16). ACM, New York, NY, USA, pp. 4884–4895 (2016). https://doi.org/10.1145/2858036.2858130
22. Wei, R., Leung, L.: Blurring public and private behaviors in public space: policy challenges in the use and improper use of the cell phone. Telematics and Informatics, vol 16, no. 1–2, pp. 11–26, ISSN 0736-5853 (1999). https://doi.org/10.1016/S0736-5853(99)00016-7
23. Drucker, S., Gumpert, G.: Public space and communication: the zoning of public interaction. Commun. Theory **14**, 294–310 (1991)
24. Vergari, M., Kojić, T., Vona, F., Garzotto, F., Möller, S., Voigt-Antons, J.-N.: Influence of Interactivity and Social Environments on User Experience and Social Acceptability in Virtual Reality.: IEEE Virtual Reality and 3D User Interfaces (VR). Lisboa, Portugal **2021**, 695–704 (2021). https://doi.org/10.1109/VR50410.2021.00096
25. Alallah, F.S., et al.: Performer vs. observer: whose comfort level should we consider when examining the social acceptability of input modalities for head-worn display? In: Proceedings of the 24th ACM Symposium on Virtual Reality Software and Technology, pp. 1–9 (2018)
26. Mai, C., Wiltzius, T., Alt, F., Hussmann, H.: Feeling alone in public: investigating the influence of spatial layout on users' VR experience. In: Proceedings of the 10th Nordic Conference on Human-Computer Interaction, pp. 286–298 (2018)
27. DIS, I. (2009). 9241–210: 2010. Ergonomics of human system interaction-Part 210: Human-centred design for interactive systems. International Standardization Organization (ISO). Switzerland
28. Gugenheimer, J.: Nomadic Virtual Reality: Exploring New Interaction Concepts for Mobile Virtual Reality Head-Mounted Displays. In: Adjunct Proceedings of the 29th Annual ACM Symposium on User Interface Software and Technology (UIST '16 Adjunct). Association for Computing Machinery, New York, NY, USA, 9–12 (2016). https://doi.org/10.1145/2984751.2984783

29. Kleinman, L.: Physically present, mentally absent: Technology use in face-to-face meetings. In: CHI'07 Extended Abstracts on Human Factors in Computing Systems, pp. 2501–2506 (2007)
30. Schleicher, D., et al.: Psychosocial stress induction in vivo vs. in virtuo and the influence of a health app on the acute stress reaction in youths: a study protocol for a randomized controlled trial. **23**, 847 (2022). https://doi.org/10.1186/s13063-022-06758-z
31. Kocur, M., et al.: Computer-assisted avatar-based treatment for dysfunctional beliefs in depressive inpatients: a pilot study. Front. Psychiatry **12**, 608997 (2021). https://doi.org/10.3389/fpsyt.2021.608997
32. Kocur, M., Kloss, M., Schwind, V., Wolff, C., Henze, N.: Flexing muscles in virtual reality: effects of avatars' muscular appearance on physical performance. In: Proceedings of the Annual Symposium on Computer-Human Interaction in Play (CHI PLAY '20). Association for Computing Machinery, New York, NY, USA, pp. 193–205 (2020). https://doi.org/10.1145/3410404.3414261
33. Kocur, M., Habler, F., Schwind, V., Woźniak, P., Wolff, C., Henze, N.: Physiological and perceptual responses to athletic avatars while cycling in virtual reality. In: Proceedings of the 2021 CHI Conference on Human Factors in Computing Systems (CHI '21). Association for Computing Machinery, New York, NY, USA, Article 519, pp, 1–18. https://doi.org/10.1145/3411764.3445160
34. Riva, G.: Virtual reality in psychotherapy: review. CyberPsychology Behav. **8**(3), 220–230 (2005). https://doi.org/10.1089/cpb.2005.8.220
35. Beat Games. Beat Saber. Game [PC, PS, Meta Quest]. Beat Games, Czech Republic (2019)

Rhythmic Stimuli and Time Experience in Virtual Reality

Stéven Picard$^{(\boxtimes)}$ and Jean Botev [ID]

University of Luxembourg, 4364 Esch-sur-Alzette, Luxembourg
{steven.picard,jean.botev}@uni.lu
https://vrarlab.uni.lu

Abstract. Time experience is an essential part of one's perception of any environment, real or virtual. In this paper, from a virtual environment design perspective, we explore how rhythmic stimuli can influence an unrelated cognitive task regarding time experience and performance in virtual reality. The task involves sorting 3D objects by shape, with varying rhythmic stimuli in terms of their tempo and sensory channel (auditory and/or visual) in different trials, to collect subjective measures of time estimation and judgment. The results indicate different effects on time experience and performance depending on the context, such as user fatigue and trial repetition. Depending on the context, a positive impact of audio stimuli or a negative impact of visual stimuli on task performance can be observed, as well as time being underestimated concerning tempo in relation to task familiarity. However, some effects are consistent regardless of context, such as time being judged to pass faster with additional stimuli or consistent correlations between participants' performance and time experience, suggesting flow related aspects. This could be of great interest for designing virtual environments, as purposeful stimuli can strongly influence task performance and time experience, both essential components of virtual environment user experience.

Keywords: Virtual Reality · UX · Time Experience · Rhythmic Stimuli

1 Introduction

While time itself is a concept, it is also something humans can perceive. However, the perception of time is subjective, and this experience is an integral part of the overall experience of any environment, with virtual environments being no exception. Therefore, acknowledging this in their conception and actively devising virtual environments to modulate the time experience of users would be an exciting design instrument. Time perception as an interdisciplinary topic is explored in numerous scientific studies in disciplines as diverse as psychology or

This project has received funding from the European Union's Horizon 2020 research and innovation programme under grant agreement No 964464 (ChronoPilot).

neuroscience. In a previous study combining cognitive science and computer science, we already examined the relationships between time perception and rhythmic stimuli with a sorting game in a two-dimensional setting, which revealed varying time experience and performance effects depending on whether single or combined stimuli were used in relation to their tempo [19]. However, that initial experiment was limited to a crowd-sourced desktop setting, and we adapted the experiment for Virtual Reality (VR), which allows for extended control of the test environment plus extending the initial set of questions to include stimuli and time experience aspects in fully immersive environments. Therefore, while our main goal with this study is to investigate and interpret anything significant by having a correlation study process, we do come with assumptions coming from our initial study, which are different effects on time perception depending on the type of stimuli present (audio, visual, or both), tempo-related time estimation errors for combined stimuli, as well as decreased task performance by the presence of visual stimuli. Before detailing the experiment in Sect. 3, analyzing the data in Sect. 4, and discussing the results in Sect. 5, we will first provide the necessary background and review related work in the following Sect. 2. Section 6 then concludes the paper with an outlook and potential impact of our findings on general virtual environment design.

2   Background and Related Work

The most common time perception model in literature is the clock model, which assumes an "internal clock" as a body system dedicated to time perception [9]. This system is usually tied to a model producing "ticks" or "units", such as an oscillator or a pacemaker model, where the body keeps track of time by counting these ticks. In these models, it is assumed that time perception can be changed either through the speed at which these ticks are produced or by skipping some, with these effects potentially resulting from external stimuli unrelated to time. Counting the ticks can be delegated to attention, making attentional resources a key element of time perception [5,6]. Attention is believed to act as a gate or switch on accounting the time units, where paying less attention to time will result in compressed time experience as time units are likely to be skipped. Another source of subjective temporal distortions can be found in the use of arousal levels, which are believed to affect the clock speed, resulting in an altered time experience [2,3,13]. However, using an internal clock model is not necessary to predict time perception accurately [22]: on the context of watching videos in different scenarios, time perception was accurately predicted by a classification network using changes in perceptual content and visual spatial attention (more specifically, gaze position). Nevertheless, it is a natural way to interpret time experience based on the focus on attention and arousal that gives initial directions to time perception studies.

In the literature, we can observe different types of timing tasks, which involve different processing mechanics. The most common aspects are time estimation (i.e., asking for a duration estimate of an event with units, such as seconds) and the feeling of time passage (i.e., judging if time passes by quickly or slowly), which is also referred to as time judgment.

This difference can be observed in depressed subjects underestimating time but judging it as passing slowly [3], with boredom-prone people judging boring tasks as passing slowly but not necessarily overestimating those [27], or with players of the game "Thumper" reporting faster time passing without time estimation errors [23].

Having defined time perception, we can discuss the state of "flow", one of the applications of time perception alterations. Flow is a psychological state of full attention on a task defined by Csikzentmihalyi, represented through nine dimensions: challenge-skill balance, action-awareness merging, clear goals, unambiguous feedback, concentration on task, sense of control, loss of self-consciousness, time transformation, and autotelic experience. The psychological state of flow is a research subject in itself, centered around one's relation to a task as it primarily relies on the challenge-skill ratio aspect [11]; it is often considered a desirable state, and time perception alterations are one of its manifestations. In social media, the manifestation of flow seems to be influenced by the positive effect of telepresence on enjoyment, concentration, challenge, and curiosity; flow would then influence the presence of time distortions [17]. Delving further into social context, it was found that the concentration and time distortion components of flow, but not enjoyment, were affected by working in a group of two compared to working individually in virtual worlds (within the social game platform Second Life) [16]. More in line with our work, several studies on flow and VR have been conducted. The previously mentioned study on Thumper compared flow states between VR and non-VR setups, finding that despite VR's technical immersion, both scenarios could lead to a flow state [23]. Within VR activities, a model ostensibly associates flow and playfulness, defined by a combination of intrinsic motivation, control, and freedom to suspend reality, this association then influences competence in the activity [21].

VR studies on time perception, however, are not limited to flow. VR itself affects our senses due to what is being conveyed through sensory channels, but also due to the devices used and the eventual physical discomfort we can get from it. Simply comparing the time perception of the same game in a VR versus a desktop setup leads to an underestimation bias for VR [15]. It also seems that time perception changes when bored or waiting in VR compared to real life [10]. In another simple study about time perception comparing the time perception between VR and desktop while doing a task ranging from 30 s to 5 min, it was observed that if both situations yielded time overestimation, the VR scenario was overestimated more [14]. However, technological immersion alone might not be a sufficient explanation, as walking in VR does not seem to affect time perception significantly [1]. In another experiment about zeitgeber on time perception while doing a task conducted both in VR and on desktop, no significant difference was observed regarding time perception, but there was a difference in task performance (with the VR participant performing better) [24]. The Thumper study also observed the effect of performing better in a VR setup compared to a non-VR one [23]. When it comes to the effect of emotional content, VR itself appears not to yield any difference to real life in time distortions when the emotional content is the same [7]. Employing VR entails possibly unique content, such as having movements represented by an avatar. Differences were observed between avatar and no-avatar conditions where avatar presence leads to, in a retrospective paradigm, a significantly faster passage of time without an effect on time estimations [25].

When considering VR and time perception, we can thus regard both the technological immersion, i.e., the effect of being in VR through its dedicated hardware, as well as the virtual environment stimuli and transformations that can be induced through VR. A specific stimulus type we want to employ in VR is rhythmic stimuli, which we already identified as having notable effects in a desktop scenario [19]. Rhythmic stimuli and music generally have a high potential to modulate one's time experience. With music, it was observed that higher tempos induce longer subjective time, but emotional valence decreases (but does not suppress) the effect of tempo and affects time perception. These effects on time perception might be due to their effect on arousal; interestingly, using a different orchestration (piano only or full orchestra) does not affect time judgment and pleasantness while affecting arousal [4]. On timing evaluations of instrumental excerpts of Disco songs (including estimation and judgment of time passage) over different tempos, it was observed that faster tempos were correlated to longer reproduction duration; however, no effect on estimations was observed alongside the necessity of a tempo difference of at least 20 BPM required for timing measurement differences to appear [8]. By varying cognitive load through tasks and arousal levels through music choice while keeping music tempo constant, it was found that (1) time is judged as passing faster under higher cognitive load (presence of a math task), (2) presence of a concurrent motor task (tapping the music's tempo) yield shorter subjective durations, and (3) for the motor task, for the same music tapping to half notes instead of eighth notes ended up with smaller time estimations and time passage rated as faster [28]. Regarding timing and spatial movement, rhythmic auditory stimuli (RAS) have been observed to improve motor performance when vision is unavailable [18].

Rhythm, however, is not only tied to music and audio. Concerning temporal judgments, audio was believed to be dominant over visuals [12]. However, a later study found visual stimuli dominance using Point-Light-Display (PLD) dance motions compared to simple audio tempos [26]. Participants were presented with both the dance motion and the audio tempo and had to give a globally fitting tempo. The result of this study suggests that under the right conditions, visual stimuli can dominate audio in terms of timing, which may be due to the quantity of temporal information on a sensory channel rather than the channel itself.

3   Experiment

We recruited 30 participants from a public, science-related event in Luxembourg City and from students and staff at the University of Luxembourg. The female-to-male ratio was 46.66%–53.33%, with ages ranging from 19 to 45 (mean age

25.63/median 24). Participants were received at the VR/AR Lab's test space at the University of Luxembourg and briefed about the experiment before the session, both verbally and via an informed consent form, in which we also collected demographic data. After the setup and familiarization phase, the participants performed the tasks, with each participant able to take breaks between trials if desired. Each session lasted a total of approximately one hour.

3.1 Trial Task and Design

Participants had to complete trials in which they had to sort three-dimensional objects according to their shape (spheres, capsules, or cubes). As shown in the screenshot sequence in Fig. 1, the objects must be grabbed with a VR controller and dragged into one of the two larger sinks, which only accept specific shapes displayed on a scoreboard above them (cf. Fig. 1a–c). Once sorted, an object disappears with a small animation, and a new object to be sorted appears in the center of the virtual environment (cf. Fig. 1d).

(a)   (b)   (c)   (d)

Fig. 1. Sorting example from trial task, in sequential order from left to right.

The sorting attempt has a predefined duration unknown to participants. After this duration, the experiment ends with a questionnaire in which the participants are asked to estimate the time in seconds and rate on two Likert scales how fast the experiment felt and how tired they were (cf. Fig. 2).

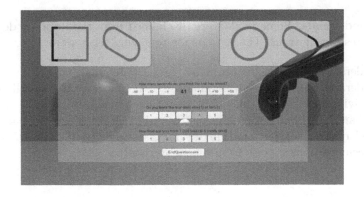

Fig. 2. Post-trial questionnaire on time estimation, time perception, and fatigue.

Trials were subjected to conditions that were a combination of these parameters:

- *trial length*: how long the trial lasted in seconds (either 40, 50, or 60)
- *tempo*: the rhythm of the audio/visual stimuli if present in beats per minute (either 100, 140, or 180; forced to 0 without stimuli)
- *visual stimuli*: whether or not there are flashing visual pulses around the object
- *audio stimuli*: whether or not metronome click sounds are produced

Each participant went through all 30 possible combinations in random order.

3.2   Technical Specifications

Participants used the VIVE Pro Eye head-mounted display (HMD) with one of its controllers, allowing them to enter VR and control virtual objects with six degrees of freedom (DoF). This particular HMD also allows for collecting precise eye-tracking data during the trials, specifically on gaze and pupil dilation. During the experiments, participants were also instructed to wear an Empatica E4 wristband to record further physiological data; our experiment included heart rate variability and skin temperature. Our custom application reads the data by receiving messages from Empatica's E4 Streaming Server software. However, the physiological data is out of the scope of this paper and will be discussed in a separate publication. The experimental application itself was developed in Unity and used SteamVR. In addition to the application, OVR advanced settings were employed to adjust the participant's height position.

4   Analysis and Results

4.1   General Methods and Data

As discussed previously, various data were collected from each trial; in this sub-section, we will describe what data we effectively used for our analysis and how.

Disclaimed Trials. Some trials were disclaimed from the data set depending on our notes during trials. The reasons for removing trials were:

- Misunderstanding of task controls by the participant.
- Misunderstanding of trial questionnaire by the participant (verbally checked when giving incoherent values such as negative time estimation).
- Disturbance or interruption during the trial, either from the participants themselves (i.e., asking a question or talking during a trial) or external sources (i.e., technical issues, noise from a nearby room).

Variables/Functions. Variables and functions extracted from trial data are:

- $t \in T$: trial identifier t from all available trials T.
- $p \in P$: participant identifier p from all available participants P.
- $trials(p)$: all trial identifiers of a participant p.
- $participant(t)$: participant identifier of a trial t.
- $correct(t)$: number of correct sorts at the end of trial t.
- $trialLength(t)$: length of trial t in seconds.
- $reportedLength(t)$: reported length of trial t in seconds.
- $reportedFatigue(t)$: self-reported fatigue of a participant after performing trial t in an ordinal scale from 1 to 5.
- $reportedSpeedPerception(t)$: subjective participant rating of trial t's speed in an ordinal scale from 1 (slow) to 5 (fast).
- $trialIndex(t)$: the index of trial t, indicates how many trials were performed before t and, therefore, global repetition from the experiment session.

Since $reportedSpeedPerception(t)$ and $reportedFatigue(t)$ are purely subjective questions to the participant, we can use these values directly. However $correct(t)$, the task performance direct variable depends on the participants' individual performance and $reportedLength(t)$, while the direct time estimation variable depends on both the trial's duration as well as the participants' individual representation of a second. Therefore, these two variables need to undergo a normalization process. Normalizing the performance variable ($correct(t)$) for our analysis goes through a three-step process involving the following extracted variables:

- $correctPerSecondTrial(t)$: average number of correct answers per second during trial t.

$$\frac{correct(t)}{trialLength(t)}$$

- $correctPerSecondParticipant(p)$: average number of correct answers per second of a participant during trials.

$$\frac{\sum_{t' \in trials(participant(t))} correct(t')}{\sum_{t' \in trials(participant(t))} trialLength(t')}$$

- $correctNormalized(t)$: amount of correct answers per second of trial t normalized with 1, i.e., the average number of correct answers per second of a participant among all performed trials.

$$\frac{correctPerSecondTrial(t)}{correctPerSecondParticipant(p)}$$

For time estimation ($reportedLength(t)$), we employed the following process:

- $secondBias(p)$: ratio of the total of seconds of a participant p's trials and the total reported time, defining what the participant considers a second.

$$\frac{\sum_{t \in trials(p)} trialLength(t)}{\sum_{t \in trials(p)} reportedLength(t)}$$

– *deltaTimePerception(t)*: averaged delta per second between reported time (accounting participant bias) and trial length of a trial *t*.

$$\frac{secondBias(p) * reportedLength(t)}{trialLength(t)} - 1$$

However, in addition to *deltaTimePerception(t)* we also use its absolute *abs(deltaTimePerception(t))* as it represents the magnitude of time perception delta of a trial.

Outcome Variables. The specific variables relevant to the analysis performed in this study are:

– *deltaTimePerception(t)*: if the difference between reported time and trial time shows too much individual bias, this variable represents a participant's variation in perception. A negative value indicates that the seconds of the trial *t* were reported as shorter than the other trial performed by this participant. A positive value means that the seconds were reported as longer.
– *abs(deltaTimePerception(t))*: instead of denoting how much longer or shorter a second is interpreted for a trial *t* compared to other trials performed by a participant, the absolute value represents the magnitude of the eventual time distortion.
– *correctNormalized(t)*: to simplify the analysis, we do not take into account negative answers to evaluate performance but only the amount of correct answers. A smaller number of correct answers would indirectly reflect the number of incorrect answers due to the time lost. Similar to a participant's variation in perception, this variable represents the variation in performance instead of the pure performance, with values <1 indicating worse and >1 better performances.
– *reportedSpeedPerception(t)*: the subjective interpretation of whether time drags or flies after performing trial *t* in an ordinal scale from 1 to 5.
– *reportedFatigue(t)*: with relatively low trial numbers, reported fatigue should mostly depend on the participants, independent of trial parameters.
– *trialIndex(t)*: the index of trial *t*, indicates how many trials were performed before *t* and, thus, is an indicator of global repetition from the experiment session.

Parameters. The parameters used in this experiment are:

– *stimulusTrial(t)*: the type of stimulus used in trial *t*, possible values are: *None, VisualsOnly, AudioOnly, Both.*
– *hasAudioTrial(t)*: whether or not the trial *t* contains an audio stimulus.
– *hasVisualTrial(t)*: whether or not the trial *t* contains a visual stimulus.
– *hasStimulusTrial(t)*: whether or not the trial *t* contains any type of stimulus.
– *tempo(t)*: the tempo in beats per minute (BPM) of a trial *t*, possible values are: 0, 100, 140, 180. a tempo of 0 means that the trial had no stimuli.

Trial Filters. When performing analyses, we may want to include only subsets of the trials to investigate specific effects. The filters used are:

- *filterAUDIOONLY*: considers only trials that only have an audio stimulus, is equivalent to saying *t where stimulusTrial(t)* == *AudioOnly*.
- *filterVISUALSONLY*: considers only trials that have a visual stimulus, is equivalent to saying *t where stimulusTrial(t)* == *VisualsOnly*.
- *filterBOTH*: considers only trials that have both audio and visual stimuli, is equivalent to saying *t where stimulusTrial(t)* == *BOTH*.

Performed Tests. Using the above variables, parameters, and filters, we performed statistical tests on various data subsets to examine the effect of a stimuli presence on performance and time estimation with the following parameters:

- *stimulusTrial(t)*: ANOVAs on *deltaTimePerception(t)*, *abs(deltaTimePerception(t))* and *correctNormalized(t)* to see if any significant difference appears between possible stimuli situations.
- *hasAudioTrial(t)*, *hasVisualTrial(t)*, *hasStimulusTrial(t)*: t-tests on *deltaTimePerception(t)*, *abs(deltaTimePerception(t))* and *correctNormalized(t)* to see if there is an effect on the presence or absence of a specific stimulus (since our t-tests are not pairwise, no t-test corrections have been performed).

To examine this effect on time judgment, we did the following as the time judgment variable is ordinal:

- *stimulusTrial(t)*: Kruskal-Wallis test on *reportedSpeedPerception(t)* to see if any significant difference appears between possible stimuli situations.
- *hasAudioTrial(t)*, *hasVisualTrial(t)*, *hasStimulusTrial(t)*: Wilcoxon test on *reportedSpeedPerception(t)* to see if there is an effect on the presence or absence of a specific stimulus.

In order to observe the effect of tempo on performance and time estimation, we performed ANOVAs between *tempo(t)* and the variables *deltaTimePerception(t)*, *abs(deltaTimePerception(t))* and *correctNormalized(t)*. The ANOVAs were also repeated across the filters *filterAUDIOONLY*, *filterVISUALSONLY* and *filterBOTH* to see if differences in tempo appear only within stimuli conditions. As for the effect of tempo on time judgment (*reportedSpeedPerception(t)*), here we again replaced the ANOVAs with Kruskal-Wallis tests, including the repeated ones under filters. Correlations between time estimation variables (*deltaTimePerception(t)*, *abs(deltaTimePerception(t))*) and performance (*correctNormalized(t)*) were investigated with Pearson tests. As the time judgment variable (*reportedSpeedPerception(t)*) is ordinal, correlation with time estimation variables (*deltaTimePerception(t)*, *abs(deltaTimePerception(t))*) as well as performance (*correctNormalized(t)*) was made through Pearson tests. The confounding effect of fatigue was investigated by considering *reportedFatigue(t)* both as a nominal and as an ordinal variable; the former allows us to eventually observe differences between specific ratings and has been considered through ANOVAs with time estimation variables (*deltaTimePerception(t)*, *abs(deltaTimePerception(t))*) and performance (*correctNormalized(t)*), the latter was considered through Spearman tests on time estimation variables, performance and time judgment (*reportedSpeedPerception(t)*). Regarding the confounding effect of trial index, *trialIndex(t)* is an ordinal data so it has been investigated with Spearman tests on time estimation variables (*deltaTimePerception(t)*, *abs(deltaTimePerception(t))*), performance (*correctNormalized(t)*) as well as time judgment (*reportedSpeedPerception(t)*). Each ANOVA with a p-value below 0.1 would lead to a subsequent Tukey HSD, Kruskal-Wallis tests would lead to subsequent paired Wilcoxon tests. Table 1 provides an overview of the different effects per subset with a significant p-value or tendency, while each is discussed in detail in the following sections. The complete data from our tests, including confidence intervals and average values, are available online [20].

Table 1. Subsets for which a significant p-value (●) or tendency (○) is observed for a combination of stimulus dimension and outcome variable group.

	Performance	Time Estimation	Time Judgment
Presence	—	—	● Full Set ● Trials 11-20 ○ Fatigue Levels 1-2 ● Fatigue Levels 3-4-5
Type	● Full Set ● Trials 1-10 ● Trials 21-30 ● Fatigue Levels 3-4-5	—	● Full Set ● Trials 11-20 ● Fatigue Levels 1-2
Tempo	○ Full Set ● Trials 11-20 ● Fatigue Levels 1-2	● Full Set ○ Trials 11-20 ○ Fatigue Levels 3-4-5	● Full Set ● Fatigue Levels 1-2

4.2   Across All Trials

Effects of Stimuli on Performance. One of the aims of this study is to investigate the effects of stimuli on task performance. Looking at performance across all trials, the ANOVA between task performance (*correctNormalized(t)*) and stimulus type (*stimulusTrial(t)*) revealed no significant difference. However, when performing a t-test between task performance (*correctNormalized(t)*) and the presence of visual stimuli (*hasVisualTrial(t)*), a significant difference ($p = 0.027$) can be observed alongside decreased performance when a visual stimulus is involved, as the mean with stimulus is lesser than without. No effect is observed when considering the t-test with the presence of an audio stimulus (*hasAudioTrial(t)*, $p = 0.167$) or any stimulus (*hasStimuluslTrial(t)*, $p = 0.431$).

Therefore, we can only observe a decrease in performance due to the presence of a visual stimulus but no effect on performance from the sole presence of any or of an audio stimulus. When stimuli have the dimension of type, they also have the dimension of tempo. The ANOVA between participant performance (*correct-Normalized(t)*) and stimuli tempo (*tempo(t)*) generally finds no effect of tempo. However, tempo might have an effect under a specific stimulus type. Therefore, we performed the same ANOVA but only considering subsets of data where trials contained either audio stimuli only (*filterAUDIOONLY*), visual stimuli only (*filterVISUALSONLY*), or both simultaneously (*filterBOTH*). We can then observe a tendency when trials have audio stimuli only (*filterAUDIOONLY, p = 0.088, F = 2.461*). The Tukey HSD of this ANOVA reveals that the effect is significant between 180-100 (*p = 0.070, diff = 0.04*), with a diff value indicating the faster tempo leads to better trial performance with audio stimuli only. In the absence of interference from visual stimuli, the faster tempo for audio stimuli may have implicitly stimulated the participant to sort objects faster.

Effects of Stimuli on Time Estimation. Similarly to performance, we evaluated the effect of stimuli type and tempo on time estimation variables. Likewise, ANOVAs were effectuated regarding the type of stimuli (*stimulusTrial(t)*) and tempo (*tempo(t)*) on both the normalized time estimation error (*deltaTimePerception(t)*) and its magnitude (*abs(deltaTimePerception(t))*). The only significant result is a tendency between time estimation error (*deltaTimePerception(t)*) and tempo (*tempo(t)*) (*p = 0.073, F = 2.328*). Tukey's HSD of this ANOVA reveals that the effect is a tendency only between tempi of 180 and 140 (*p = 0.65, diff = 0.067*), with trials under a tempo of 180 being rated with a longer time per second than trials under a tempo of 140. We performed similar ANOVAs involving tempo considering subsets of data where the trials had either only audio stimuli (*filterAUDIOONLY*), only visual stimuli (*filterVISUALSONLY*), or both at the same time (*filterBOTH*). The only significant result comes from the ANOVA between time estimation error (*deltaTimePerception(t)*) and tempo (*tempo(t)*) across trials within the AudioOnly condition (*filterAUDIOONLY*) (*p = 0.039, F = 3.288*), where the Tukey HSD follow-up reveals a near-significant difference between tempi of 140 and 100 (*p = 0.051, diff = −0.106*) and a near tendency between 180 and 140 (*p = 0.107, diff = 0.091*). This means that in the case of trials with only an audio stimulus, trials with a BPM of 140 were evaluated as faster than others, which contradicts the analysis under all types of stimuli. This contradiction may indicate the confounded effect of tempo in time perception depending on stimuli types. Finally, t-tests between our time estimation variables (*deltaTimePerception(t), abs(deltaTimePerception(t))*) and the presence of audio stimuli (*hasAudioTrial(t)*), visual (*hasVisualTrial(t)*), or any (*hasStimuluslTrial(t)*), yielded no significant result, meaning no effect of any type of stimuli present can be observed on time estimation here.

Effects of Stimuli on Time Judgment. As the time judgment variable (*reportedSpeedPerception(t)*) is ordinal, we produced Kruskal-Wallis tests between it and the type of stimuli (*stimulusTrial(t)*) and tempo (*tempo(t)*). In the case of the test between time judgment (*reportedSpeedPerception(t)*) and the type of stimuli (*stimulusTrial(t)*), we can see a significant effect ($p = 0.016$, $chi2 = 10.267$), however a follow-up paired Wilcoxon test reveals statistical difference only between the stimulus "None" and each of the other stimuli types ($p = 0.048$ for *None-AudioOnly*, $p = 0.015$ for *None-Both*, $p = 0.015$ for *None-VisualsOnly*). As for the test on tempo (*tempo(t)*), we observe another correlation ($p = 0.001$, $chi2 - 15.432$) that, after a paired Wilcoxon, shows significant differences between 0–140 ($p = 0.006$), 0–180 ($p = 0.005$), 100–180 ($p = 0.031$) as well as a tendency between 100–140 (($p = 0.064$) and a near-tendency between 0–100 ($p = 0.12$). These two tests highlight a significant difference in time judgment depending on the presence of any stimuli (both by the differences from the "None" stimulus in the first test and the "0" BPM tempo in the second, which correspond to trials without stimuli). This is also verified by the Wilcoxon test between time judgment (*reportedSpeedPerception(t)*) and the presence of any stimulus (*hasStimuluslTrial(t)*) ($p = 0.003$, *mean(TRUE)>mean(FALSE)*), considering the mean values, we can say that the presence of a stimulus has a significant impact in making a trial judged as passing faster than one without any. The same test has been done on the presence of audio (*hasAudioTrial(t)*) ($p = 0.323$) and visuals (*hasVisualTrial(t)*) ($p = 0.023$, *mean(TRUE)>mean(FALSE)*), meaning no significant difference on the presence or not of an audio stimulus is observed but a fast-inducing effect is observed on the presence of a visual one is recorded. In the case of tempo, the results of the paired Wilcoxon discussed earlier also indicate a significant between 100BPM and other (non-0) tempi across all types of stimuli. However, running the same Kruskal-Wallis test under subsets on "AudioOnly" trials (*filterAUDIOONLY*), "VisualOnly" trials (*filterVISUALSONLY*) and trials with both (*filterBOTH(t)*) highlights a significant difference only across trials with both stimuli (*filterBOTH(t)*) ($p = 0.027$, $chi2 = 7.2343$) meaning that meanwhile tempo may have an effect across all stimuli, that effect might only be due to the combined stimuli scenario. Follow-up paired Wilcoxon tests indicate a significant difference between 100–180 ($p = 0.032$) and 140–180 ($p = 0.091$), which are the same conclusion as the tests without subsets.

Correlations Between Outcome Variables. In order to investigate the correlation between outcome variables, Spearman tests were used when time judgment (*reportedSpeedPerception(t)*) was involved as the data is ordinal; otherwise, Pearson tests were used. When comparing time estimation error (*deltaTimePerception(t)*) and performance (*correctNormalized(t)*), we see no correlation ($p = 0.218$, $cor = -0.043$), but we see a significant negative correlation with the magnitude of time estimation error (*abs(deltaTimePerception(t))*) ($p = 0.016$, $cor = -0.083$). This means the performance is correlated to the magnitude of time estimation errors but not to the direction; in other words, participants may generally be more error-prone in their estimations depending on their performance. When it comes to time judgment ($reportedSpeedPerception(t)$), it is negatively correlated to time estimation errors ($deltaTimePerception(t)$) ($p = 1.724e\text{-}13$, $rho = -0.251$) and positively correlated to the magnitude of said error ($abs(deltaTimePerception(t))$) ($p = 0.002$, $rho = 0.107$). This means that the bigger the error, the faster the time is perceived and underestimated trials are rated at passing faster. As for time judgment ($reportedSpeedPerception(t)$) and performance ($correctNormalized(t)$), better performance is associated with faster passing trials ($p = 1.265e\text{-}05$, $rho = 1.50$).

Confounding Effect of Fatigue. While running the experiment, we noticed that participants were often exhausted at the end of the session. As exhaustion affects time perception and performance, we verified if it affected our outcome variables. For its effect on performance, a Spearman test between performance ($correctNormalized(t)$) and fatigue ($reportedFatigue(t)$) reveals a significant correlation ($p = 2.924c\text{-}08$, $rho = 0.190$). By considering the fatigue variable ($reportedFatigue(t)$) nominal and performing an ANOVA with performance ($correctNormalized(t)$), we retrieve this correlation ($p = 1.68e\text{-}11$, $F = 14.56$), and subsequent Tukey HSD reveals that fatigue values of "3,4,5" are statistically different from values of "1,2" as the p-value is below 0.001 in all these situations, other situations (i.e., "3-4", "1-2", ...) have a p-value above 0.48. As for time estimations, signed error ($deltaTimePerception(t)$) is not correlated if we look through a Spearman test ($p = 0.191$, $rho = 0.045$), but we retrieve statistical differences with the ANOVA ($p - 0.004$, $F = 3.86$). Subsequent Tukey HSD indicates statistical differences between "3-2" ($p = 0.001$), "5-2" ($p = 0.045$) and a tendency between "4-2" ($p - 0.06$). No correlation is observed for the absolute error ($abs(deltaTimePerception(t))$) with both the Spearman test ($p = 0.842$, $rho = 0.107$) and the ANOVA ($p = 0.893$, $F = 0.277$), however it is observed for the Spearman test with time judgment ($reportedSpeedPerception(t)$) ($p = 2.88e\text{-}11$, $rho = 0.227$). From the results of the ANOVAs involving performance ($correctNormalized(t)$) and time estimation ($deltaTimePerception(t)$), we can identify two groups of reported fatigue values which are "1-2" and "3-4-5". We thus decided to perform the same tests on subsets of our data according to these two groups on Sect. 4.4.

Confounding Effect of Trial Index. Similarly to fatigue, repeated trials can affect both performance and time perception due to learning effects and repetition. We thus evaluated correlations through Pearson tests between the number of a trial across the session ($trialIndex(t)$) as a continuous variable and time estimation variables ($deltaTimePerception(t)$, $abs(deltaTimePerception(t))$) as well as performance ($correctNormalized(t)$). When it comes to performance ($correctNormalized(t)$), the test reveals a correlation ($p = 2.626e\text{-}14$, $cor = 0.259$), which indicates a learning effect. Trial repetition also seems to affect time estimation as we retrieve a significant correlation with the signed time estimation error ($deltaTimePerception(t)$) ($p = 1.407e\text{-}04$, $cor = 0.131$) and a tendency with its absolute $(abs(deltaTimePerception(t)))$ $(p = 0.089, cor = -0.059)$. We, therefore, decided to investigate different phases (beginning, middle, end) in the experiment defined by three subsets of the data based on the trial index, as shown in Fig. 3 and discussed in detail in the following Sect. 4.3.

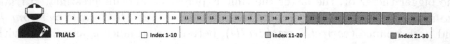

Fig. 3. Trial subset allocation for a participant by index.

4.3   Trial Index Subsets

Due to our results on the confounding effects on trial index as described in Sect. 4.2, we decided to investigate three subsets of the data based on the trial index with steps of ten (1–10, 11–20, 21–30). For each subset, we performed all the tests as on the full set of trials, which are available for download [20] and described in Sect. 4.1. However, the normalization process only considered the targeted subset when using the sum of data on trials. We go through each subset in the following subsections, focusing on the significant results.

Trials 1–10. This subset corresponds to each participant's first ten trials of the experiment, constituting a discovery phase. Regarding stimuli effects on performance, the results indicate a positive effect of audio stimulus presence (t-test performance~audiopresence, $p = 0.016$; TukeyHSD performance~stimuli, $p = 0.099$ on worse performance between visuals~both). This can be linked to the results across the entire experiment as we have seen a negative impact of visual stimulus presence and a tendency for trials with just audio to have their performance led by the tempo (see Sect. 4.2). This difference might be due to a learning effect on the trials where the participants are not proficient enough to lose enough performance from visuals but may be eased by the presence of any leading audio rhythmic stimulus for this repetitive task. As for stimuli on time estimation, here we only observe a potential novelty effect on trials without stimuli as they are rarer than trials with any stimuli (t-test time estimation error stimuli presence, $p = 0.093$). The most notable difference with the analysis on all trials regarding this aspect is the absence of the effect of tempo on the time estimations. Surprisingly, no effect of stimuli concerning time judgment is observed from any of our tests. When it comes to correlation between performance and time estimations through Pearson correlation tests, contrary to the full set of trials, we observe a (negative) correlation with the signed time estimation error $(p = 0.025, cor = -0.142)$ but not on the absolute error. Regarding time judgment concerning both time estimations and performance, we lost the correlation with the absolute time error; however, we retrieve the positive correlation from the Spearman tests with performance $(p = 0.095, rho = 0.106)$ and the signed time estimation error ($p = -0.183$, $rho = -0.184$). Finally, regarding results on confounding effects of trial index and fatigue, we retrieve correlations of fatigue on performance and time experience, correlation of performance and trial index but none between trial index and time experience. This means that with this subset, we should have isolated an experiment phase based on trials for time perception but not for performance, which is expected as the participants were likely learning how to perform better during the first few trials.

Trials 11–20. This subset corresponds to each participant's ten trials in the middle of the experiment, representing a neutral phase as they no longer learn the task while not being in the experiment long enough to be bored. Regarding performance and stimuli, in this trial, we observe a performance increase from higher tempo within trials using combined stimuli (Tukey HSD 180-100, $p = 0.044$, $diff = 0.055$; 180-140, $p = 0.075$, $diff = 0.053$) As for the effect of stimuli on time estimation, we only observed a tendency between tempo 140–100 across trials solely using a visual stimulus (Tukey HSD 140-100, $p = 0.100$, $diff = -0.083$). When it comes to time judgment, strong evidence shows that under this subset, the presence of any stimulus heavily alters it (paired Wilcoxon on time judgment and type of stimuli, $p¡0.002$ for all situations with "None"; paired Wilcoxon on time judgment and tempo, $p¡0.02$ for all cases with "0"; Wilcoxon time judgment and stimuli presence, ($p = 8.939e-05$, higher mean with stimulus). We also observe an effect of visual stimulus specifically with the same Wilcoxon test on visual stimulus presence ($p = 0.041$, higher mean with stimulus) but not on audio presence. Therefore, the effect of stimuli on time judgment in this subset is consistent with the full set regarding the effect of the present stimuli type, but we lost the effect of the tempo. This time, no correlation has been observed between time estimation and performance. However, we retrieve the time judgment correlations from the full set with Spearman tests on the performance ($p = 0.004$, $rho = 0.168$), the signed time estimation error ($p = 1.988e-04$, $rho = 0.215$) and its absolute ($p = 4.20e-05$, $rho = -0.236$). Finally, on confounding effects, we find a correlation between fatigue and time judgment, which is expected, yet we also see a correlation tendency between trial index and signed time estimation error through a Pearson test ($p = 0.071$, $cor = 0.105$). Still, the absence of correlation with performance indicates a proper subset division on the trial index.

Trials 21–30. This subset corresponds to each participant's last ten trials, representing the end of the experiment and, thus, a phase where the participant is possibly tired or bored. Here, investigation of performance suggests that when there are stimuli, the presence of visual stimulus leads to worse task performance (Tukey HSD performance between stimuli modes "Both" and "AudioOnly", $p = 0.010$, $diff = -0.045$; "VisualsOnly" and "AudioOnly", $p = 0.026$, $diff = -0.041$; t-test on performance and visual presence, $p = 1.449e-04$, lower mean when stimulus is present). Under this subset, nothing significant has been observed in the relation between stimuli (type or tempo) and time perception (time estimation and judgment). Similarly to the previous set (Trials 11–20), no correlation between time estimation and performance is observed. The relation from Spearman tests between time judgment with both performance and time estimation is similar to the subset at the beginning of the experiment (Trials 1–10), where performance is positively correlated ($p = 0.002$, $rho = 0.176$) and time estimation error is negatively correlated ($p = 4.795e\text{-}04$, $rho = -0.202$) but the absolute error is not. On confounding effect, while finding effects of fatigue on time judgment as expected, unfortunately, we see tendencies on the effects of the trial index on both time estimation error ($p = 0.067$, $cor = 0.107$) and task performance ($p = 0.073$, $cor = -0.104$) from Pearson tests. This may indicate a transition between phases of boredom and tiredness relative to the time spent in the experiment.

Fig. 4. Example trial subset allocation for a participant by fatigue.

4.4 Fatigue Subsets

Having obtained the results on the confounding effects of fatigue described in Sect. 4.2, we decided to investigate two subsets depending on the participants' answers on fatigue, one for fatigue at 1 or 2, and one for fatigue at 3, 4, or 5 (see Fig. 4). Similar to the previous subsets, for each, we performed all tests on the complete trial set, which can be found online [20], and the same modification on the variable normalization process by only considering the targeted subset when using the sum of data on trials. In the following sections, we will again focus exclusively on significant test results and will not re-elaborate the methodology.

Fatigue Levels 1–2. This subset corresponds to the participant experiencing "low" fatigue. First, concerning performance and stimuli tempo, we can observe the lesser performance of stimuli with a tempo of 100 (Tukey HSD on performance and tempo between 140 and 100 bpm, $p = 0.056$, $diff = 0.065$; 180 and 100 bpm, $p = 0.020$, $diff = 0.081$). This finding can be aligned to results from the full set (performance dependent on tempo for audio stimuli) and trials 11–20 (180 bpm leading to better performance under combined stimuli). No general effect of stimuli type on performance is observed, either from the specific situations possible or the presence of a modality. This subset yielded no significant insights regarding stimuli dimensions (type and tempo) and time estimation. Regarding time judgment and tempo, however, we observe significant differences between 180 and 100 bpm across all stimuli (Paired Wilcoxon on time judgment and tempo between 100 and 180 bpm, $p = 0.023$) as well as an effect of the presence of 180 bpm (Wilcoxon between 0 and 180, $p = 0.025$). When considering only trials with combined stimuli, the paired Wilcoxon shows a significant difference between 180–100 ($p = 0.017$) and a tendency between 100–140 ($p = 0.094$), which is consistent with the time judgment effects results on the complete set of trials. As for time judgment and stimuli type, we observe another consistent result from the full set as stimuli tend to be judged faster when there is any stimulus (Wilcoxon on the presence of any stimulus, $p = 0.073$) or if there is at least a visual one ($p = 0.020$). Looking for a correlation between performance, time estimation, and time judgment yielded similar results to the subset of Trials on index 1–10. With a tendency of a negative correlation ($p = 0.059$, $cor = -0.141$) from Pearson between time estimation error and performance, a significant negative correlation ($p = 0.022$, $rho = -0.171$) out of the Spearman between time estimation error and time judgment, a positive one ($p = 0.033$, $rho = 0.157$) between performance and time judgment, but no correlations from the absolute time estimation error. Confounding effects of trial index on performance (Pearson test, $p = 0.086$, $cor = 0.129$) are similar to trials 1–10, which is not surprising as early trials probably are low fatigue trials. A confounding effect of fatigue is not observed for both time estimation and judgment; however, we can observe it for performance (Spearman test, $p = 0.037$, $rho = 0.157$; Tukey HSD (more of a t-test considering we have two values in this subset), $p = 0.048$, $F = 3.977$, $diff2\text{-}1 = 0.046$). We can assume that higher fatigue trials in this subset would be after the learning phase when the participant would be more proficient.

Fatigue Levels 3-4-5. This subset corresponds to the participant having a higher fatigue level. Concerning performance and stimuli type, like for the full set and trials 21–30, we observe a negative impact from the presence of visual stimuli (TukeyHSD on stimuli type and performance between VisualsOnly and Audio Only, $p = 0.080$, $diff = -0.024$; t-test between performance and presence of visuals, $(p = 0.020)$). Some observations converge towards contextual effect on tempo depending on the type of stimulus of the trial (TukeyHSD on absolute time estimation error between tempos 140 and 180 for audio trials, $p = 0.086$, $diff = 0.1$; TukeyHSD on signed time error between tempos 140 and 180 across all, $p = 0.080$, $diff = 0.087$). As for time judgment and stimuli, we only found evidence indicating an effect of general stimulus presence (Paired Wilcoxon on stimuli type and time judgment, $p < 0.07$ for pairs involving "None"; Wilcoxon on time judgment and stimulus presence, $p < 0.011$; paired Wilcoxon on tempos, $p = 0.032$) between 0–140 and $p = 0.040$ for 0–180). Looking for a correlation between performance, time estimation, and time judgment yielded similar results to the full set of trials. From Spearman tests with time judgment, we retrieve the negative correlation with the time estimation error ($p = 2.217e\text{-}11$, $rho = -0.256$), the positive correlation with the absolute error ($p = 4.366e\text{-}04$, $rho = 0.136$) and with the performance ($p = 3.915e\text{-}05$, $rho = 0.159$). We do not retrieve the significant p-value on the Pearson test between performance and absolute error, but a near-tendency ($p = 0.110$, $cor = -0.062$). While we do not observe a confounding effect from the ANOVAs between fatigue and time estimation variables, we see a tendency ($p = 0.089$, $rho = 0.066$) from the Spearman test on the absolute time estimation error. The effect of fatigue is more pronounced on performance (Pearson test, $p = 0.029$, $rho = 0.085$) and from the subsequent Tukey HSD of the ANOVA ($p = 0.064$, $F = 2.768$) the difference appears to be between 3–5 ($p = 0.050$, $diff = 0.023$). Fatigue also seems to have a significant effect on time judgment ($p = 2.185e\text{-}08$, $rho = 0.215$). In this subset, the fatigue level of 3 and 5 may be significantly different on both performance and time judgment; however, this is apparently due to the normalization on the subset and was not observable across all trials. Confounding effects of the trial index observed from Pearson tests are similar to those of the full set, which is not too surprising as the subset is rather large and was not made to minimize the effect of the index.

5   Discussion

We conducted a VR experiment where participants repeatedly performed a simple sorting task subjected to different stimuli conditions, allowing us to gather numerous data, including information related to task proficiency, subjective data from questionnaires, and physiological data. The overarching goal was to explore relationships between time experience, task performance, environment/stimuli conditions, and physiological cues. However, we found that for some of the results on the complete data set, it was necessary to investigate closer multiple subsets, which we will discuss together with their implications for VR application design. Looking at the entire data set, we can observe specific effects of stimuli type and tempo on different aspects of time perception and performance, as well as some interesting correlations between those variables, which appeared to be also heavily impacted by the trial index and fatigue through the experiment. Therefore, we defined subsets of data based on the trial index and difference values from ANOVAs for fatigue. As indicated in Table 1, we can observe effects of stimuli presence, type, and tempo on performance and time experience depending on the subset. Some of the data and correlations align between subsets while others do not, which may indicate contextual effects of stimuli on performance and time experience depending on task repetition and fatigue.

5.1   Observations on Task Performance and Stimuli

A central result from the analysis of the complete set of trials is how the presence of visual stimuli negatively impacts task performance. This is coherent with our previous study and is to be anticipated as the task requires visual attention, and those stimuli may be disturbing. However, within subsets, this result is observed only for later trials (index 21–30) and high fatigue (fatigue 3-4-5). Surprisingly, we see a positive effect on performance from the presence of audio but only in the early trials (index 1–10), and no effect of stimuli type presence in-between (index 11–20). This could be interpreted as the disturbance of visual stimulus not being impacting enough when one is learning the task or not physically tired. We can also interpret the presence of audio stimuli as beneficial for this task only when the participant is in a learning phase. Effects of tempo are observed on trials within trials with only the audio stimulus when considering all trials and within trials with combined stimuli within the subset of trials from index 11–20. In both cases, the faster tempo led to faster performance, which indicates an invitation to go faster in the task from the faster stimuli; however, that interpretation from the participant depends on the context.

5.2 Observations on Time Estimation and Stimuli

Time estimation variables are defined from the difference between (normalized) participants' estimation of time taken for a trial and the actual time of a trial; we thus talk about the time estimation error and its absolute, which represents the magnitude of error regardless of if the participant under- or overestimated the length of a trial. A global effect of tempo can only be observed with the complete set of trials between 180–140 (with 180 being overestimated). As for differentiation within stimuli situations, we see a time estimation error difference on the audio stimuli for the entire trial set and for high-fatigue trials, and absolute error difference in visuals for trials 11–20 as well as on combined stimuli for high fatigue. These results show a tendency of the 140 bpm tempo leading to fewer (absolute) estimation errors and being underestimated compared to 100–180. Another overestimating effect from stimulus presence is observed for trials 1–10. Overall, we also observe context-dependent effects of stimuli as the type of stimuli will affect one's time perception differently depending on the index or fatigue.

5.3 Observations on Time Judgment and Stimuli

Time judgment or time passage refers to the subjective evaluation of a participant on whether they think a trial is going by fast or slow. It differs from time estimation as the participant gives their subjective feeling about the time spent, whereas time estimation is an attempt of the participant to be objective about time. Time judgment has semi-constant results of the presence of any stimuli inducing faster perception; this is observed across all trials for both subsets on fatigue and the subset on stimuli 11–20. We can also observe a specific fastening effect of visual stimuli on all these sets affected by the presence of any stimuli except for the high fatigue one. The absence of these observations on subsets of trials either at the beginning or at the end of the experiment might indicate the participant needing to get used and, over time, getting too used to the presence of stimuli to be noticeable, regardless of fatigue levels. Another effect observed only on the complete set and for low fatigue is a difference between tempo in general and within trials with combined stimuli.

5.4   Time Judgment, Time Estimation, and Performance Balance

Two correlations were consistent across all sets: a negative correlation between time estimation error and time judgment and a positive correlation between performance and time judgment. The first means that under-estimation of time is reflected by a subjective faster trial and the second means that when the participant rated the trial as faster than usual, they would perform better. This could directly be tied to the notion of flow as two elements of flow states are the challenge-skill balance and time transformation. The similarity between time estimation error and time judgment is indicative that our time transformation was a general time experience shift and not a side effect of disorientation (i.e., a participant judging a trial as fast because they thought it was a higher amount of time that actually passed). Among low fatigue and early trials, we also retrieve a negative correlation between performance and performance, reinforcing the flow approach. As for the time estimation error magnitude and performance, under all trials and high fatigue, it is negatively correlated, which means that possibly in a specific context, higher time transformation generally was detrimental to performance. However, this is against the flow definition, and combined with previous observations, it may imply that we are approaching flow states only with time transformations that are an underestimation. We also observed positive correlations between this magnitude and time judgment with all trials, the 11–20, and high fatigue subsets, which could be interpreted as the presence of any time transformation potentially leading to faster time passage in general.

5.5   Limitations

It is important to remember that the effect of the rhythmic stimuli in our experiment is contextualized in the particular scenario of our sorting task. We can also see some limits from the confounding effects of task familiarity and fatigue, and even with the subsets, which unfortunately implies using fewer data and thus having lesser statistical power relevance (especially in the case of low fatigue), we can isolate the effect of at most one confounding effect but not both at the same time. Individual per-participant differences are also to be considered, as through casual talks with the participants, we know of varying degrees of VR experience between participants; however, this data was not recorded and is thus not included in our analysis.

6   Conclusion

In this paper, we used a simple sorting task to explore how rhythmic stimuli affect time experience and task performance in VR. We found that the context concerning the trial index (repetition of the action) and fatigue affected these aspects of the user experience. Depending on the familiarity with the task, the presence of a particular type of rhythmic stimulus under possible tempos will affect either performance or time experience. Both aspects can contribute significantly to a flow experience or even well-being in general, and the results of this study can thus inform the design of future interactive VR applications.

While the familiarity or repetition of a task or action can be easily assessed in any interactive application, using fatigue as a modulator could be a growing opportunity for VR developers as newer HMDs incorporate advanced sensors, e.g., for eye tracking. We observed effects of rhythmic stimuli under some fatigue and task familiarity, yet the more important finding is the presence of effect variation rather than the specific effect itself, highlighting the need for studies of time perception concerning context- and subject-dependent time modulations.

References

1. Bruder, G., Steinicke, F.: Time perception during walking in virtual environments. In: 2014 IEEE Virtual Reality (VR), pp. 67–68 (2014). https://doi.org/10.1109/VR.2014.6802054
2. Droit-Volet, S., El-Azhari, A., Haddar, S., Drago, R., Gil, S.: Similar time distortions under the effect of emotion for durations of several minutes and a few seconds. Acta Physiol. **210**, 103170 (2020). https://doi.org/10.1016/j.actpsy.2020.103170
3. Droit-Volet, S., Fayolle, S., Lamotte, M., Gil, S.: Time, emotion and the embodiment of timing. Timing Time Percept. **1**(1), 99–126 (2013). https://doi.org/10.1163/22134468-00002004
4. Droit-Volet, S., Ramos, D., Bueno, J.L.O., Bigand, E.: Music, emotion, and time perception: the influence of subjective emotional valence and arousal? Front. Psychol. **4**, 417 (2013). https://doi.org/10.3389/fpsyg.2013.00417
5. Ghaderi, A., Niemeier, M., Crawford, J.D.: Linear vector models of time perception account for saccade and stimulus novelty interactions. bioRxiv (2021). https://doi.org/10.1101/2020.07.13.201087
6. Gorea, A.: Ticks per thought or thoughts per tick? A selective review of time perception with hints on future research. J. Physiol.-Paris **105**(4), 153–163 (2011). https://doi.org/10.1016/j.jphysparis.2011.09.008
7. van der Ham, I.J., Klaassen, F., van Schie, K., Cuperus, A.: Elapsed time estimates in virtual reality and the physical world: the role of arousal and emotional valence. Comput. Hum. Behav. **94**, 77–81 (2019). https://doi.org/10.1016/j.chb.2019.01.005
8. Hammerschmidt, D., Wöllner, C., London, J., Burger, B.: Disco time: the relationship between perceived duration and tempo in music. Music Sci. **4**, 2059204320986384 (2021). https://doi.org/10.1177/2059204320986384
9. Hoagland, H.: The physiological control of judgments of duration: evidence for a chemical clock. J. Gen. Psychol. **9**(2), 267–287 (1933). https://doi.org/10.1080/00221309.1933.9920937
10. Igarzábal, F.A., Hruby, H., Witowska, J., Khoshnoud, S., Wittmann, M.: What happens while waiting in virtual reality? A comparison between a virtual and a real waiting situation concerning boredom, self-regulation, and the experience of time. Technol. Mind Behav. **2**(2) (2021). https://doi.org/10.1037/tmb0000038. https://tmb.apaopen.org/pub/what-happens-while-waiting-in-virtual-reality

11. Jackson, S.A., Eklund, R.C.: Assessing flow in physical activity: the flow state scale–2 and dispositional flow scale–2. J. Sport Exerc. Psychol. **24**(2), 133–150 (2002). https://doi.org/10.1123/jsep.24.2.133

12. Lukas, S., Philipp, A.M., Koch, I.: Crossmodal attention switching: auditory dominance in temporal discrimination tasks. Acta Physiol. **153**, 139–146 (2014). https://doi.org/10.1016/j.actpsy.2014.10.003

13. Makwana, M., Srinivasan, N.: Intended outcome expands in time. Sci. Rep. **7**(1), 6305 (2017). https://doi.org/10.1038/s41598-017-05803-1

14. Mallam, S.C., Ernstsen, J., Nazir, S.: Accuracy of time duration estimations in virtual reality. Proc. Hum. Factors Ergon. Soc. Ann. Meet. **64**(1), 2079–2083 (2020). https://doi.org/10.1177/1071181320641503

15. Mullen, G., Davidenko, N.: Time compression in virtual reality. Timing Time Percept. **9**, 1–16 (2021). https://doi.org/10.1163/22134468-bja10034

16. Nah, F., Eschenbrenner, B.: Flow experience in virtual worlds: individuals versus dyads. In: SIGHCI 2015 Proceedings (2015). https://aisel.aisnet.org/sighci2015/19

17. Pelet, J.É., Ettis, S., Cowart, K.: Optimal experience of flow enhanced by telepresence: evidence from social media use. Inf. Manag. **54**(1), 115–128 (2017). https://doi.org/10.1016/j.im.2016.05.001

18. Peters, C.M., Glazebrook, C.M.: Rhythmic auditory stimuli heard before and during a reaching movement elicit performance improvements in both temporal and spatial movement parameters. Acta Physiol. **207**, 103086 (2020). https://doi.org/10.1016/j.actpsy.2020.103086

19. Picard, S., Botev, J.: Rhythmic stimuli effects on subjective time perception in immersive virtual environments. In: Proceedings of the 14th International Workshop on Immersive Mixed and Virtual Environment Systems, MMVE 2022, pp. 5–11. Association for Computing Machinery, New York (2022). https://doi.org/10.1145/3534086.3534330

20. Picard, S., Botev, J.: Rhythmic stimuli and time experience in virtual reality - complete data. Analysis (2023). https://doi.org/10.5281/zenodo.8321053

21. Reid, D.: A model of playfulness and flow in virtual reality interactions. Presence Teleoperators Virtual Environ. **13**(4), 451–462 (2004). https://doi.org/10.1162/1054746041944777

22. Roseboom, W., Fountas, Z., Nikiforou, K., Bhowmik, D., Shanahan, M., Seth, A.K.: Activity in perceptual classification networks as a basis for human subjective time perception. Nat. Commun. **10**(1), 267 (2019). https://doi.org/10.1038/s41467-018-08194-7

23. Rutrecht, H., Wittmann, M., Khoshnoud, S., Igarzábal, F.A.: Time speeds up during flow states: a study in virtual reality with the video game thumper. Timing Time Percept. **9**(4), 353–376 (2021). https://doi.org/10.1163/22134468-bja10033

24. Schatzschneider, C., Bruder, G., Steinicke, F.: Who turned the clock? Effects of manipulated zeitgebers, cognitive load and immersion on time estimation. IEEE Trans. Visual Comput. Graphics **22**(4), 1387–1395 (2016). https://doi.org/10.1109/tvcg.2016.2518137

25. Unruh, F., Landeck, M., Oberdörfer, S., Lugrin, J.L., Latoschik, M.E.: The influence of avatar embodiment on time perception - towards VR for time-based therapy. Front. Virtual Reality **2**, 658509 (2021). https://doi.org/10.3389/frvir.2021.658509

26. Wang, X., Wöllner, C., Shi, Z.: Perceiving tempo in incongruent audiovisual presentations of human motion: evidence for a visual driving effect. Timing Time Percept. **10**(1), 75–95 (2021). https://doi.org/10.1163/22134468-bja10036

27. Watt, J.D.: Effect of boredom proneness on time perception. Psychol. Rep. **69**(1), 323–327 (1991). https://doi.org/10.2466/pr0.1991.69.1.323. pMID: 1961817
28. Wöllner, C., Hammerschmidt, D.: Tapping to hip-hop: effects of cognitive load, arousal, and musical meter on time experiences. Atten. Percept. Psychophys. **83**(4), 1552–1561 (2021). https://doi.org/10.3758/s13414-020-02227-4

Designing XR Experiences

A Mixed Reality Setup for Prototyping Holographic Cockpit Instruments

Sven Liedtke[1]([⊠]) [ID], Michael Zintl[2] [ID], Florian Holzapfel[2] [ID],
and Gudrun Klinker[1] [ID]

[1] Technical University of Munich, TUM School of Computation, Information and
Technology, Boltzmannstraße 3, 85748 Garching b. München, Germany
{sven.liedtke,gudrun.klinker}@tum.de
[2] Technical University of Munich, TUM School of Engineering and Design, Institute
of Flight System Dynamics, Boltzmannstr. 15, 85748 Garching b. München, Germany
{michael.zintl,florian.holzapfel}@tum.de

Abstract. This paper discusses a possible solution to allow rapid prototyping of augmented reality content for evaluating user assistance systems. Building upon current approaches from the automotive context,
it presents options to transfer these to the aerospace context, focusing
on upcoming electric Vertical Take-Off and Landing aircraft. By showing issues of using optical-see-through glasses inside a moving simulator,
a solution for using video-see-through head-mounted displays instead is
presented. As a solution, a modular system setup that can handle different rendering sources to create contact-analog augmentations on top of a
virtual environment while using video-see-through capabilities to interact with the physical cockpit environment is presented. The main contribution is a process to avoid manual calibration between the different
coordinate systems across the involved applications. To further discuss
holographic content for vehicle-based augmentations, a first taxonomy
is discussed on locating augmentations to prototype such concepts with
the presented *Mixed-Reality-Simulator*.

Keywords: XR System Architecture · Augmented virtuality ·
Tracking and motion technologies · Contact-Analog Augmentations ·
Prototyping · Aerospace and Transport · Motion Compensation ·
Flight Simulator

1 Introduction

Mixed Reality (MR) is already utilized in many aspects of industrial applications [6]. Applications in the aviation and automotive industry [16] are mainly
based on Heads-Up Displays (HUDs). Yet, in aviation, HUDs present only

S. Liedtke and M. Zintl—contributed equally to this work
Supported by "Bayerisches Staatsministerium für Wirtschaft, Landesentwicklung und
Energie"

Bayerisches Staatsministerium für
Wirtschaft, Landesentwicklung und Energie

G. Zachmann et al. (Eds.): EuroXR 2023, LNCS 14410, pp. 79–92, 2023.
https://doi.org/10.1007/978-3-031-48495-7_5

the most crucial information about the vehicle state. They usually show little contact-analog information related to real-world positions. Following Milgram's classification of displays for augmentation [5], head-worn displays are the next level for augmentation. Head-worn displays are already technologically advanced enough to provide another means of showing and potentially overlaying relevant information directly in the user's field of view. The next logical step is to utilize a Head-Mounted Display (HMD) also for pilots to provide augmented content overlaid in the real or simulated environment, as seen for navigation purposes presented by Haiduk [4]. Under the premise that more technologically advanced HMDs will become available and licensed for aerospace usage, we can start developing Augmented Reality (AR)-based pilot assistance solutions using stereoscopic displays, reliable eye tracking, and vehicle positional data. Meanwhile, there are ideas to overcome the limitations of a built-in HUD towards more advanced augmentation concepts presented by [8,15].

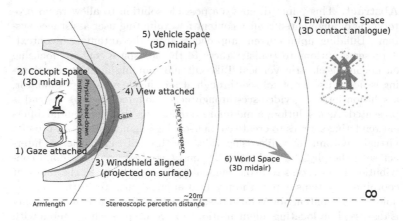

Fig. 1. *Holographic Content Spaces* showing relations between virtual content, physical cockpit, and exterior environment.

Tönnis describes the difference between augmented information displayed to a user in HMDs and real contact-analog overlays in HUDs [10]. To find suitable prototypes for in-cockpit augmentations, but also for contact-analog ones, the final concept has to be evaluated based on reliable user study data to identify usable augmentations in a 3D environment similar to Schneider et al. [8].

This paper presents a way to easily calibrate a *Mixed-Reality-Simulator (MRSim)* setup to speed up the design evaluation process for a holistic holographic cockpit experience inside a moving cockpit-based vehicle, like the electric Vertical Take-Off and Landing aircraft (eVTOL). It presents an *MRSim* setup that allows rapid prototyping to a full augmentation of the user's view, including contact-analog holograms, with multiple applications by avoiding manual calibration between the different coordinate systems while including real-world via a video feed. Our long-term goal is to identify how a holistic cockpit concept can be designed with contact-analog holograms to enhance spatial and situational awareness during flight and reduce the pilot's cognitive load.

In Sect. 2, we propose a holistic approach, defining *holographic content spaces*, considering a cockpit scenario to discuss virtual content alignment in a rapid prototyping process. In Sect. 3, we outline the setup of an MR assisted eVTOL flight simulator utilizing a motion platform to develop and test such a concept. Section 3 addresses visualization issues, requiring that several coordinate systems be merged to generate contact-analog content. In the future, this setup will be used for the rapid prototyping of holographic elements and to simulate AR content in MR, as outlined in Sect. 6.

2 Foundations of Holistic Cockpit Designs with AR

Different concepts for user interfaces and information visualization for AR applications identify various approaches to render information in the user's view. Tönnis et al. highlight the difference between *presenting* and *representing* to discuss possibilities of how content should be organized and located in an AR presentation space [11]. Following their five dimensions, *temporality, dimensionality, frame of reference, mounting and registration*, we have derived seven holographic content spaces for use in a holistic cockpit concept considering aviation contexts, shown in Fig. 1).

The seven holographic design spaces are meant to identify suitable locations depending on the pilot's tasks and the information linked to specific holographic cockpit elements for the user interface to be highly adaptive, as pointed out by Lavie et al. [9]. A final concept thus should take the current vehicle operating status, the pilot's task, and the environmental conditions into account. Possibilities for the concept spaces are derived from current AR HMDs to benefit from the tracking, head pose estimation, and depth perception using stereoscopic displays for personal space augmentation. Combined with the vehicle information about its global positioning during operation, we extend the pilot's content area by information inside the cockpit and outside the vehicle. Furthermore, midair holographic elements can visualize three-dimensional data without a physical counterpart, existing in the world coordinate system, and contact-analog holograms that ideally align perfectly with real-world geometries. As described by Tönnis [10]: AR content with a "strong dependency on the physical state and behavior of the environment. AR schemes smoothly integrate into the environment."

1. *Gaze attached*: virtual content that is gaze attached should be shown all the time, occluding other real or virtual content in the user's view. Using the gaze as a *frame of reference*, information should only be rendered in 2D at a suitable distance from the user and is intended only for high-priority content; a pilot should not overlook it. In combination with an aural alarm that could be an icon-based indication for a collision warning or engine failure, in case the pilot looks in a different direction.
2. *Cockpit Space*: The interior of the cockpit could be used for 3D and 2D content classes. As a *frame of reference*, the relative position inside the cockpit is needed, virtual content stays fixed in the cockpit. This placement aims

to reduce cognitive load by reducing the task of searching for information. All information should be connected to the user's vehicle, like acceleration, remaining range or relative to its current position, like a 3-dimensional height profile from the ground below. This space extends the traditional, but limited, space for physical instruments in a cockpit.

3. *Windshield aligned*: Content that is either in 2D or projected onto a 2D plane similar to a HUD, but with a much larger Field of View (FOV). This could be a point of interest in the environment, virtually highlighted at the user's windshield, where no depth perception is required or not possible due to large distances. This space replaces the need for a traditional HUD, which requires a lot of physical space and is limited in optical projection size. The *frame of reference* is still the cockpit and not connected to the pilot's view space. So, information is not moved if the pilot looks around.

4. *View attached*: Information that relies on the pilot's view. It contains visualizations in 2D or 3D and uses the pose of the HMD as *frame of reference*. This space is also reserved for a higher priority of information, as this may disturb the pilot in the current task or block the line of sight to important content in the vehicle's exterior. This space can direct the pilot's attention towards important information in another space, e.g., windshield aligned or environmental space.

5. *Vehicle Space*: Can be used to locate content in the exterior of the cockpit, but still using the vehicle position as *point of reference*. Information should be connected to the current vehicle state or operation. Like holograms showing the current turning rate.

6. *World Space*: This space is suitable for all content not connected to a specific physical structure on the earth's surface, but fixed on a specific geo-referenced point as *frame of reference*. Content should be presented using 3D representations, to enhance visibility in any direction. As example, a virtual gate for flying on a specific route can be floating in midair, and the vehicle can move through it, without any danger of colliding with obstacles.

7. *Environment Space*: This is used for all information connected to the earth's surface, where a contact-analog representation is needed. This can be used for any geo-referenced content, like point of interests, landing spots, and obstacles like artificial structures.

For the design of such new cockpit concepts benefiting from AR, a suitable environment for evaluation and testing must be found. Schneider et al. showed in their work on prototypes for augmented car navigation how important it is to identify design concepts that focus on reducing the cognitive load for navigation in a two-dimensional space and necessary realistic tests with augmentation-based concepts [8]. Using an optical-see-through HMD (OST-HMD), like the *Microsoft HoloLens 2*, is problematic in flight simulators. The projection on flat or curved surfaces for a dome projection leads to artifacts and adjustments on the augmented content [13,14]. The virtual content must be distorted to correctly overlay the projected outside environment. Not only does this affect the visual accuracy of objects, but it also completely removes any stereoscopic aspect of the AR visualization for geo-fixed overlays. All content is rendered at the exact distance of the projection screen to the user. Thus, any assistance relying on the stereoscopic perception of pilots cannot be correctly evaluated.

For a motion-based simulator, a projection has to cover a lot more space than in a fixed-base simulator due to the extended area of motion in comparison to just the head movement of the user. In addition, standalone AR headsets can only work reliably in a fixed environment without external forces as these can influence the internal tracking algorithm, such as the *Microsoft HoloLens 2* [14]. Deriving from these conditions, the need for controllable and safe conditions to evaluate such a complex user interface approach leads to an *MRSim*, allowing rapid prototyping and feedback loops with trained and untrained pilots.

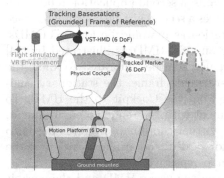

(a) Concept drawing of the *MRSim* - The physical cockpit mounted on a motion platform to have 6DoF of movement, in a ground fixed tracking environment.

(b) User's view through the Varjo XR-3 with video see-through of the physical cockpit (black area becomes see-through).

Fig. 2. *MRSim* from the side view (left) and the user's view (right). The blue line indicates content from the environment application and the green line shows content from the hologram application. (Color figure online)

3   Mixed-Reality-Simulator Environment

To properly evaluate AR concepts, a low-fidelity prototype or mock-up does not provide the required fidelity. Although Barbosa et al. [1] show advantages in the early stages of development, it is not possible to predict the outcome of a product-ready version, i.e., missing stereoscopic depth, color, or registration errors, to generate meaningful results. To overcome the limitations and artifacts of using an OST-HMD inside a physical cockpit prototype, we use a video HMD with stereo cameras to provide a real-time video-feed, streaming the actual cockpit, combined with virtual use case-specific content (see Fig. 2b).

Our *MRSim* is following the thoughts on the *Virtuality Continuum* [5], merging real environment with virtual content that correlates in location and time. This MR view allows for a relatively compact simulator since the user is provided with a full virtual 360○ surround view of the environment by the headset and there is no need for a physical screen. We used the Varjo XR-3[1] mixed reality HMD to provide a seamless integration of the real environment with the virtual one via a video-see-through HMD (VST-HMD).

To render a virtual environment suitable to fly user studies with a self-developed vehicle behavior, any *OpenVR* or *OpenXR* compatible flight simulator can be used, in this case, *X-Plane 11*[2]. Following the modular simulator setup described in [17], this software is only utilized for visualization while the flight simulation is running in a separate application.

To overlay the virtual world with holograms, a second application renders on top of the user's current view, which introduces a second virtual coordinate space independent of the environment representation as it would be for OSTHMDs. In contrast to the calibration problem for an OST-HMD as illustrated by [14] for contact-analog holograms, the *MRSim* needs to be calibrated to know the relative transformation from the tracking-reference frame, the stationary environment, to the pose of the cockpit and from the Cockpit to the HMD. To display the holograms in the correct alignment with the rendered environment, the relative transformation between both virtual coordinate systems needs to be registered. As shared knowledge, the forward direction and position of the cockpit has to be aligned to get the correct perspective for a user.

To determine the relative change between the user's HMD and the cockpit pose, an additional tracker mounted on top of the cockpit nose. This serves two purposes. First, it tracks the movement of the motion platform and, second, it is used as a shared origin for all virtual coordinate spaces as shown in Fig. 3. In this case, a *VIVE tracker* is placed in the same tracked coordinate space as the HMD. This provides a precise 6-Degree of Freedom (DoF) transformation of the cockpit for each frame, even while operating the moving platform. From this pose, we can calculate the relative pose of the HMD with respect to the cockpit tracker. Otherwise, the tracking based on the fixed exterior as a reference for the HMD would detect a motion of the user's head, although only the cockpit is moved, but the user did not change his view relative to the cockpit (see Fig. 2a).

To include the MR capabilities of the VST-HMD, a previously configured shape specifies areas in the real world, such as the physical cockpit, that should be shown through the video feed to the user and merged with the Virtual Reality (VR) view by the *Varjo SDK*. One possibility is to use a visual marker, a *Varjo* specific image marker, attached in the real world as a reference point for the blend mask and tracked constantly through the video cameras by the *Varjo* SDK. However, this method is not reliable in certain lighting conditions and varies in stability due to the camera-based approach [3]. Therefore, we propose that the MR area is also defined in the same compensated tracking space relative to the

---

[1] https://varjo.com/products/xr-3/ (accessed on 15 May 2023).
[2] https://www.x-plane.com/ (accessed on 15 May 2023).

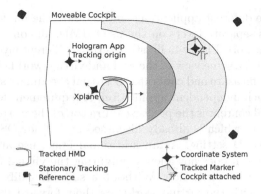

Fig. 3. Tracking setup with tracked markers and virtual origins from different applications involved in our *MRSim*.

shared anchor, being the *Vive tracker*. Following this setting in a naive way, there are four different virtual origins, the HMD tracking space, the hologram application, the *X-Plane 11* coordinate system, and the Varjo MR mask shown in Fig. 3.

To identify the relative pose between the user's view and the cockpit located in the (virtual) world, it is not possible to rely on the default tracking algorithms. While they work in a fixed-based simulator, there will be problems when operating a setup involving a motion platform. Here, any movement of the platform will also move the headset, thus resulting in a change of view for the pilot because the tracking coordinate system is fixed on the ground. Therefore, the only viable setup is to have the base stations located on the ground to provide stable tracking in all situations to overcome technical limitations by using active tracking systems in a moved environment.

To compensate for the platform movement, the view matrix calculated by *OpenVR* has to be corrected by the amount of movement caused by the platform itself. For this compensation, an open-source *OpenVR* driver, namely *OpenVR Motion Compensation*[3], can be used in *OpenVR* tracking applications.

For contact-analog holograms, more steps are necessary. As all applications share the same tracking space, handled by *OpenVR*, a stable solution for merging all applications into one virtual origin has to be found. This problem was solved by extending the aforementioned *OpenVR motion compensation* software and is described in Sect. 4.

4   Contact-Analog Merging of Mixed Reality Layers

Based on the motion compensation provided by *OpenVR motion compensation*, separate applications still use different coordinate systems, inhibiting the correct overlay of contact-analog content, as shown in Fig. 3. To align the virtual view of

---

[3] https://github.com/openvrmc/ (Accessed 15 May 2023).

the user across the different applications and to allow the rendering of arbitrary content sources as separate layers on the used HMD, all content has to be seen from the same view port. Figure 4a illustrates three different layers presented to a user, which rely on the same view of the real and virtual world. A manual process can be designed to measure and calibrate all virtual coordinate systems to a given fixed 6 DOF for each independent application. A requirement for contact-analog rendering of virtual content is the precise calibration of the virtual tracking origin for each application, which is already discussed by [12] for OSTHMDs systems and by [7] for a HUD setting. As an additional issue, use arbitrary software, like *X-Plane 11*, which does not allow configuring the virtual forward direction relative to the vehicle orientation. Without a suitable calibration, holograms would not match with the virtual world, as their forward direction does not match with the hologram's one.

To overcome this, we introduce an automated calibration process using available tracking capabilities of the *OpenVR* framework. The independent applications share the same physical display to mix virtual content with contact-analog holograms, depending on real-world states but without linked coordinate spaces. This gives the same registration issues, as in other AR scenarios, to locate the HMD view in relation to the real world. Therefore, Echtler et al. [2] show a solution to illustrate and resolve dependencies between different content elements. In Fig. 4 the different steps in the setup are illustrated and show the three

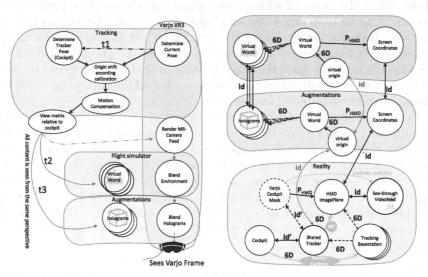

(a) Data flow of calibration with shared origin showing in between relationships (t1..t3).

(b) Proposed setup where calibration is automated using a physical tracker to unify coordinate systems along the green edges.

Fig. 4. Tracking data flow and Spatial Relationship Graph (SRG) with finally calibrated relations (green) to register independent applications to each other. (Color figure online)

coordinate systems involved in our *MRSim*. The image plane of the HMD has to present an identical view for the user as in reality (connected with green arrows) and shares the same image plane with the other applications. This derives for the SRG in Fig. 4b the need for an *identity* transformation (id) to handle the relation between the virtual content and the HMD image-plane. Other rigid transformation relationships are symbolized with 6D or with Id' if a static origin shift needs to be registered beforehand but does not change.

To achieve a valid MR user experience, a prior registration and calibration process has to be performed. For contact-analog augmentations, this calibration has to be as precise as possible and has to be repeated each time anything in the setup or tracking of *OpenVR* changes. As shown in Fig. 4 we have three major parts in the simulator that have to rely on a perfect manual calibration to visualize holographic cockpit elements with an VST-HMD. This process targets the calibration of the virtual HMD's tracking origin for each application as closest to the point of the cockpit pose relative to the user's head pose.

In the SRG shown in Fig. 4b, the *Motion Compensation (MC')* can act as a central part to reduce the number of independent coordinate systems. The limited calibration possibility of the flight simulator is mitigated by the pose of the tracker through the motion compensation driver to perform an automated registration. As the hologram application is controlled by ourselves, the Vive tracker can be integrated into the scene graph and used as a virtual origin for the reference coordinate system containing all virtual objects relative to the cockpit, which is static in all scenes. The change of tracking origin, in combination with the modified *Motion Compensation* part, to utilize the single tracker, shown as *Tr* in Fig. 2a, to work as the shared origin for each virtual coordinate system. This is achieved by changing the *Motion Compensation Driver*, to distribute the position of the *Tr* as the current HMD position and orientation. During that, all involved 3rd-party applications can now align their virtual forward direction to exactly the same orientation, by recenter to the distributed view matrix through *OpenVR*. This process can be completely automated, and the initialization is part of the start-up procedure of the *MRSim*, independent of any changes to the surround tracking system or the current HMD pose and can be reduced to just a view seconds without any involvement of a user.

With this process we can synchronize arbitrary applications with a known center position used as a reference origin for all virtual scenes. After the calibration, the headset position in world space is overwritten by the modified motion compensation driver, which calculates the HMD's pose relative to the new virtual origin, which is always identical to the physical tracker. With this very short and HMD-independent calibration process, we are able to overlay all view spaces relative to our tracking reference marker and produce a completely aligned view with independent virtual coordinate systems to allow contact-analog rendering by sharing the HMD's image-plane across different applications.

5 Evaluation of the Automated Calibration Approach

For an objective analysis of the automated implemented calibration, different approaches were integrated into the *MRSim* and tested.

Study Setup: As part of the experiment, four different approaches were implemented. Three forms of manual alignment processes and the automated solution that is proposed in this paper. Table 1 provides an overview. The setup focuses on the calibration of the orientation between the different coordinate systems. While it is expected that the positional offset is proportional to the orientation, any misalignment in the orientation is more severe for this use case. The further away the object is from the user, the more is precise orientation more important than precise translation. Therefore, world-fixed objects, such as the highlight of a landing pad, require a very precise orientation while any translational offset within the cockpit can be neglected. The calibration itself was conducted at least 10 times per calibration approach by two different experienced persons. Thus, 144 measurements in total were recorded.

The first manual process is using the built-in reset functionality of the viewpoint of the visualization engine, here *X-Plane 11*. This is both the most simplistic, but also the easiest approach regarding the implementation. The default viewpoint in *X-Plane 11* is positioned at the expected head position of the pilot. When calibrating the view, the user wearing the HMD will be asked to look straight forward and the camera position is manually reset to the default position. Therefore, if the pilots' head orientation and position match this preconfigured viewpoint, the coordinate systems are now aligned.

The second approach also involves a manual calibration step while wearing the headset. Here, a visual reference is shown through the HMD. One virtual marker is attached to the head-fixed coordinate system, while the other is located in the world-fixed simulator system. It is the task of the user to align these two markers. Then, the manual calibration is triggered and the coordinate systems should be aligned. It is based on the calibration process for OST-HMD [14].

In the third manual approach, the headset is moved to a dedicated physical location. This location can be used as a known anchor point for the manual calibration process. This physical location can be the origin of the coordinate

Table 1. Overview of the tested calibration options (Manual 1–3, Automatic: 4)

No.	Calibration approach	Operator actions	User actions
1	Approximation to default viewpoint without reference	Resets viewpoint after confirming alignment visually	Looks straight and level forwards
2	Approximation using visual reference	Triggers calibration and sets viewpoint after confirming alignment visually	Looks at calibration reference
3	Physically placing HMD to a static calibration point	Places headset into physical location and triggers calibration	none
4	Automated calibration using external tracker	None	none

system. Therefore, different coordinate systems can be aligned by placing the HMD to this position and then starting the calibration. Fourth is our proposed automated calibration process.

Table 2. Offsets in degrees with different calibration approaches

	1 Approximation	2 Visual Reference	3 Physical calibration point	4 Automatic
Variance	1,49883055	0,23491168	0,098355210	0
Mean	4,8346592	3,17905575	1,693704746	0
Std. deviation	1,13374767	0,42380653	0,223628945	0
Median	4,73958164	3,15134728	1,702962428	0

Results: The results in Table 2 show a strong deviation during a manual calibration with a worn headset. In contrast, the variance with a static calibration point is rather low, as only a small jitter during the different measures is recognizable. The quality of this calibration relies heavenly on a very good calibration point for the HMD. Figure 5 illustrates the perceived image by the pilot when comparing the average orientation offset between the four approaches. With the proposed automated approach, a zero-degree offset is possible and thus, a perfect alignment because all coordinate systems share the same anchor when the calibration is successful.

Discussion: In Fig. 5 a rather small error of 1o, which is not achieved by any calibration process with a worn headset, leads to a wrong indication for the pilot. Here is not the intended green pad marked, but already the pad 30m next to it, highlighted with pink. The Table 2 showed, that a static calibration position can result in a better calibration. Nevertheless, this needs a trained person who interrupts the current user process and needs to be done very patiently.

The small experiment showed, that a small error is always contained in a manual calibration process it is not possible to do it synchronously in time and 100% aligned with an existing reference system. Fig. 5 demonstrated that even a small misalignment can cause visible offsets and problems. The measured results are in line with the expectations when using a manual calibration process, especially when performed without a visual reference.

6   Rapid Prototyping for Simulating AR in MR

In the future, the hardware and software architecture described in this paper will enable further research into holographic cockpit elements and their evaluation. Starting with this *MRSim* for eVTOLs, we have a controlled environment for operating with trained and untrained persons to conduct user studies on various instrument content. This can be used to identify the optimal solution to decode geospatial and informational data in the user's *holographic content spaces* to assist the pilot during its tasks. With an iterative process, we can operate on a system that allows rapid prototyping in a controlled system. As an additional benefit, the concept of a *MRSim* can also be adapted to other fixed and motion-based simulators where a stationary tracking system can be applied. It is also not limited to the aerospace concept: the holographic content space can be transmitted to all kinds of vehicle operations.

We showed that it is possible to easily calibrate a complex *MRSim* to allow prototyping of content for upcoming augmented assistance systems. Unfortunately, using VR glasses with video-see-through features hides essential technical limitations that current optical-see-through HMDs have. Two major aspects, the limited FOV for virtual content is much smaller, in contrast to the 115o horizontal FOV of the Varjo XR-3. The second one is the missing functionality to fully shadow a single display pixel to allow full opaque virtual content on top of the real geometry. To allow a transfer of the design concepts to a realistic AR-supported holistic cockpit concept, these limitations have to be integrated into the application to render the holograms to the user's view in our *MRSim*. Otherwise, any evaluation performed with this setup is not applicable to the user experience when wearing AR glasses in a real aircraft.

Fig. 5. Pilot view on four landing pads with a size of 20 m x 20 m each. The correct destination is highlighted in green. Calibration misalignment is shown in pink with 1° and 3° in blue. (Color figure online)

7   Conclusion

The *MRSim* setup described in this paper allows the prototyping of holographic cockpit instruments. Following the proposed holistic concept of *holographic content spaces* throughout the view area of the pilot, arbitrary virtual content can now be designed, located, and evaluated in a realistic 3D environment. The utilization of an MR headset with video-see-through technology merges the real physical cockpit with a virtual environment and allows for a compact simulator setup incorporating a motion platform. As part of this paper, a compensation and tracking solution is introduced to merge several MR layers using a combined virtual origin for independent coordinate systems. For this purpose, a physical tracker was utilized, that is used to compensate the motion of the moving platform from the tracked HMD movement and serve as the aforementioned origin anchor. This modular simulator setup not only allows the simulation of various aircraft, but is also suitable for other concepts, where a cockpit or vehicle is involved. The same setup, e.g., by replacing the control inceptors with a steering wheel, could also be used for the evaluation of MR overlays for cars and other vehicles. This general solution to mix various application layers with a virtual origin is not restricted to any specific headset and is applicable to any environment based on *OpenVR* tracking. This would allow future usage in various use cases, ranging from contact-analog content in professional simulators to overlays in games. Furthermore, this enables the prototyping of AR content in a compact, reproducible, and virtual environment before testing the AR concept in the real-world.

References

1. Barbosa, S., et al. (eds.): Elements of XR prototyping: characterizing the role and use of prototypes in augmented and virtual reality design. ACM, New York (2022). https://doi.org/10.1145/3491102
2. Echtler, F., Huber, M.J., Pustka, D., Keitler, P., Klinker, G.: Splitting the scene graph. In: Proceedings of the International Conference on Computer Graphics Theory and Applications (GRAPP), pp. 456–459. INSTICC, Funchal, Madeira (2008)
3. Ernst, J.M., Laudien, T., Schmerwitz, S.: Implementation of a mixed-reality flight simulator: blending real and virtual with a video-see-through head-mounted display. In: Solomon, L., Schwartz, P.J. (eds.) Artificial Intelligence and Machine Learning for Multi-Domain Operations Applications V, vol. 12538, p. 125380R. International Society for Optics and Photonics, SPIE (2023). https://doi.org/10.1117/12.2664848
4. Haiduk, P.M.: Display formats for smart glasses to support pilots in general aviation. Ph.D. thesis, Technische Universität Darmstadt, Darmstadt, Germany (2017)
5. Milgram, P., Kishino, F.: A taxonomy of mixed reality visual displays. IEICE Trans. Inf. Syst. **E77-D**(12), 1321–1329 (1994)
6. Pierdicca, R., Frontoni, E., Pollini, R., Trani, M., Verdini, L.: The use of augmented reality glasses for the application in industry 4.0. In: De Paolis, L.T., Bourdot, P., Mongelli, A. (eds.) AVR 2017. LNCS, vol. 10324, pp. 389–401. Springer, Cham (2017). https://doi.org/10.1007/978-3-319-60922-5_30
7. Poitschke, T., Ablassmeier, M., Rigoll, G., Bardins, S., Kohlbecher, S., Schneider, E.: Contact-analog information representation in an automotive head-up display. In: Proceedings of the 2008 Symposium on Eye Tracking Research & Applications, ETRA '08, pp. 119–122. Association for Computing Machinery, New York (2008). https://doi.org/10.1145/1344471.1344502
8. Schneider, M., Bruder, A., Necker, M., Schluesener, T., Henze, N., Wolff, C.: A real-world driving experiment to collect expert knowledge for the design of AR HUD navigation that covers less. In: Mensch und Computer 2019 - Workshopband. Gesellschaft fur Informatik E.V., Bonn (2019). https://doi.org/10.18420/muc2019-ws-610

9. Lavie, T., Meyer, J.: Benefits and costs of adaptive user interfaces. Int. J. Hum Comput Stud. **68**(8), 508–524 (2010). https://doi.org/10.1016/j.ijhcs.2010.01.004

10. Tönnis, M.: Towards automotive augmented reality. Dissertation, Technische Universität München (2008)

11. Tönnis, M., Plecher, D.A., Klinker, G.: Representing information-classifying the augmented reality presentation space. Comput. Graph. **37**(8), 997–1011 (2013)

12. Tuceryan, M., Navab, N.: Single point active alignment method (SPAAM) for optical see-through HMD calibration for AR. In: Proceedings IEEE and ACM International Symposium on Augmented Reality (ISAR 2000), pp. 149–158 (2000). https://doi.org/10.1109/ISAR.2000.880938

13. Viertler, F.: Visual augmentation for rotorcraft pilots in degraded visual environment. Ph.D. thesis (2017)

14. Walko, C., Schuchardt, B.: Increasing helicopter flight safety in maritime operations with a head-mounted display. CEAS Aeronaut. J. **12**(1), 29–41 (2021)

15. Wiesner, C.A.: Increasing the maturity of the augmented reality head-up-display. Dissertation, Technische Universität München (2019)

16. Wiesner, C.A., Ruf, M., Sirim, D., Klinker, G.: 3D-FRC: depiction of the future road course in the head-up-display. In: 2017 IEEE International Symposium on Mixed and Augmented Reality (ISMAR), pp. 136–143 (2017). https://doi.org/10.1109/ISMAR.2017.30

17. Zintl, M., Marb, M., Wechner, M., Seiferth, D., Holzapfel, F.: Development of a virtual reality simulator for eVTOL flight testing. In: AIAA Aviation Forum 2022 (2022). https://doi.org/10.2514/6.2022-3941

AR Patterns: Event-Driven Design Patterns in Creating Augmented Reality Experiences

Philipp Ackermann$^{(\boxtimes)}$

School of Engineering, Zurich University of Applied Sciences, Winterthur, Switzerland
`philipp.ackermann@zhaw.ch`

Abstract. Augmented Reality (AR) and Mixed Reality (MR) enable superimposing digital content onto the real world. These technologies have now matured to a point where low-code/no-code editors for AR development have emerged. However, existing collections of design principles for AR often fall short, either being too generic or overly focused on low-level details. This makes it challenging to identify the essential patterns necessary for creating captivating AR experiences. This paper addresses this issue by introducing high-level AR design patterns encompassing fundamental concepts for crafting immersive AR experiences. Event-Condition-Action rules are leveraged as a generic abstraction from the reactive behavior of AR software systems to establish a unified framework. AR-specific behavioral patterns and augmentation patterns are presented in detail. Additionally, a uniform pattern diagram schema is proposed that ensures consistent presentation and technology-agnostic documentation of AR design patterns, facilitating their effective use in design and creation of AR applications.

Keywords: Augmented Reality · Design Patterns · Reactive AR · Scene Understanding · Active Rules · AR Pattern Diagram

1 Introduction

1.1 Augmented Reality Design Patterns

Design patterns are a widely accepted concept for documenting proven solutions to recurring design problems. Initially adapted from building architecture to software development by Gamma et.al. [1] in the mid-90s the idea has become a central concept in software engineering. Design patterns have been extensively applied to various aspects of software development, including system architectures and user interfaces, and have proven to be an effective tool for improving software quality, reusability, and maintainability.

Design patterns for virtual, augmented, and mixed reality have recently gained momentum [2–4]. Over the last decade, augmented reality (AR) technology has experienced strong advancements, resulting in a growing number of successful AR solutions. To capture and share this knowledge, design patterns have been proposed for developing AR applications on different levels of abstraction, including *software components*, *system architectures*, and *user interfaces*.

G. Zachmann et al. (Eds.): EuroXR 2023, LNCS 14410, pp. 93–114, 2023.
https://doi.org/10.1007/978-3-031-48495-7_6

Design Patterns for AR Software Components focus on applying generic software design patterns, such as Composite, Iterator, and Chain of Responsibility, to capture the relationships and interactions between classes or objects. These patterns can be viewed as solution templates for solving common challenges in AR software development at the object-oriented programming level.

Design Patterns for AR System Architectures center around the coordination of various subsystems, such as computer vision, rendering, interaction, and networking. One example is the Augmented Reality Framework [5] developed by the European Telecommunications Standards Institute (ETSI) which is responsible for setting telecommunications and broadcasting standards. ETSI's Industry Specification Group (ISG) has developed a functional reference architecture that defines relevant components and interfaces to ensure AR components, systems, and services interoperability. Other efforts to establish similar standards can be found in references such as [6,7].

Design Patterns for AR User Interfaces provide guidelines for implementing user interfaces and best practices for interactions in AR. These design patterns primarily focus on adapting existing design heuristics for layout, interaction, and usability to meet AR requirements. Recently, meta-analysis studies of existing UI design patterns for AR have emerged, which provide a collection of best practices [8,9].

1.2   AR Experiences Driven by Understanding Spatial Context

Creating AR experiences poses additional challenges compared to designing virtual reality (VR) and 3D content (e.g., video games). When creating VR/3D scenes, designers are in control of the virtual world they are building (even if it's programmatically generated), thus taking a sort of "god role". AR experiences take place in the uncontrolled real world, and scene understanding algorithms detect the user's spatial context. The AR experience is then driven by elements detected in the real world, without having control over their occurrence and timing during the creation process. Consequently, adapting VR and 3D design patterns to AR do not fit well due to the loss of control in the real-world environment. It is therefore worth focusing on AR-specific design patterns that reflect the dynamic scenography of AR/MR experiences.

1.3   Motivation: Unifying High-Level AR Patterns

The current generation of AR software libraries (ARKit [10], ARCore [11], MRTK [12]), WebAR toolkits (AR.js [13], 8th Wall [14]), and AR frameworks (OpenXR [15], Unity AR Foundation [16], Vuforia [17]) offer reusable system components in run-time environments that provide a working system architecture for AR applications. These tools reduce the complexity of developing AR software, allowing developers to focus more on creating engaging AR experiences. As a result, the use of design patterns has shifted from low-level software programming and system architecture to more high-level best practices that focus on the creation of compelling AR experiences.

When tackling high-level topics related to AR it is an obvious choice to focus on design patterns for AR user interaction which are already well documented [8,9]. However, while there is a large collection of UI design principles for AR/MR, they tend to be either very generic (e.g., responsiveness, consistency, personalization, learnability) or focused on low-level aspects (e.g., navigation, selection and manipulation in 3D). As a result, it is challenging to identify which of the patterns are essential for creating AR experiences. The use of large, unspecific design pattern collections are of limited help in the authoring process.

The methodological approach employed in this paper is based on the analysis of the features and functionalities offered by existing Augmented Reality Software Development Kits (AR SDKs). Special attention was given to examining generic features that can be accessed and utilized within low-code/no-code AR editors such as Apple Reality Composer [18] and Adobe Aero [19]. The assessment of these features involved identifying and validating common patterns based on the author's experience in developing a mobile AR browser [20] and its associated editor toolkits [21].

The AR patterns proposed in this paper are motivated by the following objectives:

- Focusing on high-level concepts that are relevant in creating AR experiences.
- Including only patterns that are specific to AR and related to AR (i.e., excluding generic software design patterns or VR UI patterns).
- Generalizing from specific device hardware (e.g., hand-held or head-mounted devices), AR toolkits, and programming languages, so that the patterns can be applicable in different contexts.
- Unifying the AR patterns so that they can be consistently documented and presented as diagrams, making them easy to understand and apply.

2 Event-Condition-Action Pattern as Abstraction from Reactive AR System Architectures

To design reactive systems, breaking down the system's behavior into discrete events, conditions, and actions provides a structured and modular approach. An event is a signal that something has occurred, such as the start of an AR session (on:start), a user tapping on an item (on:tap), or the detection of an image marker (on:detect). The no-code editors in [18,19] are using a trigger-action mechanism to define the behavior of an AR scenario. We propose to use more flexible Event-Condition-Action (ECA) rules that perform an action in response to an event, provided that certain conditions are met. ECA rules are widely used in event-driven and reactive systems, such as active databases [22] and workflow systems [23]. In the context of AR patterns, ECA rules provide a generic abstraction of the reactive behavior of AR software systems.

Table 1. Event categories in AR applications.

Event Category	Event Producer	Cause → Event Examples
Session Event	AR Session	State change → `on:start`, `on:locating`
Invocation Event	Rule Initiation	Invocation → `on:command`, `on:call`
Detection Event	Installed Detector	Discovery of entity → `on:detect`
User Event	App User	User interaction → `on:tap`, `on:select`
Temporal Event	Time Scheduler	Elapsed time reached → `in:time`
Data-driven Event	Data Observer	Value change → `on:altered`, `as:steady`
Response Event	Remote Request	Response of REST call → `on:response`
Notification Event	Subscribed System	System change → `on:enter`, `on:leave`

2.1 Reactive AR Using Active ECA Rules

AR systems utilize a variety of sensors, such as cameras, LiDAR, accelerators, gyroscopes, magnetometers, and microphones, along with various event producers in operating system and user interfaces. These sensors and producers generate events asynchronously, which are then handled by event-driven programs. Unlike traditional programs that make function calls to these event producers themselves (in an inner loop), an event-driven program relies on the execution environment to dispatch events to installed event handlers. Thus, control over the execution of program logic is inverted (inversion of control).

To address the reactive nature of AR applications we promote ECA rules as a means of loosely coupling AR patterns with the underlying system architecture, while also abstracting from implementation details. AR patterns are designed to be loosely bound to the specific run-time system, since events that trigger actions within AR applications are not necessarily aware of the consequences of their occurrence. As a result, creators of AR experiences are primarily responsible for defining a set of event handling rules that govern how the system responds to various arising signals and events.

2.2 Event Categories in AR Applications

In software systems, events are typically generated by a producer and triggered by various circumstances. These events can vary greatly in nature. Regarding AR systems, we organized typical events into distinct categories, as shown in Table 1. Appendix A provides a list of common events within each event category for AR applications. Compared to other interactive 3D applications, the event categories *detection events* and *data-driven events* tend to dominate in AR.

Detection events are fundamental for AR experiences. Computer vision and machine learning techniques are applied for detecting entities in 3D space and continuously track their pose [24]. The behavior of an AR application is primarily controlled by installing the necessary detectors to receive the corresponding detection events. These events are produced when a particular type of object is detected by the specialized detector, including:

- *Location Detector*: Tracks world location and device pose in environment.
- *Feature Detector*: classifies feature as video stream label.
- *Segment Detector*: tracks feature as image segment in video stream.
- *Plane Detector*: detects plane in 3D space.
- *Image Detector*: recognizes and tracks image or marker in 3D space.
- *Text Detector*: detects text matched by regular expression in video or 3D.
- *Code Detector*: detects QR/barcode matched by regex in video or 3D.
- *Object Detector*: detects object by shape in image or 3D.
- *Face Detector*: tracks facial parts of humans in video or 3D.
- *Hand Detector*: tracks hand, fingers, and gestures in 3D.
- *Body Detector*: tracks body parts and joints of humans in video or 3D.
- *Speech Detector*: recognizes voice commands.
- *Transmitter Detector*: locates signal and position of wireless sender.

Data-driven events are events that are generated as an AR session progresses and the understanding of the scene improves. The AR system may detect various entities, such as horizontal planes, vertical planes, and recognized objects. These entities can be transformed into application-specific data models, such as a floor, table, wall, door, window, or collision environment for a physical simulation. The detection and tracking of such entities has significantly improved with the use of machine learning techniques. Data changes can be observed at the key-value level and then trigger an event. When using a state machine, both value changes and state transitions can generate data-driven events, taking into account previous values (see Appendix A.5). This dynamic triggering turns ECA to active rules.

2.3   Condition Evaluation Within Spatial AR Context

The data model reflecting the AR context is exposed for condition evaluation for any ECA rule. This model typically includes the following types of data:

- *Session Data*: time, date, device data, temporary data variables, UI mode
- *Location Data*: longitude, latitude, address, country, ambience
- *User Data*: position, orientation (tilt, yaw), name, user settings
- *Detected Occurrences*: results of installed detectors
- *Augmentation Items*: model elements with visual representation (scene nodes)

Conditions are typically formulated by predicates as logical statements using an expression syntax that has access to key-values in the data model. Additionally spatial functions can be included in condition evaluations such as:

- *Existence*: does item with ID exist in AR world
- *Visibility*: is item with ID visible to user
- *Proximity*: distance in meters from user (virtual camera) to item with ID
- *Gazing*: is user gazing at item with ID
- *Geo-Distance*: distance in meters from user to place in latitude/longitude

2.4　Actions in AR Applications

Common actions in AR applications are listed by category in Appendix B. Many of these actions are concerned with manipulating augmentation items as data model (B.1) and their visual representation (B.2), or with audible feedback as well as user interface activities (B.3).

Augmentation items are visual and audible enhancements of the world that are presented in the AR application. They can be categorized as follows:

- *Visual Items*:
  - *2D View Overlay*: 2D graphics, images, and UI elements as flat overlay
  - *3D World Embedding*: spatial geometry as node in 3D scene graph
- *Audible Items*:
  - *Speech*: recorded voice or generated voice by text-to-speech system
  - *Sonification*: sound effect driven by data or by user interaction
  - *Music and ambient sound*: play-back of audio files
- *Haptic Items*: visual or non-visual items with haptic feedback on collision

Staging of augmentation items is based on the content composition principle (`do:add`). It involves assigning unique identifiers to visual and audible items and positioning them within the observed world relative to anchors of detected entities. By doing so, the AR experience becomes more immersive, as the virtual objects are seamlessly integrated into the user's physical environment.

2.5　AR Pattern Diagram Using ECA Rule Blocks

In order to provide a compact representation of active ECA rules we developed a diagram consisting of rule-reaction blocks [25]. The first line of the diagram shows the active rule as an Event-Condition-Action triple. Following the rule is a blockquoted line that depicts the changed state as reaction (see Fig. 1). If no condition is defined, it evaluates to true, and the diagram shows an immediate execution arrow (→, Fig. 2). To illustrate the use of the diagram, consider the example shown in Fig. 3, which presents an active rule triggered by a temporal event (in 20 s). If no item is found in the current AR session (the condition), the action will execute voice feedback (the reaction) using a text-to-speech system.

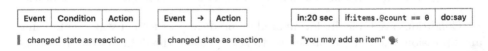

Fig. 1.　ECA　rule block.　　**Fig. 2.** Immediate EA.　　**Fig. 3.** Timed reaction rule.

An action may dynamically load and run new rules. These rules are displayed as indented block quote (see Fig. 4) consisting of several sequential lines. All rules in a block are loaded and installed in sequence, yet not (all) executed at loading time, but triggered by their corresponding event.

Fig. 4. Consecutive loading of rules.   **Fig. 5.** Indirect reaction.

The proposed AR pattern diagram has been designed to be technology-agnostic but still enable easy transformation from existing program code or declarative scripts. As demonstrated in this paper, all examples have been transformed from declarative code to the Markdown language and rendered as styled text (see Fig. 17). The mapping to Markdown is defined in [25]. With the proposed solution, AR patterns may be seamlessly incorporated into the authoring process, ultimately improving both documentation and communication.

3   Behavioral Patterns

The real world context during an AR session can be seen as stage. The dynamic behavior of an AR experience is determined by its ECA rules, which are triggered by events occurring in the actual real-world context. Table 2 lists common behavioral patterns in AR that result from ECA rules.

3.1   Instant Reaction Pattern

An instant reaction is directly triggered by the invocation of a rule and causes the immediate, singular execution of the action (see Fig. 6). It is equivalent to a function call.

3.2   Timed Reaction Pattern

Timed reactions are ECA rules that are fired after a given interval to carry out their action. Once the timed rule is initiated, an internal job scheduler triggers the rule at the time interval specified (Fig. 7)

3.3   Conditional Reaction Pattern

An ECA rule's condition is tested on the data available in the current AR session at the time of evaluation. The outcome of the condition evaluation is either true or false. Only if true the action of the ECA rule will be executed. In addition, a conditional reaction can be combined with a timed reaction (Figs. 3 and 8). Together, these reactions form the core of the continuous evaluation pattern.

Table 2. Behavioral patterns in AR applications.

Behavioral Pattern	Description	Examples
Instant Reaction Pattern	Direct execution of action triggered by invocation of rule	Immediate command of action or call of function
Timed Reaction Pattern	Temporally executed action	Delayed action or sequence of timed actions
Conditional Reaction Pattern	Execute an action only when a condition is fulfilled after being triggered by event	State-driven, asynchronous programming logic
Continuous Evaluation Pattern	Continuous polling of state changes that will triggers rules	Continuous checks on value change, existence, visibility, proximity
Publish-Subscribe Notification Pattern	Receive notifications via a message queue from a subscribed system	From speech recognition system or from WebRTC system in collaboration session
Request-Response Pattern	Remote procedure call resulting in asynchronously receiving ECA rules or media assets	REST API call to a server via a Web URL to load rules or assets (images, 3D models)
Chain Reaction Pattern	Course of events processed as indirect reactions of running subsequenced rules	Rule changing data that will trigger a rule to update an item's visual as a follow-up
Complementary Reactions Pattern	Two active rules with opposite reactions	Reacting on toggling states with two complementary active rules
Detector Reactivation Pattern	Reactivate detector with a only-once reaction	Reactivate detector after resulting augmentation is no longer existing

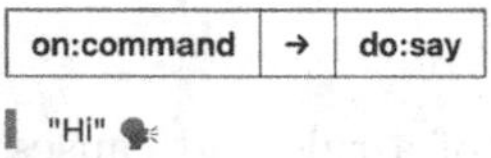

on:command	→	do:say	in:3 sec	→	do:say

▌ "Hi" 🎙

▌ "how are you?" 🎙

in:7 sec	if:location.city == 'Berlin'	do:say

▌ "Hello Berlin!" 🎙

Fig. 6. Instant reaction.

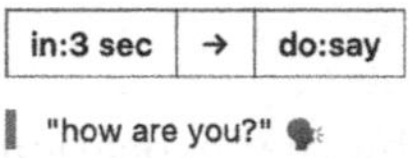

Fig. 7. Timed reaction.

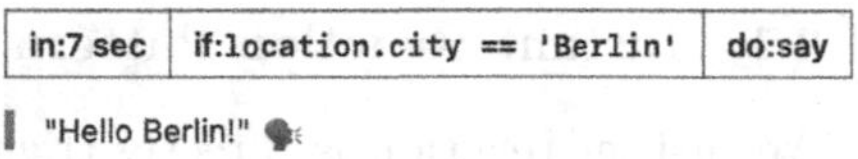

Fig. 8. Timed conditional reaction.

3.4 Continuous Evaluation Pattern

The continuous evaluation of rules can be driven by a constant time interval (first rule in Fig. 9) or by each state change of the data model (second rule in Fig. 9).

A built-in state management is observing the data model and does dispatch the processing of rules according to the data-driven events (Appendix A.5) that are bound to the ECA rules.

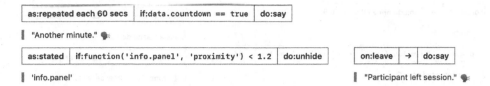

Fig. 9. Continuous evaluation pattern.   Fig. 10. Notification pattern.

3.5   Publish-Subscribe Notification Pattern

In a similar manner to monitoring changes in the data model, changes in subsystems can also generate events that trigger rules. Subsystems can be observed through a publish-subscribe notification mechanism. For instance, a speech recognition system might be initiated (by a do:listen action) and subscribed to. When a voice command is recognized, an on:voice event is published as message. Another example is the usage of a collaboration subsystem that sends notifications when a participant joins or leaves a session (Fig. 10).

3.6   Request-Response Pattern

The Request-Response Pattern is a method of communicating with remote services through non-blocking asynchronous communication. This pattern is commonly used to request media assets such as images, audio files, video streams, or 3D models, as well as scripts such as additional ECA rules (Fig. 4). Because of the temporal decoupling of request and response, an event is required to signal the arrival of the received data from the server. This allows an ECA rule to handle the result as soon as it is available.

3.7   Chain Reaction Pattern

A reaction of a rule can trigger a new event that invokes subsequent rules. In turn, these subsequent rules may have reactions that again invoke rules, leading to a chain of reactions. The Chain Reaction pattern consists of consecutive loaded rules (Fig. 4) and of indirect reactions (Fig. 5) which lead to a cascade of triggered rules with their corresponding reactions. To better illustrate this concept, consider the example shown in Fig. 16, which demonstrates how the Chain Reaction pattern can be used to detect and augment an image.

3.8   Complementary Reactions Pattern

Complementary reactions are constructed using two rules that have opposite conditions and actions with opposite results. When these two rules are evaluated continuously, they exhibit a toggling state by flipping their mutual rule execution (Fig. 11).

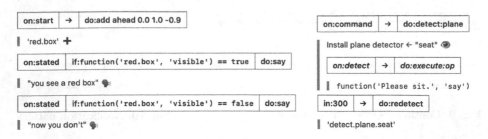

Fig. 11. Complementary reactions.   Fig. 12. Detector reactivation.

3.9 Detector Reactivation Pattern

Some detectors halt after capturing a first occurrence of an entity and need to be reactivated by a `do:redetect` action. The reactivation can be driven by a separate active rule, for instance, after a specific period of time (Fig. 12) or by assessing the existence or visibility of the item added by the detector based on a corresponding condition.

4 Augmentation Patterns

While a VR/3D designer is placing virtual objects using positions in a controlled world coordinate system, an AR content creator primarily specifies object placement intents relative to appearing anchors, which are dynamically produced by detectors. These spatial anchors serve as reference points for pinning objects. Generally in AR Patterns, the augmentation intents are formulated as ECA rules that are triggered by detector events. When a detector event occurs, ECA rule's reaction will add augmentation items to the AR scene.

Figure 13 depicts a rule that invokes an image detection action if a command event is received. As reaction, the image named 'marker.png' is requested and downloaded. Once the image is downloaded, an image detector is installed and a subsequent rule is loaded to be triggered when the image is detected in the real world. Upon detecting the image, an instant reaction pins an item with the id 'scene.3D' to the anchor of the detected image.

Another example of scene augmentation is shown in Fig. 14. In this example a detector is installed that is capturing planes of type 'seat'. When detected, this results in indirect reactions that include the creation of audible and visible augmentations.

Table 3 outlines several common placement intents for event-driven augmentation patterns that can be used to stage AR experiences. In AR, the real world serves as the spatial context for the stage, making users both spectators and performers. Their movements and perspectives influence the firing of events, leaving limited control over time and space for AR scenography (in contrast to film, theater, and VR/3D/game design). The augmentation patterns differ by the *purpose* of the added augmentation items (depicted by title), where they are *placed* (position in space), and how they are *aligned* (orientation, see Fig. 15).

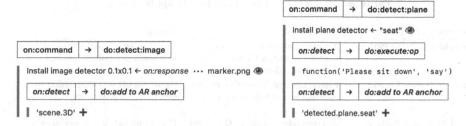

Fig. 13. Augmentation intent as ECA rule.

Fig. 14. Rules for adding audible and visual augmentations.

4.1 Geolocated Remark Pattern

A geolocated remark is a rule that is triggered by GPS location data (latitude and longitude) or by address data (i.e., country, city, street, building name). Typically, the reaction to a geolocated remark is presented as text in the 2D user interface or as audio feedback. Due to the precision restrictions of GPS signals, the reaction is not precisely placed in 2D or 3D space.

placed: *no* | aligned: *no*

4.2 Segment Overlay Pattern

By utilizing computer vision and machine learning techniques, a segment detector can recognize and track designated landmarks and image segments. The outcomes of the image segmentation process may include:

- *point (pixel)*: room corner, object corner, pupil center, ...
- *edge*: horizon line, wall-floor edge, ...
- *bounding box*: depicting rectangle border of detected text, image, face, ...
- *path (open path)*: eyebrow, body skeleton, ...
- *contour (closed path)*: face, mouth, eye, ...
- *image mask*: sky, grass, hair, ...

In the AR view, the overlay is positioned based on the pixels relative to the segment within the 2D image, on top of the video stream.

placed: *on screen at image segment* | aligned: *flat on top as overlay*

4.3 Area Enrichment Pattern

The Area Enrichment Pattern uses detected image segments to calculate the spatial 3D area resulting from perspective projection of the segment into depth of space. The calculated 3D area can then be used to populate the space with virtual items.

placed: *in 3D area at image segment* | aligned: *to area / towards user*

Table 3. Augmentation patterns in AR applications.

Augmentation Pattern	Description	Examples
Geolocated Remark Pattern	Triggering of action or of user feedback based on GPS location data or on address data	Visual or audio feedback about location-based point of interest
Segment Overlay Pattern	Presentation of 2D overlay on top of image segment detected in video stream	Attaching 2D text description to a detected image segment
Area Enrichment Pattern	Approximately placing 3D content at area of image segment	Presenting balloons in sky area
Captured Twin Pattern	Captured element of real world added to 3D data model	Captured walls and doors in an indoor AR session
Anchored Supplement Pattern	Presentation of 3D content aligned to detected entity for enhancement	Attaching visual 3D elements to a detected image (marker) or captured object
Superimposition Pattern	Presentation of 3D content replacing a detected entity	Cover a detected object with a virtual one
Tag-along Pattern	Presentation of 3D content within user's field of view while head-locked	Place 3D control panel that follows the user
Hand/Palm Pop-up Pattern	Presentation of 3D content on hand or palm while visible	Place 3D UI elements at palm of user's one hand
Ahead Staging Pattern	Presentation of 3D content ahead of user	Placing 3D item on floor in front of spectator
Pass-through Portal Pattern	Present partly hidden 3D content to force user to go through	Placing 3D scene behind a portal / behind an opening
Staged Progression Pattern	Ordered, linear story: temporal order or interaction flow of 3D presentations	Sequence of 3D content with forth and optionally back movements
Attention Director Pattern	Guide user's attention to relevant place	Use animated pointers to direct user's attention
Contextual Plot Pattern	Spatio-temporal setting that aggregates diverse AR patterns to form a non-linear plot	Scenography of dynamic, interactive, and animated AR

4.4   Captured Twin Pattern

A captured twin is a virtual replica of a physical element. It is created using data collected from sensors, cameras, and other sources. A captured twin can then, for example, be virtually visualized as a contour or as a transparent 3D bounding box to keep the real object recognizable. In Fig. 15a, a real-world chair has been detected as an object and is indicated with a virtual bounding box and a text label of the object type. A captured twin may also have no virtual representation but becomes available in the spatial data model (e.g., for collision detection or as a reference for spatial alignment).

placed: *on object* | aligned: *with object*

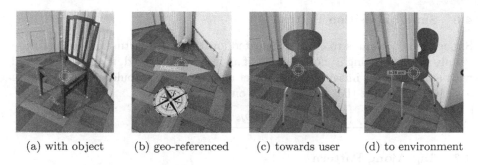

(a) with object   (b) geo-referenced   (c) towards user   (d) to environment

Fig. 15. Alignment of augmentations in 3D.

4.5   Anchored Supplement Pattern

Anchored supplements provide additional information that is aligned with a detected entity. For instance, a 3D info panel can be anchored beside a detected image, as demonstrated by the pattern diagram in Fig. 16. Similarly, a guiding sign can be anchored towards a detected door to assist with navigation.

placed: *relative to object* | aligned: *with object or towards object / user*

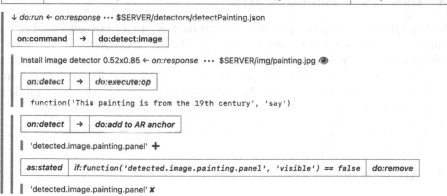

Fig. 16. Example of an anchored supplement using image detection.

In Fig. 16, an example is shown where an ECA rule is executed at the beginning of an AR session to determine whether the current location is suitable for detecting an image as a painting. If the location is a match, an image is loaded from a remote server and installed as active rule set which provides audible and visible augmentations in case of detecting the image in the real world. The visible augmentation takes the form of an info panel that is monitored by a rule which removes it when it is no longer visible from the user's perspective.

4.6 Superimposition Pattern

Superimposition aims to cover a detected entity with a virtual one rather than simply supplementing it. For example, if an image is detected, it could be covered with a downloaded image, or if an object is recognized, it could be replaced with a virtual 3D object that hides the real one.

placed: *on object* | aligned: *with object*

4.7 Tag-Along Pattern

A tag-along augmentation attempts to always stay within the user's view range, which is constrained to their eye position. To achieve this, the augmentation is typically always oriented towards the user's face using billboarding techniques. The main advantage of tag-along augmentations is that they ensure the presented interaction elements are always visible and easily accessible to the user. In AR applications for head-mounted displays, tag-along augmentations are usually designed to fit within the user's arm-length range, ensuring they can interact with the elements without stretching or straining themselves. An example is the 'Near Menu' UX component of the Mixed Reality Toolkit [12].

placed: *constraint ahead of user* | aligned: *constraint towards user*

4.8 Hand/Palm Pop-Up Pattern

The hand/palm pop-up is a prevalent design pattern used to present interaction elements for AR using head-mounted displays. Rather than constantly displaying these elements, they are shown only when the palm or back of the hand is visible (and optionally, when a hand gesture was detected beforehand). The other hand can then be used to interact with the presented 3D UI elements. An example is the 'Hand Menu' UX component of the Mixed Reality Toolkit [12].

placed: *constraint on palm* | aligned: *constraint towards user*

4.9 Ahead Staging Pattern

Ahead staging is a technique for presenting 3D content in a way that it is aligned to spectator's position and view direction. The scene is launched at a default distance (1–2m) in front of the user using a world-locked anchor, often relative to the ground floor plane. The alignment can be directed towards geolocated references (e.g., as a guide as in Fig. 15b), towards the user (Fig. 15c), or can also consider nearby objects in the environment (e.g., a wall as in Fig. 15d or the room axis). After the initial staging, users can interact with the virtual scene from their current position or move toward and around the staged content.

placed: *initial ahead of user* | aligned: *initial towards user, object, or georef*

4.10   Pass-Through Portal Pattern

A pass-trough portal is an augmentation that is initially occluded by a virtual object, which prevents the user from seeing the entire scene. This design is intended to encourage users to engage with the experience by requiring them to pass through a gateway to become fully immersed.

> placed: *initial ahead of user* | aligned: *initial towards user or object*

4.11   Staged Progression Pattern

A staged progression refers to presenting a linear story in a structured and sequential manner in AR, with an explicit beginning. This typically involves the ordered presentation of 3D content, which can be unidirectional or bidirectional (going back and forth). The story usually starts staged ahead of the user, but it can also begin at the anchor of a detected entity. The story's progress is governed by rules triggered by user events, temporal events, or data-driven events.

> placed: *initial ahead of user* | aligned: *initial towards user or object*

4.12   Attention Director Pattern

An attention director uses animated pointers (bubbles, arrows), light rays, or spatial sound to direct where users should pay attention if the relevant area is not visible or not in focus.

> placed: *initial ahead of user* | aligned: *pointing towards point of interest*

4.13   Contextual Plot Pattern

A contextual plot combines a variety of augmentation patterns and behavioural patterns to create a non-linear and immersive experience. It builds a scenography that blends seamlessly with the spatio-temporal setting of the real world. A contextual plot reacts to diverse event types, triggering rules that will dynamically control interactive and animated reactions. One of the defining features of a contextual plot is its dependence on the real-world context. The experience is affected by how the user is interacting with and exploring the scenario.

> placed: *multiple all over spatial context* | aligned: *diverse*

5   Using AR Patterns in Authoring Tool

5.1   Declarative Creation of AR Content

The proposed AR patterns were elaborated and validated during the development of the ARchi VR App [20]. Instead of using a programming language to algorithmically define how AR content should be created and behave, the app uses a declarative approach that focuses on specifying what needs to be accomplished with each AR asset. To achieve this, the app interprets declarations in JSON data structures that do not include conventional programming code, but instead use active ECA rules to define the behavior of the AR experience [21].

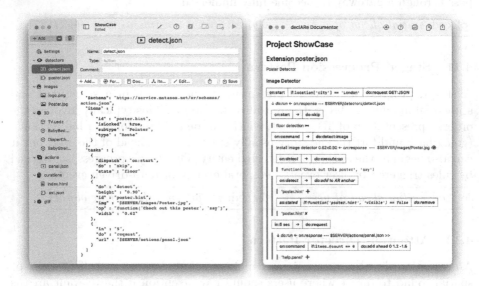

Fig. 17. Generated AR pattern diagram (right) from code (left) in an AR IDE.

5.2 Generation of AR Pattern Diagrams

When using such a declarative authoring approach many simple ECA rules are created and encoded (in case of the ARchi VR App in many separate JSON files). This helps to keep local focus when creating AR scenes, but it can be challenging to maintain an overview of the entire rule system that defines all the intents of the AR world. To address this challenge and better understand how rules are loaded and run in sequence, an integrated development environment (IDE) could support on-the-fly generation of AR pattern diagrams [25] from the encoded rules (see Fig. 17) to visualize an overall view of intended AR scenario.

6   Conclusions and Perspectives

6.1   Summary

The proposed event-driven AR design patterns have shown to be a convincing way of documenting high-level concepts in creating AR applications. AR patterns serve as a valuable means of communicating proven, reusable solutions to recurring design problems encountered during AR development. Once AR patterns are understood, learning new AR toolkits might become more accessible, as the used design patterns are familiar.

During the technical design and development process, AR patterns may also serve as a requirements catalog to clarify the specification of features and functions that an AR application should support. If an editor facilitates the creation of AR content, it might make sense to support the generation of AR pattern diagrams from code. In addition, AR design patterns may also be a useful organizational structure for providing solution templates, such as code snippets in AR authoring tools. This would allow developers to incorporate common patterns into their AR applications efficiently, improving development speed and overall quality.

6.2   Community-Driven Validation

We are strongly convinced that AR patterns can be applied to hard-coded, scripted, and no-code implementations making them widely applicable. Yet the approach was showcased in only a few development, research, and student projects. Therefore the soundness and comprehensiveness of this proposal should be further elaborated and validated:

– Do the proposed AR Patterns resonate within the AR community?
– Are common high-level AR patterns missing?
– Are the proposed AR patterns useful in the AR design process?
– How can guidelines foster learning and applying of AR patterns?
– Is the Event-Condition-Action pattern a generic abstraction mechanism?
– Can AR Pattern diagrams be in fact used "technology-agnostic"?

One way to improve the expressiveness of the proposed catalog of high-level AR patterns would be to display rendered AR user interfaces as samples and to provide implementation-specific code examples. While this paper provides a starting point, future research should further expand the catalog besides the documented behavioral patterns and augmentation patterns. Other important AR-related design patterns should be explored, e.g., covering gesture- and voice-based interactions, human-human AR collaboration [27], and human-robot AR collaboration [28]. This paper addresses the need for AR patterns in the hope that it contributes to diverse innovations ahead of us within the AR community. Contributions are welcome and are planned to be coordinated via arpatterns.dev [29] and the AR Patterns catalog repository [30].

6.3   ECA Rules as Foundation for AR Interoperability

For exchanging AR worlds between applications from different providers, open standards are in demand. The Event-Condition-Action rule could serve as a common pattern in defining standardized exchange formats for augmentation and behavior of AR content and metaverse assets (as addressed by the Metaverse Standards Forum [26]). This requires further clarifications and feasibility studies.

6.4   Generating Code from AR Patterns

A visionary idea (mentioned by a paper reviewer) is the generation of code from
AR patterns. Yet it has not even for software design patterns became a widespread approach in IDEs (although some papers appeared). Recent development
in generative AI (e.g., Co-Pilot) could be a solution to fulfill the vision of gener-
ating code from design patterns. As a prerequisite for such a generative approach
the AR community needs to establish a common understanding of AR design
patterns and has to provide sample code organized according to AR patterns.

Acknowledgement. The author would like to thank Yanick Lukic and Stefan
Schmidlin for their comments and proofreading.

A   Common AR Event Types

A.1   Session Events

- on:start: immediately after start of AR session or after loading action
- on:locating: on locating in the world (by GPS, by SLAM device positioning)
- on:stable: when spatial registration of AR device gets stable
- on:load: after loading 3D item to AR view, e.g., to animate or occlude node
- on:stop: before AR session ends

A.2   Invocation Events

- on:command: on command initiation
- on:call: on function call

A.3   User Events

- on:tap: when tapped on item
- on:press: when long-pressed on item
- on:drag: when dragging an item
- on:select: when selected from options of pop-up menu
- on:dialog: when selected from options of pop-up dialog panel
- on:poi: when selected a point of interest in a map or minimap

A.4   Temporal Events

- in:time: when elapsed time in seconds is reached
- as:always: several times per seconds
- as:repeated: like as:always, but only triggered each seconds

A.5   Data-Driven Events

- on:change: on each change of data value
- as:stated: like as:always, but action only is triggered once when if-condition result is altered from false to true
- as:steady: like as:stated, but action only is triggered when condition result stays true for a certain time in seconds.
- as:activated: like as:always, but action always is triggered when if-condition result becomes true
- as:altered: like as:always, but action always is triggered when if-condition result is altered from false to true or from true to false

A.6   Response Events

- on:response: on receiving response from request
- on:error: on error of handling request

A.7   Detection Event

- on:detect: on detecting occurrence of depicted type
- on:track: on tracked changes in occurrence of depicted type

A.8   Notification Events

- on:voice: on voice command from speech recognition system
- on:enter: on enter of participant in collaboration session
- on:message: on message from participant in collaboration session
- on:leave: on leave of participant in collaboration session

B   Common AR Actions

B.1   Item-Related Actions

Items are elements of the application model. An item can be represented as 3D object in the AR scene or as 2D overlay (sprite image, text label, UI element, ...) on top of the AR view.

- do:add at: add and anchor item at position
- do:add onto: add and anchor item onto another item
- do:add to: add item as child to another item
- do:add ahead: add and anchor item ahead to user position and orientation
- do:add overlayed: add 2D item flat on top of AR view
- do:remove: remove item from scene
- do:replace: replace item with another item at same position
- do:move to/by: move item absolute/relative to new position
- do:turn to/by: turn item absolute/relative to new orientation
- do:tint: set color of item
- do:lock/unlock: lock/unlock item to control allowed manipulation

B.2   Visual-Related Actions

Visual-related actions do change the visual representation of items in the AR scene but are not reflected or stored in the application model.

- do:hide/unhide: hide/unhide visual representation of item
- do:translate to/by: move absolute/relative
- do:rotate to/by: rotate absolute/relative
- do:scale to/by: scale absolute/relative
- do:animate key: create animation of graphical parameter (key)
- do:stop key: stop animation of graphical parameter (key)
- do:occlude: set geometry of 3D node as occluding but not visible
- do:illuminate: add additional lightning to hot spot (from above or from camera)

B.3   UI-Related Actions

Common actions to control the user interface of an AR application.

- do:prompt: show instruction in a pop-up panel
- do:confirm: get a YES/NO confirmation via an pop-up dialog panel
- do:warn: set warning or status label
- do:vibrate: vibrate device
- do:play: play system sound
- do:stream: play remote audio file
- do:pause: pause current audio stream
- do:say: say something using text-to-speech (TTS) system
- do:listen: start speech recognition system and subscribe
- do:open service: open service menu
- do:open catalog: open item catalog
- do:install: install item catalog entry or service menu entry
- do:filter: filter item catalog or service menu
- do:screenshot: take screen snapshot
- do:snapshot: take photo shot

B.4   Data-Related Actions

- do:assign: set a data variable to a value
- do:concat: concatenate a string with an existing variable
- do:select: select a value from a menu and assign to data variable
- do:eval: set a data variable by evaluating an expression
- do:fetch: fetch data from remote and map to internal data
- do:clear: delete data variable

B.5   Process-Related Actions

- do:save: save the AR scene / application model
- do:exit: end AR session
- do:execute: execute function(s)
- do:service: execute service action
- do:workflow: execute workflow action
- do:request: request action from remote server and execute

B.6   Detector-Related Actions

- do:detect type: install detector for type (feature, text, plane, image, ...)
- do:halt: deactivate detector
- do:redetect: reactivate detector

References

1. Gamma, E., Helm, R., Johnson, R., Vlissides, J.: Design Patterns: Elements of Reusable Object-Oriented Software. Pearson, London (1995)
2. Nystrom, R.: Game Programming Patterns. Genever Benning, London (2014)
3. Zollmann, S., Langlotz, T., Grasset, R., Lo, W.H., Mori, S., Regenbrecht, H.: Visualization techniques in augmented reality: a taxonomy, methods and patterns. IEEE Trans. Vis. Comput. Graph. **27**(9), 3808–3825 (2020)
4. Koreng, R., Krömker, H.: User interface pattern for AR in industrial applications. Information **12**, 251 (2021). https://doi.org/10.3390/info12060251
5. ETSI GS ARF 003: Augmented Reality Framework (ARF) - AR framework architecture (2020). https://www.etsi.org/
6. MacWilliams, A., Reicher, T., Klinker, G., Bruegge, B.: Design patterns for augmented reality systems. In: Proceedings of the International Workshop exploring the Design and Engineering of Mixed Reality Systems, Funchal, Madeira (2004)
7. Makamara, G., Adolph, M.: A Survey of extended reality (XR) standards. In: ITU Kaleidoscope-extended reality-how to boost quality of experience and interoperability, pp. 1–11 (2022). https://doi.org/10.23919/ITUK56368.2022.10003040
8. Görlich, D., Akincir, T., Meixner, G.: An overview of user interface and interaction design patterns for VR, AR, and MR applications. In: Mensch und Computer, Workshopband, Darmstadt (2022). https://doi.org/10.18420/muc2022-mci-ws06-419
9. Börsting, I., Karabulut, C., Fischer, B., Gruhn, V.: Design patterns for mobile augmented reality user interfaces - an incremental review. Information **13**(4), 159 (2022). https://doi.org/10.3390/info13040159
10. Apple ARKit: https://developer.apple.com/augmented-reality/arkit/
11. Google ARCore: https://developers.google.com/ar?hl=en
12. Microsoft MRTK: Microsoft Mixed Reality Toolkit; https://learn.microsoft.com/windows/mixed-reality/mrtk-unity/mrtk3-overview
13. AR.js - Augmented Reality on the Web: https://ar-js-org.github.io/AR.js-Docs/
14. Niantic 8th Wall: https://www.8thwall.com/products-web
15. OpenXR Standard: https://www.khronos.org/openxr
16. Unity AR Foundation: https://unity.com/unity/features/arfoundation

17. PTC Vuforia: https://www.ptc.com/en/products/vuforia
18. Apple Reality Composer: https://developer.apple.com/augmented-reality/tools/
19. Adobe Aero: https://www.adobe.com/products/aero.html
20. ARchi VR App: https://archi.metason.net
21. ARchi VR Content Creation: Technical Documentation; https://service.metason.net/ar/docu/
22. Paton, N. W. (ed.): Active Rules in Database Systems. Springer Science & Business Media, Cham (2012)
23. Müller, R., Greiner, U., Rahm, E.: AGENTWORK: a workflow system supporting rule-based workflow adaptation. Data Knowl. Eng. **51**, 223–256 (2004). https://doi.org/10.1016/j.datak.2004.03.010
24. Rambach, J., Pagani, A., Stricker, D.: Principles of object tracking and mapping. In: Nee, A.Y.C., Ong, S.K. (eds.) Springer Handbook of Augmented Reality, pp. 53–84. Springer Handbooks. Springer, Cham (2023). https://doi.org/10.1007/978-3-030-67822-7_3
25. AR Pattern Diagram: https://github.com/ARpatterns/diagram
26. The Metaverse Standards Forum: https://metaverse-standards.org
27. Pidel, C., Ackermann, P.: Collaboration in virtual and augmented reality: a systematic overview. In: De Paolis, L.T., Bourdot, P. (eds.) AVR 2020. LNCS, vol. 12242, pp. 141–156. Springer, Cham (2020). https://doi.org/10.1007/978-3-030-58465-8_10
28. Delmerico, J., et al.: Spatial computing and intuitive interaction: bringing mixed reality and robotics together. IEEE Robot. Autom. Mag. **29**(1), 45–57 (2022). https://doi.org/10.1109/MRA.2021.3138384
29. AR Patterns: https://arpatterns.dev
30. AR Patterns Catalog: https://github.com/ARpatterns/catalog

An Open-Source Fine-Grained Benchmarking Platform for Wireless Virtual Reality

Martin Danhier, Karim El Khoury[✉], and Benoît Macq

Institute for Information and Communication Technologies, Electronics and Applied Mathematics, Université catholique de Louvain, Louvain-La-Neuve, Belgium
karim.elkhoury@uclouvain.be

Abstract. Due to the improved mobility it provides, wireless virtual reality has become a promising technology used in a multitude of applications, ranging from casual gaming and film animation to remote tourism and medical assistance. However, it faces a diverse set of constraints, from both a technical and a user experience standpoint, with varying requirements depending on the application. To overcome these constraints, it is important to have a clear overview of the wireless virtual reality system as well as an in-depth understanding of the end-to-end video transmission pipeline. In this paper, we propose a plug-and-play open-source wireless virtual reality benchmarking platform that is able to perform fine-grained measurements directly within a complete pipeline. This platform can be used to detect critical bottlenecks and anomalies within the system. In addition, the platform facilitates the choice of optimal parameters for a specific application. The source code of this work is publicly available and should be seen as a first step to encourage the use of open-source benchmarking tools within the virtual reality community.

Keywords: Wireless Virtual Reality · Benchmarking · Open-Source

1 Introduction

Wireless Virtual Reality (WVR) headsets have become increasingly popular in recent years due to the improved mobility that they create for the user experience. WVR is now used in a variety of applications ranging from casual gaming and film animation to remote tourism and medical assistance [1–4]. These applications face two main types of constraints: technical constraints (mainly from a network and computational capacity standpoint) and user experience (UX) constraints (mainly from a comfort and reliability standpoint). To overcome these constraints, the WVR system would be required to provide high-efficiency video compression to be able to transmit high-quality and high-frame-rate video content while maintaining low-latency and low-bandwidth consumption. This allows the WVR application to provide a high quality, reliable and smooth user experience while reducing network and computational loads. However, the challenge lies in optimizing a WVR system to satisfy these constraints, as they differ greatly from one WVR application to another.

© The Author(s), under exclusive license to Springer Nature Switzerland AG 2023
G. Zachmann et al. (Eds.): EuroXR 2023, LNCS 14410, pp. 115–121, 2023.
https://doi.org/10.1007/978-3-031-48495-7_7

Several researchers have addressed this challenge by isolating one constraint (either technical or UX) and analyzing its impact on the system. Regarding technical constraints, Žádník et al. [5] have explored techniques and limitations of ultra-low latency video compression using standardized video codecs such as HEVC [6] and VVC [7]. They suggest that, in wireless scenarios, the unpredictability of wireless networks rather than the computational complexity of video compression is the main latency bottleneck. Tan et al. [8] have proposed three methods to minimize motion-feedback latency and jitter in bidirectional streams over WiFi in the context of WVR, most notably by limiting the aggregation size of downlink frame data transmission. Regarding UX constraints, Hu et al. [9] have defined a minimum quality of service requirements (including refresh rate, resolution and raw bitrate) in order to achieve different levels of quality of experience in accordance with Huawei standards[1]. Oculus researchers [10] have proposed an asynchronous time warping algorithm that improves UX by minimizing the impact of motion latency. This is achieved by reprojecting frames at their correct location based on the latest tracking data. Given that these constraints also impact one another, it is also interesting to analyze these constraints in a complete WVR pipeline. This is usually done by running benchmarks on a standalone headset connected wirelessly to a rendering server using a link program that handles both video compression and streaming. Zhao et al. [11] have done a series of network measurements on cloud-VR using the Virtual Desktop[2] link. Salehi et al. [12] have performed similar measurements in the context of edge computing, using the open source link AirLightVR[3] (ALVR). In both cases, the researchers gathered their measurements by sniffing packets using Wireshark[4] and analyzing the network trace.

In this paper, we propose a plug-and-play open-source wireless virtual reality benchmarking platform that is able to perform fine-grained measurements directly within a complete pipeline. Our work yields complementary results to the previously cited packet tracing methods [11,12]. The source code for the proposed platform is available on GitHub[5].

This paper is organized as follows. In Sect. 2, we present an overview of the proposed benchmarking platform as well as explain in detail the video pipeline used for measurements. In Sect. 3, we present the results of two experiments and discuss the required metric trade-offs to be made to ensure optimal performance. Finally, in Sect. 4, we summarize the paper by recapping the outcomes of our work and discussing the remaining future works.

---

[1] https://www.huawei.com/minisite/pdf/ilab/cloud_vr_network_solution_white_paper_en.pdf.

[2] https://www.vrdesktop.net/.

[3] https://github.com/alvr-org/ALVR.

[4] https://www.wireshark.org/.

[5] https://github.com/martin-danhier/wireless-vr-bridge.

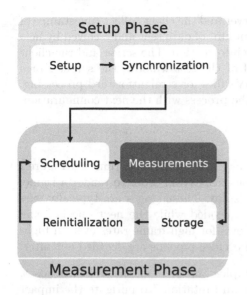

Fig. 1. Benchmarking execution flow, composed of an initial setup phase and an iterative measurement phase.

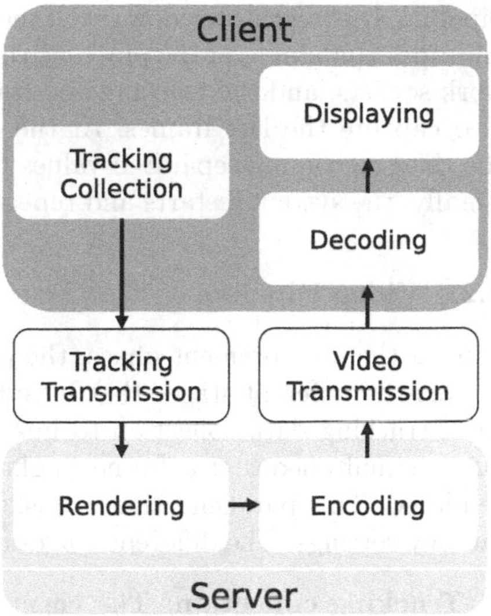

Fig. 2. Complete Client-Server-Client video pipeline from tracking to display.

2 Fine-Grained Benchmarking Platform

2.1 Overview

The proposed benchmarking platform is based on a standard link program. It is able to transmit video frames rendered on a powerful machine, called the server, to a standalone and less powerful Android WVR headset, called the client. In the opposite direction, the client streams tracking information that allows the experience to be interactive. It should be noted that our implementation differs from other open-source link programs (such as ALVR) by the fact that it was designed for the specific purpose of being a WVR benchmarking platform. Through command-line arguments, the user is able to define a series of configurations, called benchmark passes. The server will then iterate through passes, configure the client accordingly, and collect measurements. Figure 1 describes this execution flow as a state machine. At the start of the execution, the client connects to the server and shares its specifications, including resolution, frame rate, and other capabilities. It then synchronizes its clock in order to improve timestamp reliability by minimizing the error that can occur due to clock rate variations or Network Time Protocol (NTP) inaccuracy. In practice, a succession of pings is used to compute the road trip time of the network and compute the offset between the server and client clocks. Once all components are ready, the measurement phase begins. The server communicates the current configuration to the client, schedules a measurement time window, and initiates the video pipeline. During this window, both the server and the client collect timestamps of all important stages of the pipeline, the amount of data sent and received by network sockets, and the tracking and frame information. The server and the client also capture the last frames. At the end of the test window, the server stores the data in comma-separated values (CSV) files for straightforward processing. Finally, the system restarts and repeats the process with the next configuration.

2.2 Video Pipeline

During the measurement phase, the primary video pipeline is running. Figure 2 details the different stages that have to be executed in order to render a frame, from tracking data collection to image display. These stages are typically executed simultaneously: a frame might be decoded while the next one is being rendered. This parallelization of tasks allows for high frame rates even in high-latency settings. The different stages of the video pipeline are detailed hereafter:

1. **Tracking collection**: The client samples the pose of the WVR headset, mainly composed of the head position and rotation. To mitigate the impact of latency, a model is used to predict the new head location when the frame is displayed. The pose is then timestamped and cached.
2. **Tracking transmission**: The pose is sent as a packed binary format over User Datagram Protocol (UDP), which allows for the lowest latency.
3. **Rendering**: Using the latest tracking data, a frame is rendered by the application. We defer this step to SteamVR[6], which can handle compositing, user interfaces and most importantly supports a wide range of applications and games. The interface with SteamVR is achieved via a custom driver.
4. **Encoding**: The rendered frame is compressed to reduce the amount of data that will have to be transmitted over the network. For encoding, we mainly focused on the HEVC codec [6] for which efficient hardware-accelerated encoders are provided by NVIDIA[7]. Moreover, the use of the FFMpeg libavcodec library[8] allows the user to add support for other codecs quickly. Custom codecs can also be defined through a plug-in system.
5. **Video transmission**: The encoded frame is packetized, transmitted over the network over Transmission Control Protocol (TCP), and depacketized. The use of TCP allows for reliable and codec-independant transmission.
6. **Decoding**: The frame is decoded with the same codec used for encoding via Android's MediaCodec[9] library. Other decoders can also be defined.
7. **Display**: The decoded frame is submitted to the headset alongside the tracking pose that was used to render it. The image is then reprojected to its correct location using the asynchronous time warping algorithm [10] and displayed on the screen.

---

[6] https://www.steamvr.com/.
[7] https://developer.nvidia.com/video-codec-sdk.
[8] https://ffmpeg.org/libavcodec.html.
[9] https://developer.android.com/reference/android/media/MediaCodec.

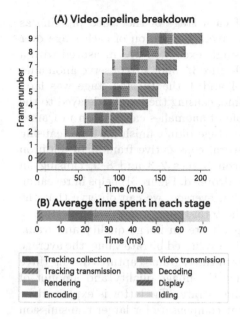

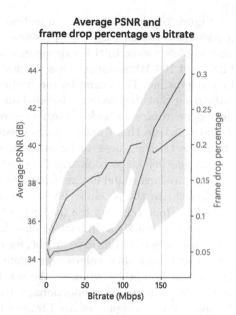

Fig. 3. Frame-by-frame timeline highlighting each stage of the video pipeline. (A) Detailed parallel execution of the first ten frames. (B) Average duration of each stage over an entire video.

Fig. 4. Peak signal-to-noise ratio (PSNR) and frame drops evolution with respect to bitrate increment.

3 Results and Discussion

Using our proposed benchmarking platform, we collected a series of measurements using a Meta Quest 2[10] headset as a client and a desktop computer as a server. The server ran on Windows 11 with a RTX 3070 GPU, an i7-9700KF CPU, and 16GB of RAM. The two devices were connected via a dedicated Wi-Fi 6 router[11]. However, the server was connected to the router via a cable in order to minimize reliance on unstable wireless transmissions. It is also important to note that this Wireless Local Area Network (WLAN) was entirely dedicated to the WVR link and was disconnected from the Internet. Regarding video encoding, all measurements were performed using HEVC [6] with the NVENC hardware encoder and a Qualcomm hardware decoder. The encoder was configured using the default preset, a group of picture (GOP) size of 0, no overlapping frames, and no reordering delay. The transmitted video was of 2880×1584 pixels in size with a frame rate of 90 frames per second (FPS). These settings were chosen to provide low-latency encoding while still maintaining a high image quality.

---

[10] https://www.meta.com/quest/products/quest-2/.
[11] https://www.tp-link.com/fr/home-networking/wifi-router/archer-ax55/.

Figure 3A shows the decomposition of each stage of the video pipeline as a parallel timeline. Figure 3B presents the average duration of each stage over an complete video. In this experiment, a single execution was measured with a bitrate of 100 Mbps during a 4-s window. Figure 3A allows to observe anomalies in the pipeline. For example, for frames 4 and 9, the *Display* stage was late, indicating that they weren't decoded on time, causing them to be delayed to the next synchronization tick. Another example of anomalies can be seen in frames 4 and 6, where the *Tracking transmission* stage didn't finish on time, causing the same tracking pose to be used for several consecutive frames. In addition the *Rendering* stage took too long between frames 2–3 and 8–9, causing an accumulated delay and forcing frames to be dropped. Figure 3B helps in revealing bottlenecks in the pipeline. For instance, on average, we can observe that the *Decoding* stage takes up the majority of the total frame transmission delay.

Figure 4 shows the impact of encoding bitrate on image quality and frame drop proportion. In this experiment, for each evaluated bitrate value, the average PSNR and frame drop values were taken from thirty frame captures during three executions over a 4-s window. We see that the image quality and amount of frame drops increased proportionally to the bitrate. The latter is explained by the preventive dropping of aged frames that compensate for larger transmission delays induced by high bitrates. This experiment allows us to find a compromise between image quality and FPS. For example, an application requiring high visual quality but only allowing up to 10% of frame drops, can use a bitrate of up to 110Mbps.

4   Conclusion

In summary, we proposed a plug-and-play open-source WVR benchmarking platform. We showed that the use of precise measurements in the video pipeline allows to solve both technical and UX constraints. The detection of anomalies, such as late tracking data and frame drops, in addition to the identification of the major bottlenecks, such as decoding time, allows detection of critical issues in the video pipeline. Measurements also enable the user to select the most appropriate encoding parameter values for the application at hand in order to achieve an optimal user experience. Moreover, the open-source nature of the proposed platform will enable the future integration of further features, such as motion controller inputs, sound support, outside-in tracking, and additional metrics, as well as more advanced video algorithms such as fixed foveated rendering [13]. Future work can also explore optimizations to reduce decoding delay, the current main bottleneck, for example through the use of alternative video codecs or other hardware-accelerated decoders.

References

1. Zong, B., Fan, C., Wang, X., Duan, X., Wang, B., Wang, J.: 6g technologies: key drivers, core requirements, system architectures, and enabling technologies. IEEE Veh. Technol. Mag. **14**(3), 18–27 (2019). https://doi.org/10.1109/mvt.2019.2921398
2. Lei, D., Kim, S.H.: Application of wireless virtual reality perception and simulation technology in film and television animation. J. Sens. **2021**, 1–12 (2021). https://doi.org/10.1155/2021/5041832
3. Mirk, D., Hlavacs, H.: Virtual tourism with drones (2015). https://doi.org/10.1145/2750675.2750681
4. El Raghibi, L., et al.: Virtual reality can mediate the learning phase of upper limb prostheses supporting a better-informed selection process. J. Multimod. User Interfaces. **17**(1), 33–46 (2022). https://doi.org/10.1007/s12193-022-00400-7
5. Žádník, J., Makitalo, M., Vanne, J., Jääskeläinen, P.: Image and video coding techniques for ultra-low latency. ACM Comput. Surv. **54**(11), 1–35 (2022). https://doi.org/10.1145/3512342
6. Sullivan, G.J., Ohm, J.R., Han, W.J., Wiegand, T.: Overview of the high efficiency video coding (HEVC) standard. IEEE Trans. Circuits Syst. Video Technol. **22**(12), 1649–1668 (2012). https://doi.org/10.1109/tcsvt.2012.2221191
7. Bross, B., et al.: Overview of the versatile video coding (VVC) standard and its applications. IEEE Trans. Circuits Syst. Video Technol. **31**(10), 3736–3764 (2021). https://doi.org/10.1109/tcsvt.2021.3101953
8. Tai Tan, D., Kim, S., Yun, J.H.: Enhancement of motion feedback latency for wireless virtual reality in IEEE 802.11 WLANs (2019). https://doi.org/10.1109/globecom38437.2019.9013507
9. Hu, F., Deng, Y., Saad, W., Bennis, M., Aghvami, A.H.: Cellular-connected wireless virtual reality: requirements, challenges, and solutions. IEEE Commun. Mag. **58**(5), 105–111 (2020). https://doi.org/10.1109/mcom.001.1000511
10. van Waveren, J.M.: The asynchronous time warp for virtual reality on consumer hardware (2016). https://doi.org/10.1145/2993369.2993375
11. Zhao, S., Abou-zeid, H., Atawia, R., Manjunath, Y.S., Sediq, A.B., Zhang, X.P.: Virtual reality gaming on the cloud: a reality check (2021). https://doi.org/10.1109/globecom46510.2021.9685808
12. Li, Y.C., Hsu, C.H., Lin, Y.C., Hsu, C.H.: Performance measurements on a cloud VR gaming platform (2020). https://doi.org/10.1145/3423328.3423497
13. Albert, R., Patney, A., Luebke, D., Kim, J.: Latency requirements for foveated rendering in virtual reality. ACM Trans. Appl. Percept. **14**(4), 1–13 (2017). https://doi.org/10.1145/3127589

Collaborative VR Anatomy Atlas Investigating Multi-user Anatomy Learning

Haya Al Maree[1]([✉]), Roland Fischer[1], René Weller[1], Verena Uslar[2], Dirk Weyhe[2], and Gabriel Zachmann[1]

[1] University of Bremen, Bremen, Germany
haya@uni-bremen.de
[2] University Hospital for Visceral Surgery, University of Oldenburg, PIUS-Hospital, Oldenburg, Germany

Abstract. In medical education, anatomy is typically taught through lectures, cadaver dissection, and using replicas. Advances in VR technology facilitated the development of specialized VR tools for teaching, training, and other tasks. They can provide highly interactive and engaging learning environments where students can immersively and repeatedly inspect and interact with virtual 3D anatomical structures. Moreover, multi-user VR environments can be employed for collaborative learning, which may enhance the learning experience. Concrete applications are still rare, though, and the effect of collaborative learning in VR has not been adequately explored yet. Therefore, we conducted a user study with $n = 33$ participants to evaluate the effectiveness of virtual collaboration on the example of anatomy learning (and compared it to individual learning). For our study, we developed an UE4-based multi-user VR anatomy learning application. Our results show that our VR Anatomy Atlas provides an engaging learning experience and is very effective for anatomy learning, individually as well as collaboratively. However, interestingly, we could not find significant advantages for collaborative learning regarding learning effectiveness or motivation, even though the multi-user group spent more time in the learning environment. Although rather high for the single-user condition, the usability tended to be lower for the multi-user group. This may be due to the more complex environment and a higher cognitive load. Thus, more research in collaborative VR for anatomy education is needed to investigate, if and how it can be employed more effectively.

Keywords: Virtual Reality · Anatomy · Education · Anatomy Atlas · Collaborative Learning

1 Introduction

The teaching of human anatomy is fundamental in medical education as it forms the basis for the development of clinical and surgical knowledge among professionals [17,30], and influences the design of the medical curriculum [14]. Classically, anatomy teaching is done using dissection, prosection, anatomical models,

G. Zachmann et al. (Eds.): EuroXR 2023, LNCS 14410, pp. 122–135, 2023.
https://doi.org/10.1007/978-3-031-48495-7_8

and lectures. Dissection offers a hands-on approach to examining anatomical specimens, enhancing students' understanding of anatomy [32], prosection reinforces students' comprehension of complex structures and relationships, and anatomical 3D models help to visualize anatomical structures. However, dissection is costly and time-consuming, prosection relies heavily on the anatomist's skill and expertise [9], and lectures may not be effective in promoting active learning and engagement compared to more interactive approaches. Also, the availability of human cadavers and animal specimens for dissection is limited [4].

Thus, virtual reality (VR) has become increasingly prevalent in recent years and is considered a valuable tool in education [23,27]. The technology offers several advantages, such as safe, controllable, immersive 3D environments and natural interaction, making the learning experience more intuitive and engaging [2,31]. However, most current VR-based learning applications are limited to single-user usage, and there is minimal research on the effectiveness of collaborative VR-based learning. Collaborative learning, in general, has been shown to have positive effects on learning outcomes [6,15,19] and to provide numerous other benefits, though. For instance, a higher problem-solving performance, a shared understanding of meanings and a shared sense of achievement [28], increased productivity, positive interpersonal relationships [24], better psychological health, higher social competence, and self-esteem [20].

To investigate if collaboration in VR (anatomy learning) also provides benefits and more positive outcomes than individual VR learning, we developed a multi-user VR anatomy learning application. We conducted a user study to evaluate its effectiveness. Concretely, we examined the participants' learning progress, usability, and motivation when using our VR learning environment, individually and in groups. With our results, we provide valuable insights into this sparsely-researched area.

2   Related Work

Virtual reality (VR) is a rapidly expanding field that holds promise for a variety of applications in healthcare, most importantly for education and training. Accordingly, the use of VR in medicine got much attention lately [25]. For example, Falah et al. [11] developed a VR and 3D visualization system for anatomy teaching that offers an interactive, real-time 3D representation of the human heart and various self-assessment tools. Similarly, Fairen et al. [10] developed and evaluated a VR anatomy teaching tool that provides real-time, interactive 3D representations of various anatomical structures that were augmented with additional information. An evaluation with anatomy students showed very positive results. Codd and Choudhury [7] evaluated the use of 3D virtual reality and compared it with traditional anatomy teaching methods (dissection and textbooks) on the example of a human forearm. Interestingly, they found no significant learning advantages using VR. In contrast, Kurul et al. [18] also conducted a study on anatomy training comparing immersive, interactive 3D VR with classical teaching methods and found the former to lead to significantly higher test scores. Another example highlighting the benefits of VR to anatomical education is the Immersive 3D Anatomy Atlas by Gloy et al. [13]. It provides a realistic 3D model of the human body in an immersive environment and allows users to explore individual anatomical structures interactively. An evaluation showed that the VR group took significantly less time to answer anatomical questions and had significantly better test results than students that learned using textbooks. The use of VR in the medical area is not limited to education, though. Other promising application domains are surgery planning and training. For instance, Reinschluessel et al. [26] developed a VR-based surgery planning tool that provides a 3D view of medical data. They found that planning in VR had many advantages, such as improving the surgeons' spatial understanding and identifying anatomical structures.

Most VR tools for medical education and training are limited to single-user usage only, though. Only a few works enable collaboration and even fewer investigate its effects and benefits. Works that do provide shared VR environments are, for example, the one by Kaluschke et al. [16], who presented a multi-user haptic VR system for dental surgical skill training, and the one by Fischer et al. [12], who presented a system for real-time volumetric medical image visualization with support for multi-user VR interactions. Boedecker et al. [3] also developed an immersive VR application for liver surgical planning that was later extended by Schott et al. [29] to allow for collaborative usage. It provides various teaching scenarios for collaborative and cooperative training in different group sizes. An exploratory study with medical students and surgery lecturers indicated positive outcomes for usability and presence. Another immersive VR learning environment that supports collaboration of multiple users was developed by De Back et al. [1,8]. Its effectiveness was shown through two empirical studies that revealed that collaborative learning provided greater learning gains compared to conventional textbook learning, particularly among participants with low spatial ability. For a more detailed overview and review of VR for anatomy education, we refer to the work by Lee et al. [21].

3   Our Collaborative VR Anatomy Atlas

For our work, we decided to use the Immersive Anatomy Atlas by Gloy et al. [13] as a basis. It already provided a good implementation of a VR anatomy learning application and was based on the modern Unreal Engine 4. The latter made it easy to extend for our purposes, mainly, multi-user functionality. Thus, our Collaborative VR Anatomy Atlas allows multiple users to meet, interact, and collaboratively learn within a shared environment, see Fig. 1. The user interface is the same for the single- and multi-user condition and consists of the HMD and controllers for interaction and room-scale and teleportation for locomotion. Each user is represented by an avatar consisting of a virtual HMD and a pair of hands with which they are able to grab, move, rotate, and interact with the organs. When an organ is grabbed, it gets highlighted and its name is shown on a label. We decided on this avatar model, as it doesn't require complicated scanning setups, is computationally cheap, and is not prone to distracting or glitchy behavior. We use a client-server model based on the network functionality provided by the Unreal Engine 4, which allows for shared learning sessions between users in the same local network or over the internet. Our application can be started as either a listen or a dedicated server. The avatars, body parts, and other interactive objects, such as the operation table, instruments, and tablets, get replicated (synchronized) between users using RPCs. Specifically, when an object is moved (significantly) or its state is changed by a user (client), an RPC is sent to the server, which then executes a multi-cast RPC to all connected clients. In our implementation, we prevent updates on the client that initiated the change. Additionally, we optimized the replication process by employing struct replication, delta replication, caching, and careful selection of reliable/unreliable replication channels, reducing the data to be transmitted to a minimum. We also developed and integrated additional features such as a model of the human circulatory system that simulates the pulsatile blood flow, and extensive logging functionality to enable researchers to track user interaction and behavior within the virtual environment. Lastly, we developed a VR quiz (post-test) to evaluate participants' anatomy knowledge after their learning session. To access the quiz level, users can click on a 3D button located on an interactive tablet, which also provides access to other functions and controls.

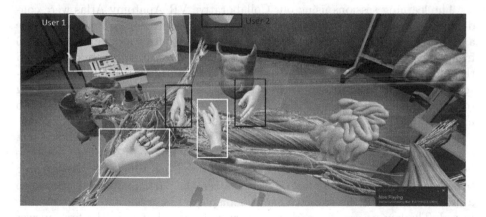

Fig. 1. Two users within our Collaborative VR Anatomy Atlas examining anatomy. Each user has an avatar consisting of a virtual HMD and one pair of hands (light blue, highlighted in black and white boxes). (Color figure online)

4   User Study

4.1   Research Questions

The purpose of our study is to investigate the effectiveness of collaborative anatomy learning in VR, specifically, using our collaborative VR Anatomy Atlas, and to compare it to individual learning. Moreover, we are also interested in assessing its impact on learning motivation and its usability. Thus, we formulated the following research questions that we intend to answer with our study: (R_1) Is the Collaborative VR Anatomy Atlas effective for anatomy learning? Based on prior research that found benefits in collaborative learning [20, 24], we want to investigate if (R_2) collaborative learning in VR also leads to better learning outcomes than individual VR learning. Additionally, we want to evaluate the usability (R_3) and user experience/motivation (R_4), in general, and especially if there are any differences between individual and collaborative learning.

4.2   Design and Setup

For our study we employed a between-subject design, hence, we divided the participants randomly into two groups: one group testing the single-user condition and the other group testing the multi-user condition. Multi-user sessions always consisted of two participants and each condition was performed an equal number of times, thus, the number of participants testing the multi-user learning condition was twice as large. We limited ourselves to groups of two, in order to still get meaningful results while having a manageable sample size. The study was conducted in our laboratory and, in the case of the multi-user condition, both participants were in the same room and could communicate verbally.

The learning sessions using our Collaborative VR Anatomy Atlas were conducted using HTC VIVE Pro HMDs including a pair of controllers. To provide a good user experience, we ensured that the frame rate was maintained at 90 frames per second. In the virtual environment, the participants were represented through avatars (see Sect. 3) and were able to freely move around using room-scale VR and teleportation. The virtual environment resembled an operating room and included a virtual anatomic 3D model that they were supposed to interact with and explore in order to learn about the anatomy.

To evaluate the learning effectiveness, we designed a multiple-choice test consisting of 8 anatomy questions. This test was conducted two times: one time before the learning session on paper (pre-test), and one time after the learning session directly in VR (post-test). For the latter, the participants transitioned to a quiz level. There, the correct answer is displayed in green and incorrect ones in red. The key presses for each answer were logged, but only the first answer entered was evaluated. Thus, the participants could learn the correct answer and improve their knowledge without affecting the validity of the study, even if they initially answered incorrectly. By comparing the results of the two tests, we calculate the learning progress. Additionally, we employed questionnaires on usability and motivation. Specifically, the System Usability Scale [5] and an adapted version of the questionnaire on motivation for cooperative and playful learning strategies (CMELAC) [22]. We customized the latter by removing the "Teamwork" factor as it was not applicable in the single-user condition and we wanted to ensure equivalence between both conditions. However, we believe it to be still valid and reliable. We also added a question to gauge the participants' interest in learning in a virtual reality environment. To analyze the participants' behavior, we tracked the time they spent in VR, video recorded the sessions, and employed extensive data logging using our custom implementation.

4.3 Procedure

The procedure of our study is depicted in Fig. 2. First, the participants were informed about the study and its goal, read and signed a consent form, and had time to ask questions. Then, the participants were asked to complete a demographical questionnaire about age, gender, previous experience with VR, etc. To determine the anatomical pre-knowledge, the participants were then asked to complete our pre-test questionnaire consisting of 8 anatomical questions (on paper). Following this, the Collaborative VR Anatomy Atlas application, its features, and its usage were briefly explained. Lastly, the participants were given up to three minutes to freely explore the VR environment and familiarize themselves with it.

Once the participants were ready, the learning session was started in which they had to explore the virtual anatomic model and complete various tasks with which we aimed to mimic classical non-VR learning. Specifically, the tasks were discovering the human anatomy, searching for specific organs (e.g. the spleen, pancreas, liver), and finding answers to the pre-test questions. The tasks were solvable individually as well as team-wise (in the multi-user condition), however, we expect the latter to be more effective, as in traditional learning. No assistance was given during task completion, but the tasks were repeatable. Figure 2 (left) shows an example of a multi-user learning session. Participants were given an unlimited amount of time.

Upon completion of the tasks, the participants were transitioned to the quiz level and took our anatomy post-test. There, they had to answer the shown questions by pressing the corresponding 3D buttons. After the post-test, and while their memories were still fresh, the participants had to complete the questionnaires about usability and motivation (on paper). They were also asked if they experienced any motion sickness and to provide subjective feedback. The procedure was identical for both conditions, with the exception that the participants of the multi-user group were explicitly instructed to work together on the anatomical tasks and to learn collaboratively. However, at the VR quiz level, they were required to complete the post-test independently.

5 Results

In this section, we present demographic data, the results of the anatomy pre-test and post-test as well as the results of the questionnaires on motivation and usability. As the data was, as expected, normally distributed, we conducted independent samples t-tests to test for statistically significant differences between the single and multi-user groups.

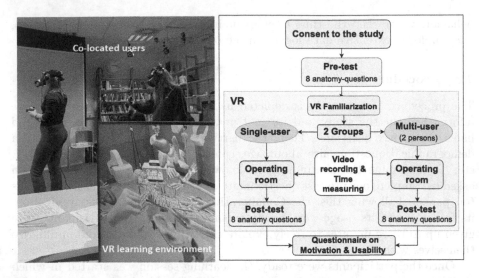

Fig. 2. Left: Multi-user learning session. In this case, both participants were in the same physical room. The virtual operating room with the anatomical model can be seen on the monitor in the foreground. Right: Flow diagram of the study procedure.

5.1 Demography

The study was conducted with $n = 33$ participants who were randomly divided into two groups for the two different learning modalities: 11 participants experienced solo learning (single user) and 22 participants experienced shared learning (multi-user) in random pairs. We selected participants that were roughly in the same age group as typical medical students. However, as they were mostly university students form various subjects, they had no particular medical experience. The single-user group was made up of 2 female (18.2%) participants and 9 male (81.8%) participants while the multi-user group was made up of 14 men (63.6%) and 8 women (36.4%). Moreover, a substantial percentage of single users (54.5%) and a smaller percentage of multi-users (22.7%) reported having extensive experience with VR, a significant percentage of single users (36.4%) and multi-users (31.8%) reported having used VR before, while a minority of single users (9.1%) and a substantial percentage of multi-users (45.5%) had no experience with VR. We also asked about the preferred learning setting: By chance, a higher percentage of single users (45.5%) preferred learning alone than in a group (9.1%) while for the multi-user group, the ratio was more balanced (45.5% each).

5.2 Anatomy Knowledge and Learning Progress

The results of the anatomy pre-test with 8 anatomical questions (conducted before the VR learning session) are depicted in Fig. 3 (left). The mean pre-test score for the single-user group was 2.091 ($SD = 1.375$) and the one for the multi-user group was 2.727 ($SD = 1.518$). Although the means are similar, there is a slight advantage for the multi-user group. However, the difference is not statistically significant $(t(31) = -1.170, p = 0.251)$.

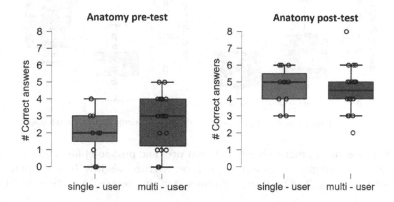

Fig. 3. Results of the anatomical knowledge pre-test conducted before the study (left) and the post-test conducted after the study (right). The multi-user participants had, on average, slightly more pre-knowledge. In the post-test, both groups scored better than before and fairly similar, with a slight advantage for the single-user group.

The results of the anatomy knowledge post-test (conducted after the study) are depicted in Fig. 3 (right). Both groups visibly improved compared to the pre-test and answered more questions correctly. Between the groups, the results are again similar, this time, with just a slight advantage for the single-user group. The mean score for the single-user group was 4.727 ($SD = 1.104$) and the mean score for the multi-user group was 4.545 ($SD = 1.371$). We, again found no significant differences between the groups ($t(31) = 0.381, p = 0.705$).

In order to better investigate the learning effectiveness, we compute the participants' learning progress as the difference (delta) between the pre- and post-test results, see Fig. 4 (left). The single-user group, on average, did have slightly higher learning progress: the mean score was 2.636 ($SD = 1.859$), whereas the multi-user group's mean score was 1.818 ($SD = 1.140$). The median, however, is more similar between the groups. A t-test resulted in: ($t(31) = 1.569, p = 0.127$). However, the result is still above the usual threshold of p ≤ 0.05 for statistical significance.

The time spent in the VR learning session, divided by single- and multi-user group, is depicted in Fig. 4 (right). The mean time for the single-user group was 22.130 min, whereas it was 33.774 min for the multi-user group. We found that the single-user group spent significantly less time in the VR environment than the multi-user group ($t = -3.783, p < 0.001$).

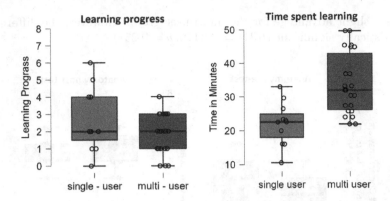

Fig. 4. Left: Learning progress (delta between pre- and post-test) for single- and multi-user groups. The single-user group learned, on average, slightly better. Right: Time spent learning in VR. The multi-user group spent, on average, more time in VR.

5.3   Questionnaires on Motivation and Usability

The results of the questionnaire on motivation for cooperative and playful learning strategies (measuring the factors of motivation, learning, and flow) are depicted in Fig. 5 (left). The average scores between the single- and multi-user groups are similar and both very positive. Concretely, on motivation, the means scores were 4.429 ($SD = 0.564$) (single user) and 4.253 ($SD = 0.612$) (multi-user), on learning 4.091 ($SD = 0.628$) (single user) and 4.164 ($SD = 0.564$) (multi-user), and on flow 3.97 ($SD = 0.69$) (single user) and 3.788 ($SD = 0.739$) (multi-user). The standard deviations indicate that the scores were relatively consistent within each group. We found no significant differences between the single-user and multi-user groups in terms of motivation ($t(31) = 0.795, p = 0.433$), learning ($t(31) = -0.336, p = 0.739$), or flow ($t(31) = 0.681, p = 0.501$).

The perceived usability of the Collaborative VR Anatomy Atlas was measured using the System Usability Scale. The SUS scores were calculated using the standard methodology and are depicted in Fig. 5 (right). Overall, the participants provided positive feedback and moderate to high ratings. The mean SUS score for the single-user group was 75.227 ($SD = 8.976$) and for the multi-user group 66.364 ($SD = 14.15$). The t-test revealed that there is a noticeable difference in means between the single-user and multi-user groups, although the usual threshold of $p = 0.005$ for statistical significance was just not reached ($t(31) = 1.887, p = 0.069$).

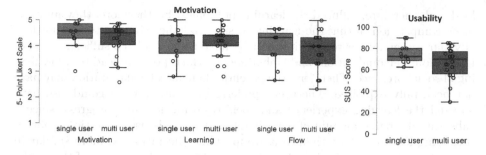

Fig. 5. Left: Results of the motivation questionnaire (factored into motivation, learning, and flow). The averages between the single- and multi-user groups are similar and both very high. Right: The System Usability Scale scores. The scores are generally high but the single-user group's feedback is more positive.

6 Discussion

Looking at the results, the post-test scores show a substantial improvement compared to the pre-test scores, for both groups, single-user and multi-user. Accordingly, on average, the participants had high learning progress. These positive results may come due to the VR learning environment allowing the participants to interact with the content in an immersive, engaging, and interactive way, which could have helped them better retain the information and recall it more easily during the post-test. The VR environment also allowed learners to visualize and explore anatomy in a three-dimensional way, which could have been helpful to understand the subject matter and the spatial relations between anatomical structures. With these results, we can answer our first research question R_1: our Collaborative VR Anatomy Atlas is, generally, effective in enhancing the knowledge and understanding of anatomy. This result is in line with prior research [23,27], that found learning using VR to be beneficial.

Interestingly, the learning progress and post-test scores are not higher for the collaborative learning condition. In fact, they tend to be slightly (but not statistically significant) lower than the ones for the single-user group. Thus, we could not find VR learning to be more effective in collaboration than individually, which answers our research question R_2. This result is interesting as we would have expected advantages for the multi-user group since collaborative learning is generally considered beneficial [6,15,19]. A potential explanation for the higher (or at least similarly high) single-user learning outcomes could be that the single-user group had on average slightly less prior knowledge about anatomy (see the pre-test scores). This means that the single-user group had more learning potential. Another possible reason for these results may be that the participants that learned individually could better focus on the task than the participants in the shared environment. The participants in the latter group were possibly more distracted by each other and the more complex multi-user environment, which provides additional social cues and requires communication and coordination between users. This may have increased their cognitive load and, therefore, reduced the learning outcomes. Furthermore, they may felt more competition during the learning session and the VR post-test. Additionally, our chosen avatar representation may have not provided a sufficient level of immersion, personalization, and embodiment, which possibly lead to a low feeling of social presence. Therefore, the potential benefits of collaboration may have not been fully exploited. The users' preferred learning setting could also have affected the learning experience and their resulting learning progress, since a substantially higher amount of participants in the single-user condition reported preferring learning alone than in a group, while the ratio was more similar in the multi-user group. This may have influenced the results in favor of the single-user group for this study. We also have to consider the option that the task of anatomy learning in VR may be one that is not benefiting from collaboration.

Our results regarding the time spent learning in VR show that the multi-user group stayed significantly longer in the learning sessions. On one hand, this could be an indicator of a more engaging, positive user and learning experience, which multiple participants suggested after the study. On the other hand, the increased time may indicate slower learning progress and reinforce the assumption of a more complex, distracting environment for the multi-user group.

Regarding our research question R_3, we found that the results of the usability questionnaire are generally positive, especially for the single-user group. This shows that our Collaborative VR Anatomy Atlas provides a good user experience. The score for the multi-user group is noticeably lower, though. This reinforces our assumption that participants in the multi-user condition perceived the environment as more complex and demanding, potentially leading to a higher cognitive load. Thus, the lower usability may be a central reason for the lower learning progress for the multi-user group. We also got very positive average scores in our motivation questionnaire for both the single-user and multi-user groups, which indicates high levels of motivation and engagement when using our Collaborative VR Anatomy Atlas. The scores for all three factors (motivation, learning, flow) were similar between the groups, which answers our research question R_4. This result is somewhat surprising, as, after analyzing the other results, we would have expected the multi-user group to fare slightly worse to be in line with the lower usability results and our theories about the more complex, distracting shared environment and increased cognitive load. The subjective feedback given by the participants during and after the learning session was generally very positive, too. They found the Collaborative VR Atlas to be an effective, useful, and enjoyable anatomy learning tool. Especially the collaborative scenario was often noted to provide an engaging, fun user and learning experience. Moreover, no participant experienced any signs of cybersickness.

7   Limitations

One limitation of this study is related to the adapted CMELAC questionnaire. Although we assume it to be still valid and reliable, we did not formally reassess it. In addition, the number of participants was relatively small and usability ratings were mediocre, so the study's power may be limited.

8 Conclusions and Future Work

In order to investigate the effectiveness of collaborative learning in VR, we developed the Collaborative VR Anatomy Atlas, a virtual reality system for anatomy education, and evaluated it by conducting a user study with $n = 33$ participants in which we compared individual learning to collaborative learning. Our application is based on the Unreal Engine 4 and provides an immersive multi-user learning environment in which users can interactively explore detailed anatomical structures including a model of the circulatory system. The results show that our Collaborative VR Anatomy Atlas was effective in anatomy learning for both single and multi-user scenarios. Moreover, the participants found the learning experience engaging and motivating and reported moderate to high usability scores. However, we could not find significant advantages (or differences) for the collaborative learning scenario, neither regarding learning effectiveness, nor motivation. The usability even tended to be slightly lower. We suspect this to be due to the more complex shared environment and a higher cognitive load. Other reasons could be that the used avatars were not immersive enough, leading to low social presence, or that learning anatomy in VR is a task that does not necessarily benefit from collaboration. Nonetheless, we believe that, like in real-world learning situations, collaborative VR settings can be effective and efficient for learning complex spatial knowledge. However, our results demonstrate that more work-needs to be done to determine the best 3D interaction techniques and forms of collaboration in VR to achieve these goals.

In the future, we plan to further enhance the usability and user experience, especially regarding multi-user usage, by developing improved interaction techniques and integrating more comfort features, such as different colors for each avatar's hands. It would also be important to normalize the learning progress based on pre-existing knowledge and formally revalidate the adapted CMELAC questionnaire. Moreover, we want to conduct further studies to compare the effectiveness of the Collaborative VR Anatomy Atlas to traditional (collaborative) anatomy education methods and examine the impact of presence, cognitive load, more immersive avatars, and co-located vs remote collaboration. Future research could also focus on exploring larger group sizes and potential correlations between learning progress and gender mix-up within groups/age ranges. Lastly, comparing traditional VR setups with Mixed Reality setups may be interesting.

Acknowledgment. We express our gratitude to Dr. Verena Uslar and Prof. Dr. med. Dirk Weyhe for their assistance with the anatomy-related questions and tasks. The software used in the study was built on top of the virtual anatomy atlas by Gloy et al. [13].

References

1. de Back, T.T., Tinga, A.M., Nguyen, P., Louwerse, M.M.: Benefits of immersive collaborative learning in CAVE-based virtual reality. Int. J. Educ. Technol. High. Educ. **17**, 1–18 (2020)

2. Barfield, W., Zeltzer, D., Sheridan, T., Slater, M.: Presence and performance within virtual environments. In: Virtual Environments and Advanced Interface Design, pp. 473–513 (1995)
3. Boedecker, C., et al.: Using virtual 3D-models in surgical planning: workflow of an immersive virtual reality application in liver surgery. Langenbecks Arch. Surg. **406**, 911–915 (2021)
4. Bonali, M., et al.: Surgical instruments and preparation of the specimen. In: Bonali, M., Presutti, L., Marchioni, D. (eds.) Comparative Atlas of Endoscopic Ear Surgery, pp. 9–27. Springer, Cham (2021). https://doi.org/10.1007/978-3-030-47005-0_2
5. Brooke, J.: SUS: a retrospective. J. Usability Stud. **8**(2), 29–40 (2013)
6. Casey, A., Goodyear, V.A.: Can cooperative learning achieve the four learning outcomes of physical education? A review of literature. Quest **67**(1), 56–72 (2015)
7. Codd, A.M., Choudhury, B.: Virtual reality anatomy: is it comparable with traditional methods in the teaching of human forearm musculoskeletal anatomy? Anat. Sci. Educ. **4**(3), 119–125 (2011)
8. De Back, T.T., Tinga, A.M., Louwerse, M.M.: Learning in immersed collaborative virtual environments: design and implementation. Interact. Learn. Environ., 1–19 (2021)
9. Estai, M., Bunt, S.: Best teaching practices in anatomy education: a critical review. Ann. Anat.-Anatomischer Anzeiger **208**, 151–157 (2016)
10. Fairén González, M., Farrés, M., Moyes Ardiaca, J., Insa, E.: Virtual reality to teach anatomy. In: Eurographics 2017: Education Papers, pp. 51–58. European Association for Computer Graphics (Eurographics) (2017)
11. Falah, J., et al.: Virtual reality medical training system for anatomy education. In: 2014 Science and Information Conference, pp. 752–758 (2014)
12. Fischer, R., Chang, K.-C., Weller, R., Zachmann, G.: Volumetric medical data visualization for collaborative VR environments. In: Bourdot, P., Interrante, V., Kopper, R., Olivier, A.-H., Saito, H., Zachmann, G. (eds.) EuroVR 2020. LNCS, vol. 12499, pp. 178–191. Springer, Cham (2020). https://doi.org/10.1007/978-3-030-62655-6_11
13. Gloy, K., et al.: Immersive anatomy atlas: learning factual medical knowledge in a virtual reality environment. Anat. Sci. Educ. **15**(2), 360–368 (2022)
14. Guimarães, B., Dourado, L., Tsisar, S., Diniz, J.M., Madeira, M.D., Ferreira, M.A.: Rethinking anatomy: how to overcome challenges of medical education's evolution. Acta Med. Port. **30**(2), 134–140 (2017)
15. Johnson, D.W., Johnson, R.T., Stanne, M.B.: Cooperative learning methods: a meta-analysis (2000)
16. Kaluschke, M., Yin, M.S., Haddawy, P., Srimaneekarn, N., Saikaew, P., Zachmann, G.: A shared haptic virtual environment for dental surgical skill training. In: 2021 IEEE Conference on Virtual Reality and 3D User Interfaces Abstracts and Workshops (VRW), pp. 347–352. IEEE (2021)
17. Keyes, O., Peil, B., Williams, R.M., Spiel, K.: Reimagining (women's) health: HCI, gender and essentialised embodiment. ACM Trans. Comput.-Hum. Interact. (TOCHI) **27**(4), 1–42 (2020)
18. Kurul, R., Ögün, M.N., Neriman Narin, A., Avci, Ş., Yazgan, B.: An alternative method for anatomy training: immersive virtual reality. Anat. Sci. Educ. **13**(5), 648–656 (2020)
19. Kyndt, E., Raes, E., Lismont, B., Timmers, F., Cascallar, E., Dochy, F.: A meta-analysis of the effects of face-to-face cooperative learning. Do recent studies falsify or verify earlier findings? Educ. Res. Rev. **10**, 133–149 (2013)

20. Laal, M., Ghodsi, S.M.: Benefits of collaborative learning. Procedia. Soc. Behav. Sci. **31**, 486–490 (2012)
21. Lee, J.E., Han, I.H., Kim, S.H., Kim, K.S.: Effectiveness of virtual reality-based learning for anatomy education: a systematic review and meta-analysis. Anat. Sci. Educ. **14**(5), 587–600 (2021)
22. Manzano-León, A., et al.: Development and validation of a questionnaire on motivation for cooperative playful learning strategies. Int. J. Environ. Res. Public Health **18**(3), 960 (2021)
23. Markant, D.B., Ruggeri, A., Gureckis, T.M., Xu, F.: Enhanced memory as a common effect of active learning. Mind Brain Educ. **10**(3), 142–152 (2016)
24. Nokes-Malach, T.J., Richey, J.E., Gadgil, S.: When is it better to learn together? Insights from research on collaborative learning. Educ. Psychol. Rev. **27**, 645–656 (2015)
25. Preim, B., Saalfeld, P., Hansen, C.: Virtual and augmented reality for educational anatomy. In: Uhl, J.-F., Jorge, J., Lopes, D.S., Campos, P.F. (eds.) Digital Anatomy. HIS, pp. 299–324. Springer, Cham (2021). https://doi.org/10.1007/978-3-030-61905-3_16
26. Reinschluessel, A.V., Muender, T., Salzmann, D., Döring, T., Malaka, R., Weyhe, D.: Virtual reality for surgical planning-evaluation based on two liver tumor resections. Frontiers Surg. **9** (2022)
27. Roh, T.H., et al.: Virtual dissection of the real brain: integration of photographic 3D models into virtual reality and its effect on neurosurgical resident education. Neurosurg. Focus **51**(2), E16 (2021)
28. Rutherford, S.M.: Collaborative Learning: Theory, Strategies and Educational Benefits. Nova (2014)
29. Schott, D., et al.: A VR/AR environment for multi-user liver anatomy education. In: 2021 IEEE Virtual Reality and 3D User Interfaces (VR), pp. 296–305 (2021)
30. Singal, A., Bansal, A., Chaudhary, P.: Cadaverless anatomy: darkness in the times of pandemic covid-19 (2020)
31. Slater, M.: Immersion and the illusion of presence in virtual reality. Br. J. Psychol. **109**(3), 431–433 (2018)
32. Smith, J., Jones, S.: Anatomy education: classical techniques and modern advancements. Med. Educ. J. **10**(2), 50–60 (2020)

3D Molecules Visualization with XRmol: An AR Web Tool for Mobile Devices

Sara Corazza[iD], Fabio Pittarello[(✉)][iD], and Marta Simeoni[iD]

Università Ca' Foscari Venezia, Venice, Italy
{pitt,simeoni}@unive.it

Abstract. We present XRmol, a prototype web application, based on the WebXR standard, for visualizing 3D proteins and nucleic acids. The work represents a contribution to the investigation of the potential stemming from the AR paradigm coupled with the use of personal smartphones and features a number of solutions for improving access, portability, and use in different contexts. A first pilot study with 14 volunteers outlines its potential for integration into daily lab activities and use in educational contexts.

Keywords: AR · Education · Molecular Graphics Tool · Pilot Study · WebXR

1 Introduction

3D representation of molecules offers interesting opportunities for researchers, teachers, students, and citizens to comprehend and manipulate these structures better. Researchers have used different interaction paradigms over the years to achieve this goal. While visualization for desktop systems has always been the mainstream solution, technology advances in the so-called mixed reality continuum, which, according to Milgram and Kishino [14], includes all the different mixtures of real and virtual worlds, have progressively widened the focus to immersive visualization. One of the most complete and updated surveys [13], related to the use of immersive environments for representing molecular structures, underlines that despite the achievements reached in research related to molecular visualization, there are still open issues. In the mixed reality continuum, most work has been done in the virtual reality domain. David et al. [13] suggest that the reason may be attributed to the fact that molecular structures exist on a different scale, and therefore there isn't a direct relation with reality. However, Patterson et al. [16] state that an immersive environment can lead to high cognitive loads because the user is placed in an unknown environment. Concerning education, not all the researchers agree on the benefits of mixed reality for producing better educational outcomes [1,3,4,30]. Besides, the choice of technologies brings consequences in terms of user experience but also on the real possibility of using the application in different contexts, facing questions of portability, immediate availability and costs.

G. Zachmann et al. (Eds.): EuroXR 2023, LNCS 14410, pp. 136–149, 2023.
https://doi.org/10.1007/978-3-031-48495-7_9

Overall, there are reasons for investigating further the mixed reality domain, focusing more on other segments of it. While head-mounted displays (HMDs) for augmented reality (AR) are less diffused and cost even more than VR HMDs, an interesting type of experience can be granted by AR applications for smartphones. These personal devices have great potential for computing power, immediate availability, and the possibility to simultaneously arrange an AR experience for many people, like in a lab or a classroom context. The work presented in this paper is meant to contribute to this investigation. We present XRmol, a web-based protein structure viewer prototype that provides an interactive 3D display of proteins and nucleic acids in different environments, including desktop computers and devices supporting AR.

XRMol is meant for public release and free to use, and it is currently accessible on the web (https://xrmol.dais.unive.it/index.html).

XRmol has been developed to be computationally lightweight and is supported also by mobile devices. Moreover, XRmol has been designed to offer an attractive and intuitive user interface to minimize the need for preliminary training. XRmol provides all the typical functions of molecular graphics software, which include different types of visualization of protein structures (space-fill, wireframe, secondary structure, ball and rods), surface calculation and the use of a wide range of colors, as well as the ability to read any PDB file that complies with the latest PDB standard [18]. The various functions can be experienced through the usual desktop screen and AR. VR mode is currently in progress and it is considered for inclusion in the next releases of the platform. Overall, the main research questions that guided the design and the implementation of XRmol are:

- How to provide seamless and fast access to a complete dataset of proteins for desktop and mobile paradigms?
  How to provide a flexible approach for visualizing the molecules in different contexts of use, including educational and research activities, fostering collaboration among colleagues and integration with research procedures?

Concerning the first question, XRmol allows accessing any molecule available in the PDB Databank [2], the most complete dataset of proteins, by simply specifying its PDB identifier. For the AR paradigm, XRmol adopts a marker-less approach, which doesn't require the preliminary creation of a physical marker for each protein to visualize. Implementing these two features represents a relevant contribution w.r.t. the existing solutions in the literature. Concerning the second question, XRmol implements two modalities for mobile devices, paving the way for the tool's use (even collaborative) in various contexts where computers with large screens may not be accessible (e.g., classrooms, research labs, libraries, travel). Besides, the mobile AR solution improves the application's usability by translating zooming and rotating operations into physical gestures, which are more intuitive and retain the connection with the real environment.

This work will focus mainly on the AR paradigm coupled with personal smartphones, which seems to have great potential for several of the issues cited above, including the interaction in a well-known real environment and the availability for many potential users. The use of web technologies for this project brings additional advantages in terms of the immediate availability of the application. Portability is further increased by using standards like WebXR [29], which is available for different classes of devices. The platform has been built to investigate the potential for research and education, and in this work we also report the results of an initial evaluation study, targeted to researchers, teachers and students, which was very useful for obtaining feedback about the work done and improve the application for wider use.

2   Related Work

Many solutions for representing molecules in a 3D space are available in the literature: stand-alone applications, web applications and plug-ins written in various programming languages (Python, Java, JavaScript, etc.) and with a wide range of features.

Stand-Alone Applications: Stand-alone applications are the most widespread type of software for the 3D visualization of molecules. Among the most famous for desktop environments we find PyMol [22], UCSF Chimera [17] and Swiss-PDB viewer [11]. An ample and very recent survey [13] cites the most interesting projects related to the VR paradigm, such as UCSF ChimeraX [10]. Additional details and citations can be found in the survey itself. While research on AR interfaces for molecular visualization is less developed, there are some interesting stand-alone applications worth noting, as Stereochem [24] and Jmol [12].

Stand-alone solutions require the installation of specialized software that often is not available for all operating systems. This represents a strong limit for portability and immediate accessibility of the software functionalities, in a scenario that nowadays has become even more complex for the availability of different types of target devices (e.g., desktops and laptops, mobile devices, head-mounted displays). This situation led our project to focus on web technologies.

Web Applications: Displaying 3D objects on the web makes them accessible to all interested people, like scientists, educators, and students, not just experts with access to dedicated (and possibly expensive) software. Specifications for representing 3D objects on the web have been available since the beginning of the web itself. The standardization effort led initially to define VRML97 [26], a high-level language for specifying objects and behaviors. The X3D specification [31] followed, and permitted to represent all the VRML97 entities with an XML language. Initially, the deployment of 3D scenes for the web required the use of external plugins, like Java applets that were good in performance but had security problems and could be tedious to install on web browsers. In the latest year, technological advances have permitted to move to solutions fully based on software layers based on WebGL [27], supported by most modern web browsers. WebGL is a low-level graphics library that requires the use of additional layers for authoring the interactive 3D scene. In recent years its functionalities have been integrated by WebVR [28] and WebXR [29]. The former had added the possibility to visualize the 3D interactive scenes on VR devices. The latter, a W3C specification, has replaced WebVR, adding support for augmented reality.

There are different solutions for desktop environments. LiteMol [23] is a free web library/plugin for 3D visualization of molecules and other related data written in Typescript. As a library, it provides a parser and data representation for molecular data. NGL Viewer [20,21] is a complete web application for the visualization of complex 3D molecular structures. Its main feature is scalability since it is able to parse and render very large structures in a few seconds. GLmol [15] is a 3D molecular viewer based on WebGL and JavaScript used to embed molecular models in web pages without the need for Java or other plugins. It is meant for desktop browsers and Android devices that support WebGL. Jsmol is the JavaScript version of Jmol [12], an open-source Java applet for the visualization of 3D structures. It has all the typical functionalities of a protein viewer. Being a plugin, Jsmol needs to be embedded in a web page for use. Miew [8] is a high-performance web tool for advanced visualization and manipulation of molecular structures. It works as a stand-alone Javascript/HTML5 web application or integrates as a component into web pages. Miew is supported by all the latest versions of WebGL-enabled desktop and mobile OS (IOS, Android).

VRmol [32,33] and ProteinVR [5] add to the desktop mode the VR mode. Windows Mixed Reality, HTC Vive or Oculus Rift can be used to access VR mode in VRmol. VRmol can parse PDB files uploaded from the local filesystem or retrieved from the PDB databank [2] and displays the result in various structural representation styles. VRmol has structure editing functionalities and a *fragment* mode, with which one can emphasize some specific regions by presenting them in diverse styles. ProteinVR is a web-based application that displays 3D molecular structures within built-in biological environments (intracellular, lipid bilayer etc.). Its strength is the wide range of VR headsets and operating systems supported. ProteinVR can read PDB files directly from the PDB databank [2], parse and then display them in the pre-processed environment.

Also for web applications AR research is less developed, but there are some interesting web platforms to focus on. The first one is BioSIM [9], a free web application available for most desktop and mobile operating systems, based on A-Frame and AR.js. Currently, 70 molecules can be visualized using smartphones or desktop cameras, after the recognition of one of the physical markers provided by the platform. MoleculARweb [19] is a widely diffused web platform for visualizing molecular models in virtual and augmented reality. Markers are used in augmented reality not only for visualizing molecular representations but also for highlighting, through the direct manipulation of the markers themselves, interactions between different structures. In this platform, some of the visualization features can be launched using the WebXR functionality that detects flat surfaces and superimposes the models on top of them, instead of using markers.

Because of the success of this tool, the authors have proposed later a tool for overcoming the limits of the initial set of molecules mapped to the markers. This online tool [7] permits users to generate VR/AR models compatible with the platform, starting from a PDB file. The output of the processing is sent by mail to users who can decide to use it for a marker-based or marker-less visualization.

3   XRmol

The analysis of the available literature determined the design directions for the XRmol project described in this paper. As anticipated, we decided to use web technologies to grant immediate accessibility and ease the integration with other web tools and libraries. The choice of relying on the web-based, cross-platform WebXR standard, was done for augmenting the portability across devices and operating systems and for granting longevity. In this respect, the history of interactive 3D visualizations for the web has demonstrated the superiority of standards (e.g., VRML, X3D) to proprietary solutions. WebXR, although still in development, represents the most advanced API that brings also the possibility to design for different paradigms: inline (desktop and mobile screens), VR and AR. This grants flexibility and it is also an interesting opportunity for making comparisons. As anticipated, this work has a special focus on AR, which is a less explored paradigm, as underlined in [13], but has great potential in terms of integration in the flow of research and educational activities in labs and classrooms and collaboration with colleagues. Besides, the choice of privileging a solution based on personal smartphones improves portability and immediate access and permits the arrangement of educational experiences with a large number of students. Most of the examined AR works take advantage of physical markers for triggering the visualizations. Although this may represent a point of strength in the case of advanced interactions like in the MoleculARweb platform, it is also a point of weakness because it limits the number of molecules that can be visualized. For this reason, we decided to go for the marker-less solution and we complemented this choice with seamless access to the huge PDB dataset, a feature that is missing or requires some kind of intermediate manual pre-processing in most of the AR solutions examined.

XRmol is fully written in Javascript, HTML and CSS. It is composed of three modules: a *parsing module* to retrieve and parse PDB files from Protein Data Bank [2] or uploaded from the user's device; a *rendering module* to generate and render 3D models of molecular structures and an *interaction module* to analyze and interact with them in three different environments: inline (desktop/mobile screens), immersive VR and AR. XRmol makes use of external API/libraries for rendering 3D molecules in the three environments, namely WebGL [27], Three.js [25] and WebXR [29]. The XRmol inline visualization mode is supported by all browsers while the AR and VR modes strictly depend on WebXR, which fully supports the latest releases of Chrome, Opera and Firefox. At the moment, we mainly focused on the inline mode because it grants the widest portability, and on the AR mode for the potential in educational and research settings, and for the challenges it poses. An additional reason is related to the COVID pandemic, which brought issues for sharing devices (i.e. HMD) that usually are not owned by many persons. On the contrary, inline and AR modes could count the wide availability of devices for personal use. However, the implementation of the VR mode is in progress, and it will be considered for release in future versions of the platform.

The XRmol graphical user interfaces (GUI) for desktop and mobile devices are shown in Fig. 1. They have been designed following a user-centered design approach. Three categories of users have been identified who may be interested in using XRmol: students, teachers and researchers. For each category or *User Personas* [6], the User Stories and User Flows have been developed, in order to describe features appreciated by a user using software and to derive from them a possible structure for the application. For example, Johanna Lee is a 38-year-old teacher with a PhD. in biology, whose main goals are to be a good teacher and train future biology experts. The main barriers to her activity are the difficulties in explaining chemical concepts and permitting students to manipulate molecular models. The related User Flows for this Persona describe how to show protein different colors to capture the students' attention, how to display bonds for explaining secondary and tertiary structures, how to show nucleic acid structures for explaining base pairing, and how to take advantage of AR for engaging students and permitting them to have a better comprehension of molecular structures. Once the different functionalities were established, the interfaces for the inline mode (desktop and mobile, see Fig. 1), as well as for the AR mode (see Fig. 2), were developed. The graphical style and rendering of molecules are the result of a trade-off between expressiveness and quality of representation in order to obtain fast visualization on mobile devices.

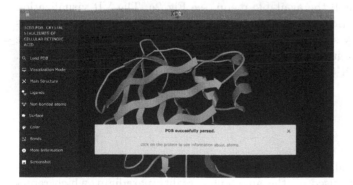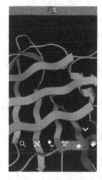

Fig. 1. Left: Desktop devices GUI; Right: mobile devices GUI

AR interaction for smartphones takes advantage of a two-level horizontally scrollable menu placed at the bottom of the interface (see Fig. 2). This solution, stemming from an initial prototyping work, is meant to minimize the occlusion of the real scene by the visual widgets currently in use. The first level is characterized by the use of icons for minimizing the horizontal width of the menu and for offering a visual cue that can be easily learned to speed up interaction. The second-level menu is semi-transparent and uses only textual labels. While most application functionalities can be accessed from this menu, the control of the molecule representation in terms of translation, rotation and scaling takes advantage of different mechanisms. Touch interaction is used for establishing the position of the molecule on the selected horizontal plane (see Fig. 2c). Rotation can be adjusted by manipulating a spherical widget with shares its center with the center of the molecule (see Fig. 2, from d to h). Finally, scaling can be operated with a pinch gesture. In addition, users can change their position to see the molecule from other directions or get near to examine the molecule's details.

When XRmol is first opened, the 1CBS protein is taken from the PDB databank and rendered by default. We proceed by briefly describing the various interactions, with the help of screenshots taken from a mobile device to show the AR mode rendering.

Users can render molecules in XRmol in two ways: by uploading their own file in PDB format [18] or by searching for it in the PDB Bank [2] using its four-letter identifier, as shown in Fig. 2a. Once the protein is shown, its structure can be explored in four different display modes: *Wireframe* (see Fig. 2b), *Ball and Rod* (see Fig. 2d), *Sphere* (see Fig. 2e) and *Secondary Structure* (see Fig. 2f). Ligands and water molecules can be added to the scene, for instance, Fig. 2g shows the secondary structure of a protein and its water molecules as spheres. XRmol also allows for representing the protein surface in different ways, for instance, Fig. 2h shows the Van Der Waals surface of the protein under study. Moreover, XRmol offers a wide range of colors for molecules. For instance, the classical color scheme is used for showing atoms (see Figs. 2d and 2e), residues (see Fig. 2f) and chains (see Fig. 2g). Finally, The VR or AR visualization modes can be activated through the available menu, see Fig. 2c. The VR visualization mode is currently under development and will be considered for the next releases of the tool. Instead, by selecting the immersive AR mode, the users can decide where to place the protein as the WebXR Hit Testing module has found a surface. Once it is positioned, it can be rotated and resized, but not moved.

4   Pilot Study

4.1   Volunteers

The prototype was evaluated with a pilot study that involved 14 volunteers aged 25–60 and was focused on the augmented reality paradigm, which represents the most innovative interaction modality of the project. The volunteers included chemists, physicists, biochemists and biologists in different stages of their careers (teachers, researchers and PhD students). All test participants had already used protein viewers in the past, e.g. PyMol [22] in particular. In addition, one candidate also had experience in programming molecular viewers. None of them had tried augmented reality viewers before this test.

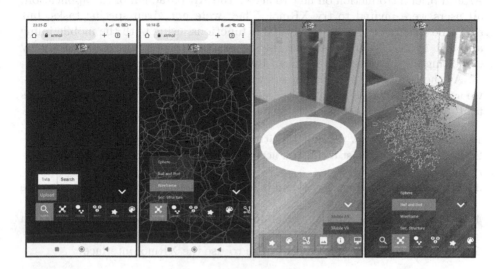

(a) Search/upload a PDB file (b) Wireframe visualization (c) AR mode: placing the protein (d) Ball and rod colored by elements

(e) Sphere visualization colored by residues (f) Ribbon visualization colored by residues (g) Ribbon colored by chain and water molecules as spheres (h) Protein with the Van der Waals surface

Fig. 2. XRmol examples in mobile inline and AR modes

4.2 Study Setup

After a brief introduction on how to access the AR paradigm of the application, all users were invited to try XRmol. They were not given specific tasks, but everyone was free to try all the available functions, using both the mobile inline and AR modes. Volunteers were able to explore the protein under study by exploiting all the possibilities offered by XRmol.

At the end of the test, volunteers were asked to fill in a survey. First of all, we asked the participants to give an answer to 5 questions related to the factors that, according to Jacob Nielsen, define usability:

1. **Learnability:** How difficult was it to learn to use the system?
2. **Efficiency:** How fast could you accomplish your task with the XRmol interface?
3. **Memorability:** How easy would it be to remember how to interact with the interface in future sessions?
4. **Error Tolerance:** How much helpful was XRmol for informing you, through dedicated messages, about your errors?
5. **Satisfaction:** How much did you like to use the XRmol interface?

Then, in order to have additional insights about the two different interaction modalities for mobile devices (inline and AR modes), we asked the volunteers to evaluate the simplification of zooming and rotation operations and the additional connection with the real environment permitted by the AR mode.

For all the questions mentioned above, the participants were asked to give a score using a 5-point Likert scale. The closed questions were complemented by two open questions focused on the main points of strength and weakness of the interface.

4.3 Results

The Tukey box plot displayed in Fig. 3) summarizes the answers to the closed questions. Three quartiles out of four are associated with the minimum score (1, i.e., very easy) measuring the difficulty of learning, and with the 4–5 score range for the other four usability parameters.

All the users assigned a score in the 4–5 range to the parameters that measure the simplification of interaction brought by the AR paradigm. Finally, most users appointed a score in the 3–5 range to the connection with the real world added by the AR paradigm. Only a single user appointed a score equal to 2 for this parameter.

The points of strength cited in the answers to the first open question included:

1. the ease of visualization;
2. the rapid visualization of crystallographic structures;
3. the immediate access without the need to download software or data sets;
4. the integration with the PDB databank;
5. the access from a personal smartphone;

6. the fact that augmented reality permits to access visualization without losing contact with colleagues and the lab environment;
7. the great potential for research, teaching, and stimulating citizens' awareness.

The points of weakness cited in the answers to the second open question included:

1. the fact that XRMol is rapid, but it requires fast smartphones for visualizing the most complex structures;
2. the lack of an initial tutorial, useful for non-experts (students and citizens);
3. the lack of color personalization;
4. the difficulty to export hi-res images.

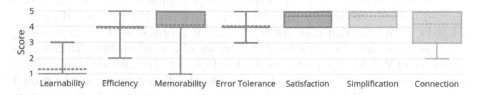

Fig. 3. The results for the five usability questions (green boxes) and the two additional questions related to simplification and connection issues (yellow boxes). The dashed lines represent the means for each parameter. (Color figure online)

4.4   Discussion

The evaluation study displays that XRMol has an interesting potential. The rest of the section discusses the results for each of the considered parameters and the answers to the open questions.

Learnability. All the users agreed on the fact that the system has a high degree of learnability, as outlined by the very low scores obtained for the difficulty of learning. All the volunteers were able to use XRmol and didn't ask for support after the initial briefing. The use of specialized terms was not a problem because the participants all had experience with protein viewers, as they are part of their daily work tools, and were therefore already familiar with the terminology and functions used by this type of software. However, some volunteers outlined in the open questions the potential of XRmol as an educational tool for students and even for citizens, and therefore they suggested that, in this scenario, it would be useful to provide an initial tutorial.

Efficiency. The speed of rendering of the protein structures and the speed with which it was possible to apply changes allowed an optimal user experience in many situations, even if one user mentioned that complex visualizations could be an issue for low-performance smartphones and therefore assigned a 2 score.

Memorability. Volunteers esteemed that remembering how to use the application after the initial trial would have not caused trouble. This stems not only from the generally very high scores but also from the open questions, where the ease of use of the interface was mentioned.

Error Tolerance. The good score obtained for this parameter is most probably due to the fact that most interactions are based on the selection of functionalities from a two-level menu placed in the lower part of the interface and this grants the possibility to explore options and to recover readily from unwanted situations. Besides, in the AR interface, traditional view adjustments like panning or zooming, were converted to physical actions by the user which manipulated the smartphone and also this feature granted an easy recovery from unwanted situations. Other situations that require direct user input or the availability of the network connection were managed through dedicated error messages that directed the user toward the solution of the problem. For example: if the user entered a PDB code that does not exist, XRmol informed her by recommending to try another one. For the sake of clarity, we also mention that XRmol takes advantage of WebXR [29] that is under development. The available implementation sometimes caused unexpected errors, like the disappearance of the protein from the scene, which occurred when it was no longer framed by the smartphone or when the user got too close. Users were advised about this possibility and asked not to take into account this issue when assigning the error tolerance score.

Satisfaction. At the end of the tests all the users were very satisfied with XRmol. In particular, as outlined in the answers to the open questions, they showed enthusiasm for the possibility of viewing the molecules in augmented reality. They appreciated the intuitive AR interaction that helped to understand the structure of the molecules. Besides they focused on the advantages of using immediately personal devices without the need to install special tools and without losing contact with colleagues and the working environment. AR was considered very useful both for safety reasons (labs can be dangerous places) and the possibility to discuss and to use the other tools that are part of the working routine. The request to add the possibility to export hi-res images underlines the interest in inserting XRmol in the daily workflow. According to [13], the task of extracting data, images, or video from a 3D molecular representation is one of the activities that help its integration into the workflow of scientists. The functionality has already been integrated into the current version of XRmol.

Simplification of Zooming and Rotation Operations with AR. The high scores assigned by the users underline the appreciation for the simplification brought by the AR paradigm. Converting zooming and rotation operations to the physical manipulation of the device permitted to hold it with a single hand in many situations, consulting books or taking notes with the other hand.

Connection with the Real Environment. Also the additional connection permitted by the AR received a positive evaluation by the users, although less .- Some users outlined in additional comments the feeling of lively navigating the proteins and the engagement triggered by this modality, considered important for students and non-experts.

Answers to the open questions related to the points of strength and weakness of XRmol outlined the appreciation for the direct access to the PDB repository, a feature not available in the other AR platforms. Also, the other qualifying features of the platform, like immediate access without the need to download the software, the use of the personal smartphone, and the possibility of using the AR application without losing contact with the real environment were positively mentioned by the volunteers. Concluding, all the test users concluded that XRmol is a tool they would surely use during their research.

Critical remarks were mainly related to the request for additional features. Besides, in spite of the fact that all the volunteers recognized the speed of visualization of XRmol, they underlined the need for fast smartphones. Finally, the request for an initial tutorial for non-experts underlines again the interest of the University researchers in the educational potential of XRmol.

5 Conclusion

XRmol is a web platform under development that permits the representation of molecules taking advantage of different interaction paradigms. In this work, we have focused on the AR paradigm, whose potential has been extensively outlined. The user study has given initial feedback that outlines the interest of the potential users in inserting the tool into the daily workflow of research activities. Besides, all the users underlined the educational interest of the platform and requested additional features, like an initial tutorial, to support it. Future work will consider not only VR implementation but also additional exploration of the potential of AR technology for collaboration in real settings. As outlined in [13], HMDs can be helpful for remote collaboration, but they isolate the user from the real world and therefore probably are not the best choice for performing other complementary actions, like manipulating other lab tools or collaborating in presence. In this respect, AR has a potential worth exploring, because it permits direct human communication, including non-verbal communication like pointing to the 3D representation for outlining issues, annotating or even modifying its structures.

References

1. Bennie, S.J., et al.: Teaching enzyme catalysis using interactive molecular dynamics in virtual reality. J. Chem. Educ. **96**(11), 2488–2496 (2019). https://doi.org/10.1021/acs.jchemed.9b00181
2. Berman, H., et al.: The protein data bank. Nucleic Acids Res. **28**, 235–242 (2000)
3. Brůža, V., Byška, J., Mičan, J., Kozlíková, B.: VRdeo: creating engaging educational material for asynchronous student-teacher exchange using virtual reality. Comput. Graph. **98**, 280–292 (2021). https://doi.org/10.1016/j.cag.2021.06.009, https://www.sciencedirect.com/science/article/pii/S0097849321001242

4. Brown, C.E., Alrmuny, D., Williams, M.K., Whaley, B., Hyslop, R.M.: Visualizing molecular structures and shapes: a comparison of virtual reality, computer simulation, and traditional modeling. Chem. Teacher Int. **3**(1), 69–80 (2021). https://doi.org/10.1515/cti-2019-0009

5. Cassidy, K.C., Šefčík, J., Raghav, Y., Chang, A., Durrant, J.D.: ProteinVR: web-based molecular visualization in virtual reality. PLoS Comput. Biol. **16**(3) (2020). https://durrantlab.pitt.edu/pvr/

6. Cooper, A.: The inmates are running the asylum, pp. 17–17. Vieweg+Teubner Verlag, Wiesbaden (1999). https://doi.org/10.1007/978-3-322-99786-9_1

7. Cortés Rodríguez, F., Dal Peraro, M., Abriata, L.A.: Online tools to easily build virtual molecular models for display in augmented and virtual reality on the web. J. Mol. Graph. Model. **114**, 108164 (2022). https://doi.org/10.1016/j.jmgm.2022.108164, https://www.sciencedirect.com/science/article/pii/S1093326322000432

8. EPAM Systems, I.: Miew - 3D Molecular Viewer, https://miew.opensource.epam.com/

9. Fernandes, H.S., Cerqueira, N.M.F.S.A., Sousa, S.F.: Developing and using biosimar, an augmented reality program to visualize and learn about chemical structures in a virtual environment on any internet-connected device. Journal of Chemical Education 98(5), pp. 1789–1794, May 2021. https://doi.org/10.1021/acs.jchemed.0c01317

10. Goddard, T.D., et al.: UCSF ChimeraX: meeting modern challenges in visualization and analysis. Protein Sci. **27**(1), 14–25 (2018). https://doi.org/10.1002/pro.3235

11. Guex, N., Peitsch, M.C.: Swiss-model and the swiss-pdbviewer: an environment for comparative protein modeling. Electrophoresis **18**, 2714–2723 (1997). https://spdbv.vital-it.ch/

12. Jmol: an open-source Java viewer for chemical structures in 3D. http://www.jmol.org/

13. Kuvták, D., et al.: State of the art of molecular visualization in immersive virtual environments. Comput. Graph. Forum n/a(n/a) (2023). https://doi.org/10.1111/cgf.14738

14. Milgram, P., Kishino, F.: A taxonomy of mixed reality visual displays. IEICE Trans. Inf. Syst. **77**(12), 1321–1329 (1994)

15. Nakane, T.: GLmol - molecular viewer on WebGL/Javascript, Version 0.47 (2012). http://webglmol.sourceforge.jp/index-en.htmll

16. Patterson, K., Lilja, A., Arrebola, M., McGhee, J.: Molecular genomics education through gamified cell exploration in virtual reality. In: Proceedings of the 17th International Conference on Virtual-Reality Continuum and Its Applications in Industry. VRCAI 2019, Association for Computing Machinery, New York, NY, USA (2019). https://doi.org/10.1145/3359997.3365724

17. Pettersen, E.F., et al.: UCSF chimera - a visualization system for exploratory research and analysis. J. Comput. Chemistry **25**(13), 1605–1612 (2004). http://www.cgl.ucsf.edu/chimera

18. Protein Data Bank Contents Guide: Atomic Coordinate Entry Format Description 3.30: (2008)

19. Rodríguez, F.C., et al.: MolecularWeb: a web site for chemistry and structural biology education through interactive augmented reality out of the box in commodity devices. J. Chem. Educ. **98**(7), 2243–2255 (2021). https://doi.org/10.1021/acs.jchemed.1c00179

20. Rose, A., Hildebrand, P.: NGL viewer: a web application for molecular visual-izationngl viewer: web-based molecular graphics for large complexes. Nucl Acids Res **43**(W1), W576–W579 (2015). http://proteinformatics.charite.de/ngl-tools/ngl/html/ngl.html, https://doi.org/10.1093/nar/gkv402

21. Rose A.S., Bradley A.R., Valasatava, Y., Duarte J.M., Prlić, A., Rose, P.W.: NGL viewer: web-based molecular graphics for large complexes (2018). http://proteinformatics.charite.de/ngl-tools/ngl/html/ngl.html, https://doi.org/10.1093/bioinformatics/bty419

22. Schrödinger, LLC: The PyMOL molecular graphics system, version 1.8, November 2015

23. Sehnal, D., et al.: Litemol suite: interactive web-based visualization of large-scale macromolecular structure data. Nat. Methods, **14**, 1121–1122 (2017). https://doi.org/10.1038/nmeth.4499, https://www.litemol.org/Viewer/

24. Swamy K.L., N., Chavan, P.S., Murthy, S.: StereoChem: augmented reality 3d molecular model visualization app for teaching and learning stereochemistry. In: 2018 IEEE 18th International Conference on Advanced Learning Technologies (ICALT), pp. 252–256 (2018). https://doi.org/10.1109/ICALT.2018.00065

25. Three.js: https://threejs.org/

26. VRML97 Specification - ISO/IEC 14772-1:1997: https://www.web3d.org/documents/specifications/14772/V2.0/index.html (2006)

27. WebGL specification. https://www.khronos.org/registry/webgl/specs/latest/2.0/

28. WebVR - Specification Draft. https://immersive-web.github.io/webvr/spec/1.1/ (2017)

29. WebXR augmented reasuitey module - Level 1. https://www.w3.org/TR/webxr-ar-module-1/

30. Won, M., Mocerino, M., Tang, K.-S., Treagust, D.F., Tasker, R.: Interactive immer-sive virtual reality to enhance students' visualisation of complex molecules. In: Schultz, M., Schmid, S., Lawrie, G.A. (eds.) Research and Practice in Chemistry Education, pp. 51–64. Springer, Singapore (2019). https://doi.org/10.1007/978-981-13-6998-8_4

31. X3D specification - ISO/IEC-19775-1. https://www.web3d.org/documents/specifications/19775-1/V3.3/index.html (2013)

32. Xu, K., et al.: VRmol: an integrative cloud-based virtual reality system to explore macromolecular structure. bioRxiv (2019). https://doi.org/10.1101/589366, https://www.biorxiv.org/content/early/2019/03/27/589366.1

33. Xu, K., et al.: VRmol: an integrative web-based virtual reality system to explore macromolecular structure. Bioinformatics (2020). https://doi.org/10.1093/bioinformatics/btaa696

Human Factors in VR: Performance, Acceptance, and Design

Correlations of Flow, Usability, Workload, and Presence with Task Performance in a Spatially Distributed Memory Task

Jan P. Gründling[(✉)][ID], Nico Feld[ID], Daniel Zielasko[ID], and Benjamin Weyers[ID]

Trier University, Universitätsring 15, 54296 Trier, Germany
{gruendling,feldn,weyers}@uni-trier.de, daniel.zielasko@rwth-aachen.de

Abstract. It requires an elaborated set of measurements to assess how the performance of tasks conducted in VR is composed. Flow is a measurement widely used in other domains as a predictor of performance and has been shown to be positively correlated with performance. However, some previous works indicate that flow might bring different results in VR than in traditional environments. It is not well known for VR environments how this phenomenon relates to usability, workload, and presence. Therefore, this work reports on an experiment that allows positioning flow among the other measurements, using a spatially distributed task. The results suggest that flow correlates negatively with performance, workload, and presence, which supports VR-specific previous work while it contradicts findings from other domains. Flow is positively correlated with usability in this experiment, which is in line with expectations from previous work.

Keywords: Flow experience · Transitions · Usability · Workload · Presence

1 Introduction

Application areas for virtual reality (VR) go beyond simply replicating physical environments, as illustrated by Wexelblat [41]. For example, the simulation of manufacturing processes as described by Mujber et al. [28] or virtual and augmented reality scenarios for data analysis [39,46]. Especially for application fields like immersive analytics (IA), Skarbez et al. [34] denote that it is a matter of performing tasks as well as possible, which raises the need to understand in the best possible way what psychological states induced by the virtual environment (VE) contribute to the performance shown in tasks.

Purely assessing the performance provides information about whether the user is doing the task well or poorly. However, it only gives a limited indication of which aspects of the virtual environment lead to this performance. To identify these aspects, a deeper understanding of the mechanisms by which interaction with VR impacts the psychological state of the user and how these mechanisms

G. Zachmann et al. (Eds.): EuroXR 2023, LNCS 14410, pp. 153–165, 2023.
https://doi.org/10.1007/978-3-031-48495-7_10

can be further developed to derive the greatest possible benefit from the use of VEs for work tasks is necessary. Flow experience as characterized by Csikszent-mihalyi [9] emerges whenever there is an optimal fit of human skills and task demands. It seems to be a promising candidate, as it is usually positively cor-related to task performance and even counts as a solid predictor for it in cases where users do not interact with VEs [1,20,29]. Furthermore, other measures from the VR domain and broader Human-Computer Interaction (HCI) research are associated with task performance. These include workload, usability, and presence. Usability is considered to be the gold standard to measure the quality of use in interfaces (c.f. ISO 9241-11 [2]) and can be measured by question-naires as e.g., the System-Usability-Scale (SUS) [6]. Workload is the degree to which a task requires the user's cognitive resources [42]. Another widely used metric in the VR domain is presence, usually described as the feeling of "being there" introduced [37] and later extended by Slater [36] to place and plausibil-ity illusion. In the form of two unstandardized items, presence has also already been investigated in the context of VR scenarios with transitions [18]. While the workload, usability, and presence have found some breadth in the evaluation of VR environments, rather little research has been done in previous literature on how flow relates to VR environments and performance. This raises the research question:

How does flow compare to existing measurement methods for examining psycho-logical states during task processing in VR environments?

The present work contributes to the answer to this question with an explo-rative investigation of flow experience as a psychological measure known from other contexts for its connection with interaction and task performance. It is assessed in a laboratory study in which participants had to complete a task with transitions. It is then analyzed for correlations with task performance alongside workload, usability, and presence.

The goal of this analysis is twofold: On the one hand, it investigates if previous findings about the flow-performance relationship are reproducible in the VR domain. On the other hand, there might be aspects of the psychological states accompanying tasks in VR, that can be more thoroughly explained by combining flow with other measurements.

The main contribution of this paper is to provide insights into the character-istics that flow shows in relation to task performance next to workload, usability, and presence as a potential basis for future research hypotheses in the field.

2   Background and Related Work

The selection of correlates considered here is based on a search for measures that already show a relationship to task performance in known situations. In the literature research conducted for this purpose, workload, flow experience, and usability in particular stood out. Additionally, we consider presence, as it is an established measure in VR research [32]. In the following, the connections to performance found in the literature are presented.

2.1   Workload, Usability, and Presence

Workload, or task load can be described as the amount of mental effort required to complete a task in consideration of limited cognitive resources [42]. Apart from the secondary-task paradigm [30], a common technique to assess workload induced by a task is the NASA-TLX questionnaire, developed by Hart and Staveland [17]. It has been used in a wide range of investigations, including, but not limited to, robotics, teleoperation, and computer use [16]. Longo et al. [26] find that workload predicts performance in non-VR scenarios. Because of its strong relation to task performance and user satisfaction, workload is an important metric to be included in this work.

Usability is a concept that has enduring relevance in HCI because it represents a universal measure of whether or not a system is usable in principle [15]. It is commonly measured using the System-Usability-Scale developed by Brooke [6]. Usability has been considered in different situations and relations. This is also the case in the context of performance. Longo [26] finds that usability is a variable related to performance independently of workload, while Lin et al. [25] find that subjective usability-related measures are linked to task performance. However, when it comes to usability in the context of work, for instance, Seeliger et al. [33] find that although users think they would need less time for a task when using augmented reality (AR) with high usability scores for a task, they did not need more or less time compared to other technologies. This contradicts findings from the web domain, where, e.g., Leporini and Paternò [24] find that increased usability shortens the time needed to navigate certain web pages. The aforementioned findings about usability show that more work on clarifying the relations to other measurements can help with putting results in the right context, which is why we include usability in the study at hand.

A widely used measure in the context of VR is the construct *presence*, which was designed with the idea that a VE fulfills its purpose of embedding a user into a digital world if it gives the user the feeling of actually "being there" [37]. However, the nature of the construct implies that this method can only be meaningful and effective if the core concern of the VE does exist in the participant [35] and the application's purpose is to make the users believe that they are in the VE. This is why Slater extended the concept to place and plausibility illusion [36]. There are questionnaires of different lengths to measure presence. For example, the Slater-Usoh-Steed questionnaire [40] consists of 6 questions. To quickly assess presence, it is desirable to keep questionnaires as short as possible, which is why sometimes shorter or even single-item questionnaires are used as in e.g., Zielasko et al. [44] ("I felt physically present in the virtual world"), Zielasko and Law [45] ("How present ('really there') did you feel during the last level?"). Husung and Langbehn [18] use a novel, short method for assessing presence in the context of transitions using two questions taken from Men et al. [27], answered on a 7-Point scale ("The transition technique reminded me that I was in a virtual world." and "The transition technique made the virtual world become less real."). We observe the advantage that the two questions are context-related, while quick and easy to answer for the participants, which is especially helpful for studies where participants have to answer several question-naires. Presence as a measure related to virtual environments is omnipresent [13] and it would therefore be incomplete not to consider this aspect when looking at correlates in VEs. That being said, there are some interesting observations in the literature about presence in combination with task performance in VR. For example, Cooper et al. [7] find that presence and performance are negatively correlated in a wheel-changing task on a virtual car. This contrasts with find-ings by Youngblut and Huie [43], who report a significant positive correlation between presence and performance. Also, Lackey et al. [23] report that in a mil-itary training task, certain facets of presence can serve as a predictor of task performance. As there seems to be a need for more data regarding the relation between presence and task performance, we add to this by including presence in the investigation.

2.2   Flow

According to Csikszentmihalyi [8], flow experience is characterized as an optimal fit of human skill and task demands, which results in a highly motivating and enjoyable feeling for the person experiencing it. Csikszentmihalyi further states that experiencing flow may make humans conduct a task even if it means high costs. Usually, this also is accompanied by better performance. For example, in athletics, Jackson et al. [19] find that flow correlates with the performance of athletes with r =.18 to r =.48. Engeser et al. [11] find that flow predicts the outcome of a university course ($\beta = .32$, $p < .01$) In research with expert users, Batch et al. [1] employ performance, space utilization, and presence to rate their IA application ImAxes. The authors discovered that the test participants had an intense sensation of presence. Noticeable is the fact that during usage, a psychological state developed that caused the user to lose track of time and appeared to be a key component of the good experience. The test subjects rated this occurrence as being especially encouraging and helpful for the data analysis procedure. Even though Batch et al. do not expressly call it that, the description of this condition is very similar to Csikszentmihalyi's [9] flow experience.

In contrast, research findings by Bian et al. [3] indicate a weakening of the normally assumed positive relationship between flow and performance when the task is performed in a virtual environment. This, in turn, raises the question of how a strongly perceived flow experience should then be interpreted. The authors suggest that this could be due to a lack of congruence between the interaction methods and the task requirements [4] or to the presence or absence of distractors [5].

Due to the scarcity of findings in the literature concerning the relationships between flow, workload, presence, performance, and satisfaction in spatially dis-tributed VR tasks, we decided not to formulate any specific hypotheses in this study but rather to contribute to the data pool through an exploratory method. In light of the presented literature, we specify the research question from the introduction further: *Is flow experience poorly related to performance or biased by other psychometric measures in a spatially distributed memory task?*

3   User Study

To investigate our research question of how flow experience compares to other psychometric measures in the context of VR, an experimental design was needed that lets users process a moderately demanding task, including a calibrated amount of interaction with the VE. This way, the chance of coming as close as possible to an optimal fit of the participant's skill and task demands, hence the chance of experiencing flow, would be highest.

3.1   Task

To achieve a calibrated amount of interaction, we chose a memory task that required participants to solve a memory game in which ten different pairs of objects were hidden under boxes in two environments (cf. [12]). The two environments were an office and a farm environment. The boxes that hid the object pairs were placed as shown in Fig. 1. The positions of the objects were not congruent in the two environments, i.e. neither the boxes nor the hidden objects were in the same places in both environments. In the farm environment, pairs of farm-related objects were hidden under the crates (pumpkin, beehive, apple crate), while in the office environment, office-related objects (pencil cup, folder, lamp) were hidden. In addition, objects related to pirates (skull, compass, bomb, treasure map) were placed in such a way that the other item in each pair could only be found in the other environment. This forced the additional interaction for the transition between the environments so that the intended circumstances for observing flow, usability, workload, and presence were created. Further, participants were instructed to solve the memory task with the least amount of errors and should take their time to do so, thus, experiencing no time pressure.

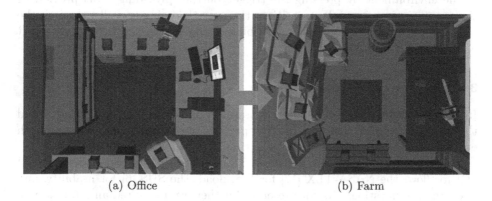

(a) Office   (b) Farm

Fig. 1. Used environments from bird's eye view.

3.2 Transitions

Using the described task, a laboratory experiment with six conditions was performed in a within-study design. The conditions differed in the method used to transition between environments. While the task types were the same for all conditions, they were not the exact same task each time. The tasks that a subject completed differed between trials in that the hidden objects were in different locations in each condition. This reduced learning effects. The transitions used were cut, dissolve, fade, transformation, orb, and portal, as described by Husung and Langbehn [18]. While cut, dissolve, and fade were inspired by filmmaking, transformation, orb, and portal were inspired by existing VR applications. A cut is the most common transition in movies [10] and was implemented as an instant teleport to the target environment without any visual animation. The dissolve transition is a transparent crossfade over $1.3s$ and is often considered an alternative to cut that provides a higher continuity but requires more time [18]. The fade transition is similar to the dissolve transition, but instead of a transparent crossfade, the user perceives a short fade to black over $1.3s$ while they get teleported to the target environment. With the transformation transition, the user perceives a rift that expands around them over $1.3s$, revealing the target environment, and was introduced by Husung and Langbehn. This transition aimed to utilize VR-specific features and was inspired by the "NVIDIA VR Funhouse" application. All these four transitions could be triggered by pressing the trigger button of a controller at any time. With the orb transition, the user could create a floating orb ($d = 0.2\,\mathrm{m}$) above their controller by pressing the trigger button, providing a 3D preview of the target environment. To transition to the target environment, the user had to move the orb closer to their head. This transition was inspired by the VR applications "The Lab" and "Budget Cuts". Lastly, with the portal transition, the user can spawn a portal ($1\,\mathrm{m} \times 2.25\,\mathrm{m}$) in the center of the environment by pressing the trigger button, providing a 3D preview of the target environment. To transition, the user then simply walks through the portal. The portal is a common transition in video games, like "Portal", and VR applications [14,22,38].

3.3 Procedure

In each condition, the participant was assigned one of six transitions and solved the memory task. To find all pairs, the participant had to switch between both environments multiple times, i.e. every time a pirate object was uncovered.

After each condition, the participant filled out the Flow Short Scale (FSS) [31] for flow, the NASA-TLX [17] for Workload, the SUS [6] for usability, and two presence questions [18] for presence. Further, we measured an error rate on how many wrong boxes the participant revealed against better knowledge as an indicator of task performance.

3.4   Apparatus

The HTC Vive Pro with a wireless adapter was used, and the study was implemented with Unity 2021.3 and the XR Interaction Toolkit 2.0.4.

3.5   Sample

An a priori power analysis with $\alpha = .05$, $1\text{-}\beta = .65$, and $\rho = 0.4$ indicated a required sample size of 24 Participants. The sample in this experiment has 24 participants whose ages ranged from 20 to 41 years with $M = 25.71 \pm 4.667$. 15 (62.5%) identified as male, 8 (33.3%) as female and 1 (4.2%) as diverse. 22 (91.7%) stated to be right-handed and 2 (8.2%) left-handed. Further, 18 (75%) had prior experience with VR, and 14 (58.3%) with 3D video games. To assess motion sickness, the Fast Motion Sickness (FMS) [21] scale was used. Participants reported low scores for motion sickness ($M = 1.1$, SD $= 1.45$, range $= 0$–9).

4   Results

The results obtained for flow, workload, usability, and presence are described below. All statistics have been calculated in *IBM SPSS Statistics*. Table 1 shows Pearson correlation coefficients for all captured measurements. As displayed, the NASA-TLX measurements correlate moderately with all other measurements except presence, which is why workload is considered a potential confounding variable in further analysis.

Table 1. Correlations for all captured measurements, not controlled for workload

	Flow	Perf	TLX	Presence	SUS
Flow	1				
Performance	0.03	1			
TLX	-0.37^*	-0.45^*	1		
Presence	-0.25^*	0.15	0.02	1	
SUS	0.41^*	0.13	-0.37^*	-0.27^*	1

$^*p < 0.05$

The standard correlation coefficient for flow and performance across all transition methods is not significant ($p > .815$). However, partial correlation with workload as a control variable reveals a small negative correlation of flow and performance (r $= -.166$, $p = .048$). Looking at the results within each condition as displayed in Table 2, a moderate correlation occurs in the cut transition condition (r $= .437$, $p = .033$). However, no significant correlation coefficients between flow and performance are observed within the remaining experimental conditions (all $p > .14$). A different picture emerges when controlling for perceived workload. As can be seen from Table 3, a moderate negative correlation (r = −.505, p = .014) occurs in the Transformation condition when controlling for workload. All other correlation coefficients for flow and performance do not appear to be significant when controlled for workload (all p > .112).

Table 2. Table showing the correlation coefficients for all transitions, not controlled for workload

Transition		Flow (p)	Performance (p)
Cut	Performance	.437 (.033)[*]	
	Sus	.090 (.677)	−.050 (.815)
Dissolve	Performance	−.113 (.598)	
	Sus	.408 (.048)[*]	.306 (.146)
Fade	Performance	−.235 (.270)	
	Sus	.073 (.736)	.435 (.034)[*]
Orb	Performance	.039 (.858)	
	Sus	.676 (.001)[*]	.025 (.908)
Portal	Performance	.310 (.140)	
	Sus	.371 (.074)	-.016 (.941)
Transformation	Performance	−.308 (.144)	
	Sus	.317 (.131)	.164 (.445)

[*]$p < 0.05$

As seen in Table 1, flow shows a moderate correlation with **usability** all conditions combined, which even persists when controlling for workload (r = −.32, p < .001). However, the correlation coefficients for each individual transition, as shown in Table 2 and Table 3 respectively, reveal that this might mainly be driven by the Orb condition.

Moreover, without controlling for workload, flow correlates negatively with the **presence** measure used in this work (c.f. Table 1). The same applies when controlling for workload (r = −.25, p = .002). Furthermore, when controlling for workload, presence shows a small correlation with performance (r = −.17, p = .037).

There is a moderate negative correlation between **workload** and flow (r = −.37, p < .001) which persists when controlling for all other measurements (r = −.31, p < .001). Regarding the relation of workload and performance, there is a negative correlation between workload and performance across all transition types (r = −.447, p < .001), which is also found within the individual groups. The only exception is the orb transition, where no significant correlation was found (r = −.052, p = .08).

Table 3. Table showing the correlation coefficients for all transitions, controlled for workload

Transition		Flow (p)	Performance (p)
Cut	Performance	.253 (.245)	
	Sus	.004 (.987)	−.031 (.887)
Dissolve	Performance	−.341 (.112)	
	Sus	.319 (.138)	.137 (.534)
Fade	Performance	−.269 (.214)	
	Sus	.104 (.638)	.194 (.374)
Orb	Performance	.014 (.950)	
	Sus	.586 (.003)[*]	.002 (.991)
Portal	Performance	.069 (.754)	
	Sus	.296 (.170)	−.273 (.207)
Transformation	Performance	−.505 (.014)[*]	
	Sus	.298 (.167)	.047 (.831)

[*]$p < 0.05$

5   Discussion and Future Work

The correlations found provide insight into how psychometric measures and performance are related. It is apparent that the correlations between performance on the one hand and flow, presence, and usability on the other are confounded by workload. This is shown by the finding that workload correlates with performance and all psychometric measures, except presence in this investigation. The main finding, however, is that in the context used here, flow appears to have a negative partial correlation with performance. This appears contradictory to theoretical assumptions from other contexts that would assume that flow is positively correlated with performance. Simultaneously it seems to support other findings from the VR domain that also find a weaker relation of flow and performance in sports and learning environments [3] Since this correlation is only found here when controlling for workload, it could hypothesized that perceived workload plays a role in the bias here. According to the flow theory [8], the perceived workload should be optimal at high flow, which would lead to better performance. The opposite appears to be the case in this experiment. This observation leads to the question: What is the primary source for perceived flow and workload while using VR? One hypothesis, that would need to be tested in future work, is that a higher perceived workload might not be related to the task but to the interaction. Likewise, it can be hypothesized that perceived flow could be less related to the task and more to the interaction. If the participant is put into a state of flow by the mere interaction, this could push the actual task into the background, which in turn could lead to poorer performance. Another task for future research is to find out how these findings can be used for the development of future VR applications. Is there an optimal style that interactions should have such that they do not interfere with the user's cognitive resources for the task, and if yes, how would they differ between use cases?

5.1 Limitations

As the task here was a memory game, the result's generalizability can be improved by repeating similar investigations with other use cases, for example, data analysis tasks or games. Moreover, although the method to assess presence here seems to be appropriate for the use case, comparability with other studies regarding presence could have been enhanced by adding a commonly used questionnaire e.g., the Slater-Usoh-Steed questionnaire [35]. Furthermore, it should be noted that the present work exploratively investigates the relationships between the mentioned measures. This implies that no definite conclusions should be drawn based on the results reported here. Rather, it is a data basis on which hypotheses can be formed that should subsequently be tested in future work using appropriate empirical methods.

6 Conclusion

In the present study, correlations between flow, usability, presence, and performance during task processing in VR environments with location transitions were investigated. The correlations found allow the positioning of the individual measures in relation to each other and give indications that measures such as flow, which are known from conventional task processing environments for positive correlations with performance, could change their meaning in VR. This is an important indication for those who use these measures to evaluate their VR environments. Future research should investigate if the different meanings in VR derive from the amount or type of interaction and how to circumvent biased measurements of psychometric variables in VR.

Acknowledgements. This work has received funding by the European Union's Horizon 2020 research and innovation programme under grant agreement No. 871260

References

1. Batch, A., et al.: There is no spoon: evaluating performance, space use, and presence with expert domain users in immersive analytics. IEEE Trans. Visual Comput. Graphics **26**(1), 536–546 (2020). https://doi.org/10.1109/TVCG.2019.2934803
2. Bevan, N., Carter, J., Harker, S.: ISO 9241-11 revised: what have we learnt about usability since 1998? In: Kurosu, M. (ed.) HCI 2015. LNCS, vol. 9169, pp. 143–151. Springer, Cham (2015). https://doi.org/10.1007/978-3-319-20901-2_13
3. Bian, Y., et al.: Exploring the weak association between flow experience and performance in virtual environments. In: CHI (ed.) CHI 2018, pp. 1–12. ACM, New York, NY (2018). https://doi.org/10.1145/3173574.3173975

4. Bian, Y., Zhou, C., Chen, Y., Zhao, Y., Liu, J., Yang, C.: The role of the field dependence-independence construct on the flow-performance link in virtual reality. In: Symposium on Interactive 3D Graphics and Games, pp. 1–9. ACM Digital Library, Association for Computing Machinery, New York, NY, United States (2020). https://doi.org/10.1145/3384382.3384529

5. Bian, Y., Zhou, C., Liu, J., Geng, W., Shi, Y.: The effect of reducing distraction on the flow-performance link in virtual experiential learning environment. Virtual Reality 26(4), 1277–1290 (2022). https://doi.org/10.1007/s10055-021-00621-3, https://link.springer.com/article/10.1007/s10055-021-00621-3

6. Brooke, J.: Sus: a 'quick and dirty' usability scale. In: Jordan, P.W., McClelland, I.L., Thomas, B., Weerdmeester, B.A. (eds.) Usability evaluation in industry. CRC Press, an imprint of Taylor and Francis, Boca Raton, FL (1996)

7. Cooper, N., Milella, F., Pinto, C., Cant, I., White, M., Meyer, G.: The effects of substitute multisensory feedback on task performance and the sense of presence in a virtual reality environment. PLoS ONE 13(2), e0191846 (2018). https://doi.org/10.1371/journal.pone.0191846

8. Csikszentmihalyi, M.: The Psychology of Optimal Experience. Harper and Row, New York (1990)

9. Csikszentmihalyi, M.: Flow and the Foundations of Positive Psychology. Springer, Dordrecht (2014). https://doi.org/10.1007/978-94-017-9088-8

10. Cutting, J.: Event segmentation and seven types of narrative discontinuity in popular movies. Acta Physiol. (Oxf) 149, 69–77 (2014). https://doi.org/10.1016/j.actpsy.2014.03.003

11. Engeser, S., Rheinberg, F., Vollmeyer, R., Bischoff, J.: Motivation, flowerleben und lernleistung in universitären lernsettings 1dieser beitrag wurde unter der geschäftsführenden herausgeberschaft von joachim c. brunstein akzeptiert. Zeitschrift für Pädagogische Psychologie 19(3), 159–172 (2005). https://doi.org/10.1024/1010-0652.19.3.159

12. Feld, N., Bimberg, P., Weyers, B., Zielasko, D.: Keep it simple? evaluation of transitions in virtual reality. In: Proceedings of ACM CHI Conference Extended Abstracts on Human Factors in Computing Systems (2023). https://doi.org/10.1145/3544549.3585811

13. Felton, W.M., Jackson, R.E.: Presence: a review. Int. J. Hum.-Comput. Interact. 38(1), 1–18 (2022). https://doi.org/10.1080/10447318.2021.1921368

14. Freitag, S., Rausch, D., Kuhlen, T.: Reorientation in virtual environments using interactive portals. In: 2014 IEEE Symposium on 3D User Interfaces (3DUI), pp. 119–122 (2014). https://doi.org/10.1109/3DUI.2014.6798852

15. Goundar, M.S., Kumar, B.A., Ali, A.B.M.S.: Development of usability guidelines: a systematic literature review. Int. J. Hum.-Comput. Interact. 1–19 (2022). https://doi.org/10.1080/10447318.2022.2141009

16. Hart, S.G.: Nasa-task load index (NASA-TLX); 20 years later. Proc. Hum. Fact. Ergon. Soc. Ann. Meeting 50(9), 904–908 (2006). https://doi.org/10.1177/154193120605000909

17. Hart, S.G., Staveland, L.E.: Development of NASA-TLX (task load index): results of empirical and theoretical research. Adv. Psychol. 52(1), 139–183 (1988). https://doi.org/10.1016/S0166-4115(08)62386-9

18. Husung, M., Langbehn, E.: Of portals and orbs: an evaluation of scene transition techniques for virtual reality. In: Alt, F. (ed.) Proceedings of Mensch und Computer 2019, pp. 245–254. ACM Digital Library, Association for Computing Machinery, New York, NY, United States (2019). https://doi.org/10.1145/3340764.3340779

19. Jackson, S.A., Thomas, P.R., Marsh, H.W., Smethurst, C.J.: Relationships between flow, self-concept, psychological skills, and performance. J. Appl. Sport Psychol. **13**(2), 129–153 (2001). https://doi.org/10.1080/104132001753149865

20. Jin, S.A.A.: I feel present. Therefore, I experience flow: a structural equation modeling approach to flow and presence in video games. J. Broadcasting Electr. Media **55**(1), 114–136 (2011)

21. Keshavarz, B., Hecht, H.: Validating an efficient method to quantify motion sickness. Hum. Factors **53**(4), 415–426 (2011)

22. Kunert, A., Kulik, A., Beck, S., Froehlich, B.: Photoportals: shared references in Space and Time. CSCW 2014, Association for Computing Machinery, New York, NY, USA (2014). https://doi.org/10.1145/2531602.2531727

23. Lackey, S.J., Salcedo, J.N., Szalma, J.L., Hancock, P.A.: The stress and workload of virtual reality training: the effects of presence, immersion and flow. Ergonomics **59**(8), 1060–1072 (2016). https://doi.org/10.1080/00140139.2015.1122234

24. Leporini, B., Paternò, F.: Applying web usability criteria for vision-impaired users: Does it really improve task performance? Int. J. Hum.-Comput. Inter. **24**(1), 17–47 (2008). https://doi.org/10.1080/10447310701771472

25. Lin, T., Imamiya, A., Hu, W.: An empirical study of relationships between traditional usability. Australas. J. Inf. Syst. **13**(2) (2006). https://doi.org/10.3127/ajis.v13i2.45

26. Longo, L.: Experienced mental workload, perception of usability, their interaction and impact on task performance. PLoS ONE **13**(8), e0199661 (2018). https://doi.org/10.1371/journal.pone.0199661

27. Men, L., Bryan-Kinns, N., Hassard, A.S., Ma, Z.: The impact of transitions on user experience in virtual reality. In: 2017 IEEE Virtual Reality (VR), pp. 285–286. IEEE, Piscataway, NJ (2017). https://doi.org/10.1109/VR.2017.7892288

28. Mujber, T.S., Szecsi, T., Hashmi, M.: Virtual reality applications in manufacturing process simulation. J. Mater. Process. Technol. **155–156**, 1834–1838 (2004). https://doi.org/10.1016/j.jmatprotec.2004.04.401

29. Nakamura, J., Csikszentmihalyi, M.: The concept of flow. In: Flow and the Foundations of Positive Psychology, pp. 239–263. Springer, Dordrecht (2014). https://doi.org/10.1007/978-94-017-9088-8_16

30. Park, B., Brünken, R.: Secondary task as a measure of cognitive load. In: Cognitive Load Measurement and Application, pp. 75–92. Routledge, November 2017. https://doi.org/10.4324/9781315296258-6

31. Rheinberg, F., Vollmeyer, R.: Flow-erleben in einem computerspiel unter experimentell variierten bedingungen (2006)

32. Riches, S., Elghany, S., Garety, P., Rus-Calafell, M., Valmaggia, L.: Factors affecting sense of presence in a virtual reality social environment: a qualitative study. Cyberpsychol. Behav. Soc. Netw. **22**(4), 288–292 (2019). https://doi.org/10.1089/cyber.2018.0128

33. Seeliger, A., Netland, T., Feuerriegel, S.: Augmented reality for machine setups: task performance and usability evaluation in a field test. Procedia CIRP **107**, 570–575 (2022). https://doi.org/10.1016/j.procir.2022.05.027

34. Skarbez, R., Polys, N.F., Ogle, J.T., North, C., Bowman, D.A.: Immersive analytics: theory and research agenda. Front. Robot. AI **6** (2019). https://doi.org/10.3389/frobt.2019.00082

35. Slater, M.: How colorful was your day? why questionnaires cannot assess presence in virtual environments. Presence **13**(4), 484–493 (2004)

36. Slater, M.: Place illusion and plausibility can lead to realistic behaviour in immersive virtual environments. Philos. Trans. R. Soc. B Biol. Sci. **364**(1535), 3549–3557 (2009)
37. Slater, M., Wilbur, S.: A framework for immersive virtual environments (five): speculations on the role of presence in virtual environments. Presence Teleoperators Virtual Environ. **6**(6), 603–616 (1997). https://doi.org/10.1162/PRES.1997.6.6.603
38. Steinicke, F., Bruder, G., Hinrichs, K., Steed, A.: Gradual transitions and their effects on presence and distance estimation. Comput. Graph. **34**, 26–33 (2010). https://doi.org/10.1016/j.cag.2009.12.003
39. Su, S., et al.: Virtual and augmented reality applications to support data analysis and assessment of science and engineering. Comput. Sci. Eng. **22**(3), 27–39 (2020). https://doi.org/10.1109/MCSE.2020.2971188
40. Usoh, M., Catena, E., Arman, S., Slater, M.: Using presence questionnaires in reality. Presence Teleoperators Virtual Environ. **9**(5), 497–503 (2000). https://doi.org/10.1162/105474600566989
41. Wexelblat, A.: Virtual reality: applications and explorations. elsevier reference monographs, s.l., 1. aufl. edn. (2014). https://ebookcentral.proquest.com/lib/kxp/detail.action?docID=1876828
42. Wickens, C.D., Tsang, P.S.: Workload. In: Boehm-Davis, D.A., Durso, F.T., Lee, J.D. (eds.) APA Handbook of Human Systems Integration, pp. 277–292. American Psychological Association, Washington (2015). https://doi.org/10.1037/14528-018
43. Youngblut, C., Huie, O.: The relationship between presence and performance in virtual environments: results of a verts study. In: IEEE Virtual Reality, 2003, Proceedings. pp. 277–278. IEEE Comput. Soc (2003). https://doi.org/10.1109/VR.2003.1191158
44. Zielasko, D., Horn, S., Freitag, S., Weyers, B., Kuhlen, T.W.: Evaluation of hands-free HMD-based navigation techniques for immersive data analysis. In: Proceedings of IEEE Symposium on 3D User Interfaces, pp. 113–119 (2016). https://doi.org/10.1109/3DUI.2016.7460040
45. Zielasko, D., Law, Y.C., Weyers, B.: Take a look around - the impact of decoupling gaze and travel-direction in seated and ground-based virtual reality utilizing torso-directed steering. In: Proc. of IEEE Conference on Virtual Reality and 3D User Interfaces (VR), pp. 398–406 (2020). https://doi.org/10.1109/VR46266.2020.00060
46. Zielasko, D., et al.: Remain seated: towards fully-immersive desktop VR. In: Proceedings of IEEE 3rd Workshop on Everyday Virtual Reality, pp. 1–6 (2017). https://doi.org/10.1109/WEVR.2017.7957707

Evaluating the Worker Technology Acceptance of a Mixed Reality Technical Documentation

Enricoandrea Laviola⬤, Sara Romano⬤, Michele Gattullo(✉)⬤,
and Antonio Emmanuele Uva⬤

Department of Mechanics, Mathematics, and Management, Polytechnic University of Bari,
Via Orabona, 4, 70125 Bari, Italy
{enricoandrea.laviola,michele.gattullo}@poliba.it

Abstract. Mixed Reality (MR) technology has gained popularity in the manufacturing industry over the last few decades. In the maintenance field, it helps workers in document analysis and decision-making during operations. While numerous studies have demonstrated the empirical benefits of MR, few have examined its applicability in a real industrial context. Among them, many focus on user performance. The novelty of our work is to evaluate mainly the acceptance of MR technology by experienced technicians using smart glasses for maintenance tasks in a real industrial context. We conducted a user study involving 7 workers who were asked to follow the instructions provided by an MR Technical Documentation (MRTD) developed considering authoring guidelines already validated in the literature but only in a laboratory context. The industrial operators performed both navigation tasks within the menu of the MRTD and a disassembly task, following the instructions displayed on the smart glass. The evaluation in the real working scenario showed that MRTD is highly appreciated by workers even if they have no previous experience with smart glasses. These results allow us to confirm the goodness of the design guidelines followed for the authoring of the MRTD.

Keywords: Mixed Reality · User Acceptance · Technical Documentation · Smart Glasses · Industrial Operator Support

1 Introduction

This research focuses on the behavior and attitude that industrial workers might have if they are supposed to use Mixed Reality Technical Documentation (MRTD) using smart glasses during real industrial maintenance tasks. Mixed Reality (MR) has become a promising technology in the manufacturing industry during the last decades [1, 2]. In particular, it proves a great added value in maintenance since it helps workers manage complex, worker-centric processes and heavy cognitive load by providing visual information, simplifying document analysis, and facilitating decision-making during operations [1].

MR is a technology that promotes seamless interaction between real and virtual environments [3], allowing workers to manipulate objects through a tangible interface

G. Zachmann et al. (Eds.): EuroXR 2023, LNCS 14410, pp. 166–180, 2023.
https://doi.org/10.1007/978-3-031-48495-7_11

metaphor and transition effortlessly between reality and virtuality. In other words, MR not only enables operators to benefit from the added value provided by AR, which overlays virtual information onto real-world components to offer visual cues and simplified step-by-step guidance, but it also allows them to interact with a non-referenced AR interface by customizing it for their individual needs [4].

Although MR benefits are empirically proven and widely acknowledged by workers [5], we still observe occasional usage in real industrial contexts. Many studies attributed this shortcoming to the lack of knowledge regarding which technology is best suited for certain tasks [6] or to the absence of optimal features (e.g., content authoring, interaction, hardware capability, ergonomics) of the used technology in a specific task [7]. However, nowadays, these barriers are no longer a challenge thanks to the rapid technological advances [8]. Wireless commodity smart glasses, in fact, are becoming commercially available. Specifically, the current most advanced Optical See-Through (OST) Head-Mounted Display (HMD) Microsoft HoloLens 2 [9] offers the chance to engage in hands-free work without holding a device such as a smartphone or tablet. Moreover, its commercial availability and unique features [4, 8] allow to make it highly demanded by companies as well as create more reliable guidelines. Therefore, in the literature, most of the works discuss the optimal approach to convey maintenance instructions in MRTD [10, 11] and the best MR interface to improve workers' performance [12]. However, the study on the learning skill and acceptance of an industrial worker when confronted with this new technology is often overlooked.

Although MR was introduced almost several decades ago, MR applications for maintenance tasks with smart glasses were mostly limited to laboratory research. For example, Aransyah et al. [13] developed an application for HoloLens to optimize the pipeline of a maintenance procedure. They mentioned the benefits about the inspection speed and accuracy. However, only a focus group tested the application in a laboratory-controlled environment without worrying about how operators might react to this technology. Schlagowski et al. [14] developed a prototype analyzing the user needs of a real industrial scenario, but also in this case, they focused only on the user performance improvement that can be obtained. Very few studies involve workers in a real industrial context focusing on performance or ergonomic aspects rather than investigating the operators' attitude towards this technology [15, 16]. Even fewer works, finally, are interested in operators' acceptability regarding this new technology. In [17], for example, a usability study was performed to test a predictive maintenance system reliability. According to the authors, workers understood the useful features of the MR application, but they required a training to comprehend its usage fully. Therefore, further studies on users' attitude are necessary. Understanding why individuals embrace information technologies is crucial, as it can aid in enhancing design, evaluation, and predicting how users will react to a novel technology [18]. Neglecting these potentials may trigger unforeseen outcomes, such as the counterintuitive result that paper-based technical documentation leads to better results than the MR technology in experimental studies [19].

In this work, we intend to focus on the behavior and attitude of industrial operators if they are supposed to use MRTD using smart glasses in a real industrial maintenance context rather than in a laboratory one. Therefore, we turned our attention primarily to the experienced technicians' ability to accept MR technology with unfamiliar interactions to them rather than evaluating only the improvement in their performance while carrying out routine maintenance operations. For this purpose, we chose the Microsoft HoloLens 2 as HMD because of the system commercial availability and unique features that attract companies nowadays. Therefore, the following research question is investigated: "in an industrial maintenance context, how much is the workers' acceptance towards a MR technology using a HMD in their daily work life?". To answer our research question, we conducted a user study in which we evaluated the user's attitude towards this emerging technology by adopting the Technology Acceptance Model (TAM), which enables to identify the factors that promote the system usage [20]. The case study is the maintenance of a real machine with which operators are used to work without changing the boundary conditions, such as light and position of the equipment. After an initial training, real workers were asked to interact with the Graphical User Interface (GUI) of a developed MRTD of a gas-fired radiant heating system to perform navigation tasks within the menu and a disassembly task. Then, their task completion time was measured and compared with that of a focus group composed of MR experts to evaluate the impact of the training on workers' learning skills, especially from an interaction perspective. Feedback was also collected to understand the operators' opinions more closely regarding the use of a MRTD. Another contribution of this study, finally, is also to confirm, in a real industrial scenario, guidelines validated in previous laboratory tests, such as those regarding a user-friendly interface [8], the readability of information with an OST display [21], and the MRTD authoring [10].

2 MRTD Design for the Case Study

2.1 Definition of User Needs

As a case study, we chose a real maintenance scenario of the company Upgrading Services SpA. We were engaged in a research project aimed at designing and developing a MRTD for a gas-fired radiant heating system (Fig. 1). Therefore, we were given access to both the machine and its maintenance manual in PDF format and native language.

Fig. 1. Machine (gas-fired radiant heating system) that the designed MRTD refers to.

After understanding the functionality of the machine, we defined the main user needs, listed in Table 1, together with the company managers and experienced technicians. Based on the user needs, we defined the MRTD content distinguishing the sections where AR has added value in maintenance operations (referred to as "AR scenes") from those where AR does not appear to have added value but is still essential for providing a complete manual (referred to as "MR scenes") to respect UN-005. We designed the MRTD for this specific use case. However, the framework can be reused for other cases by simply replacing the pages of the new manual as to the MR section. As for the AR section, after adapting the content according to the required task type, the visual assets used for the same information types can be replicated.

As for the device, we chose the Microsoft HoloLens 2 to respect UN-006 and UN-007. Unity 3D Engine is the software used to implement the MRTD, including Mixed Reality Toolkit packages and Vuforia Engine for tracking. An image target was designed and placed inside the right panel of the machine in order for the "AR scenes" content to work properly. The complete 3D CAD model of the equipment was imported into Unity to create the "AR scenes."

Table 1. User needs deriving from the brainstorming with company managers and technicians.

ID	User Need	Source
UN-001	Identify the machine components	Technicians
UN-002	Localize the machine components	Technicians
UN-003	Understand the functionality of the machine components	Technicians
UN-004	Facilitate understanding of elementary maintenance operations	Technicians
UN-005	Provide all the information available in the PDF manual without exclusion	Technicians, managers
UN-006	Intuitive and easy-to-use device	Technicians, managers
UN-007	Be hands-free during maintenance tasks	Technicians, managers

2.2 Definition of MRTD Content

We considered "MR scenes" those that do not require the information registration on the real components involved in the tasks. Thus, they only require a navigation interface to read information or select the "AR scene" to be viewed. Therefore, the developed "MR scenes" are used for the following purposes: login the operator; provide instructions on how to access "AR scenes" and how to view their contents with a natural feature; access all content that does not require an AR scene such as warnings, machine technical data, wiring diagrams, and calibration tables. Figure 2 shows an example of a "MR scene."

Regarding "AR scenes," we considered included in this category all scenes that required the information registration on the real components involved in the tasks. We identified 3 sections in the manual where AR technology can provide high-added value.

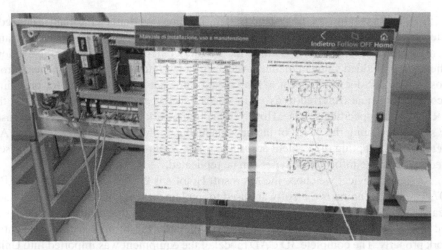

Fig. 2. Example of a "MR scene" of the developed MRTD with machine technical data.

The first "AR scene" is about gas flow adjustment with the following features: identify the components of the flow regulator; understand their functionalities for calibration. The second "AR scene" concerns the adjustment of the mixing damper with the following features: identify the components of the mixing damper; understand their positioning for calibration. The third "AR scene" concerns the disassembly of the thermal unit components with the following features: identify and remove the components of the burner, electrodes, and recirculation motor. Figure 3 shows an example of an "AR scene."

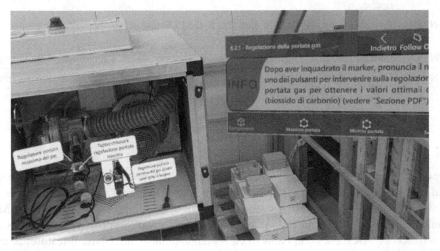

Fig. 3. Example of an "AR scene" of the developed MRTD about gas flow adjustment.

All AR information provided was designed following the "Minimal AR" authoring approach that we presented in [10], for the optimization of visual assets to convey work instructions in manufacturing. According to this approach, if a work instruction only includes the identity of a component, a drawing is used as a visual asset. If the location of the component is also required, an auxiliary model is used. Finally, in cases where the orientation of the component must also be conveyed, product models are exploited.

2.3 Graphical User Interface

Following the guidelines provided by [8], the fundamental principles that should be followed for a user-friendly GUI are affordance, feedback, consistency, non-destructive operations (e.g., undo), discoverability, scalability, and reliability. To comply with these features, we designed the GUI of the developed MRTD as described in the following paragraphs.

For both "AR scenes" and "MR scenes," an interface layout was designed and divided into 3 sections, each with buttons having the icons proposed by Microsoft (see Fig. 2 and Fig. 3). The first section shows the title of the scene with an undo button to return to the previous section, one to return to the "Home" and another button to enable/disable the mode by which the interface can follow the user so as not to lose sight of it. The second section presents only the textual content necessary to provide all supporting information to the user, including the instruction for each step in the "AR scenes," but also information such as technical data, wiring diagrams, and calibration tables for "MR scenes." Finally, the third section is for "AR scenes" only and shows a toolbar used for buttons to filter AR information regarding different calibration configurations and component identification or to change step.

For both "AR scenes" and "MR scenes," the location, orientation, and size of the interface are customizable by the user through anchors placed along the contour of the interface as proposed by the Mixed Reality Toolkit packages. This choice ensured maximum user comfort based on the work area and user preferences. Users can exploit this interaction also during the experiment. As for text, readability has been assured by backgrounds with high-contrast colors: black or white on a blue background [21]. The same applies to labels and buttons. In addition, after the buttons are pressed, they change color by lightening slightly to give user feedback.

The allowed interactions are the standard ones offered by the HoloLens: near pointer gesture, far pointer gesture, and voice command. For the latter, the acceptable words are the button names readable even under their icon. Since these interactions do not interfere with each other, we decided to leave the users free to choose the one they prefer to study their behavior.

3 Design of Experiment

To answer the research question of this work ("in an industrial maintenance context, how much is the workers' acceptance towards a MR technology using a HMD in their daily work life?"), we designed an experiment targeted to expert technicians who frequently perform maintenance tasks with the case study machine.

Due to the nature of this research on a selective population, the number of participants and the sample assortment provided by the company were limited. We recruited

7 participants (7 males, 25–47 years old, mean = 35, SD = 8) with experience in the maintenance field for more than 5 years. On a 7-point Likert rating item (1: Not at all familiar – 7: Extremely familiar), the familiarity level with MR was rated 2.0 on average (SD = 1.31, Median = 1, Min = 1, Max = 4), and with smart glasses 1.86 on average (SD = 1.12, Median = 1, Min = 1, Max = 4).

The trial carried out for each user was divided into two parts: a session on using the developed MRTD on the gas-fired radiant heating system and a subjective questionnaire. Figure 4 summarizes the procedure of the experiment. In the first phase, after a training in which users were able to try out all the interactions proposed by the HoloLens on an interface model similar to the one proposed in the MRTD, they were asked to perform specific tasks listed as follows: log in the MRTD (T1); read and understand the instructions on how the image target works (T2); find a specific section of the included PDF (T3); access the first "AR scene" and view all button features (T4); access the second "AR scene" and view all button features (T5); access the third "AR scene," perform step 1 manually, and view all AR info of the following steps (T6). To evaluate the impact of the training on the workers' learning skills, particularly in terms of interaction, their task completion time was measured and compared to a focus group consisting of 4 MR experts (2 females, 26–34 years old, mean = 29, SD = 3). On a 7-point Likert rating item (1: Not at all familiar – 7: Extremely familiar), the familiarity level with MR was rated 6.5 on average (SD = 0.50, Median = 6.50, Min = 6, Max = 7) and with smart glasses 6.0 (SD = 0.71, Median = 6.00, Min = 5, Max = 7). Unlike the workers, they had no previous experience with the machine under experiment.

During the second phase, operators were asked to fill out a subjective questionnaire. It consists of four sections: demographic characteristics (i), TAM factors (ii), HoloLens interaction feedback (iii), and recommendations on how to improve the MRTD (iv). The user acceptance was measured by 29 selected TAM questions using a 7-point Likert rating item (1: Strongly disagree – 7: Strongly agree). The questions used were derived from validated questionnaires [22–25] used in previous research and modified according to the purpose of our study. As regards the HoloLens interaction feedback, on a 7-point Likert rating item (1: Strongly disagree – 7: Strongly agree), the near pointer gesture was rated 4.29 on average (SD = 2.19, Median = 5, Min = 1, Max = 7), the far pointer gesture 5.71 (SD = 1.03, Median = 6, Min = 4, Max = 7), and the voice command 3 (SD = 2.27, Median = 2, Min = 1, Max = 7).

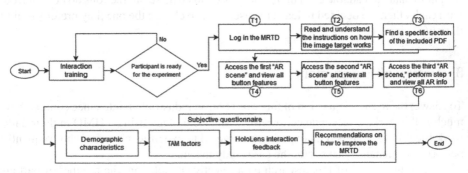

Fig. 4. Experiment procedure.

It was ensured that all the users were not color-blind. They were allowed to wear eyeglasses along with the HoloLens. For each participant, the experiment lasted on average 40 min. The data collected for each participant during the experiment are errors manually checked by the experimenters and participants' feedback.

4 Results

The statements of the TAM questionnaire and the descriptive statistics for each statement are presented in Table 2. Factor analysis was used to examine the construct validity of six factors: Device Interaction (DI), Device Ergonomics (DE), Perceived Ease of Use (PEU), Perceived Usefulness (PU), Attitude Towards using the system (AT), and Intention to Use (IU). Three to eight items were included in the TAM questionnaire to measure each factor. A factor analysis score of at least 0.6 reflects satisfactory survey validity [26]. Almost all factor analysis scores surpassed this threshold, underscoring the robust validity and reliability of the TAM survey. Afterwards, the internal consistency of the items concerning the same factor was analyzed through Cronbach's Alpha reliability analysis. A Cronbach's alpha value of 0.7 or higher is commonly deemed acceptable in terms of reliability [27]. In this study, all Cronbach's alpha values exceeded 0.7, indicating high internal consistency and reliability among the items. All mean values for each factor are within a range of 5.36 and 6.14. The standard deviation ranges from 0.89 to 1.86.

Table 2. Descriptive statistics of TAM factors for the MRTD acceptability with the HoloLens.

Factors	ID	Item	Factor analysis	Cronbach's alfa	Mean (SD)
Device Interaction	DI 1	HoloLens interaction is not frustrating	0.733	0.704	5.67 (1.34)
	DI 2	HoloLens interaction is fun to use	0.610		
	DI 3	HoloLens interaction is simple	0.907		
	DI 4	Doing the procedure by HoloLens is simple	0.413		
	DI 5	The MRTD would gain value adding audio/video	0.667		

(*continued*)

Table 2. (*continued*)

Factors	ID	Item	Factor analysis	Cronbach's alfa	Mean (SD)
	DI 6	Overall, the MRTD interaction is easy and simple	0.907		
Device Ergonomics	DE 1	The HoloLens is comfortable	0.684	0.891	5.43 (1.86)
	DE 2	The virtual element rendering is clear	0.966		
	DE 3	I am not tired due to the HoloLens after the tasks	0.739		
	DE 4	The HoloLens did not cause me any side effects	0.832		
	DE 5	The HoloLens did not strain my eyes	0.819		
Perceived Ease of Use	PEU 1	Learning how to use MRTD is easy for me	0.784	0.703	5.36 (1.49)
	PEU 2	Remember how to do the task using the MRTD is easy for me	0.384		
	PEU 3	I was able to access all the features of the MRTD without the help of an experienced technician	0.403		
	PEU 4	I was able to understand the entire MRTD system without prior knowledge of MR	0.572		
Perceived Usefulness	PU 1	It is easy to get from the MRTD what I want	0.633	0.914	5.88 (1.28)

(*continued*)

Table 2. (*continued*)

Factors	ID	Item	Factor analysis	Cronbach's alfa	Mean (SD)
	PU 2	Using MRTD improves my performance	0.727		
	PU 3	With the MRTD, I learn maintenance tasks faster	0.441		
	PU 4	With the MRTD, I learn maintenance tasks easier	0.383		
	PU 5	The MRTD supports me in individual understanding of more complex instructions	0.988		
	PU 6	The MRTD interface is easy for me to follow	0.691		
	PU 7	The association between real component and virtual element in the "AR scene" is good	0.318		
	PU 8	Overall, I find the MRTD useful	0.958		
Attitude Towards using the system	AT 1	Using the MRTD raises my interest in my work	0.828	0.852	6.14 (0.89)
	AT 2	I was able to understand what MR technology is using the MRTD	0.987		
	AT 3	Using the MRTD increases my motivation in performing the task	0.626		

(*continued*)

Table 2. (*continued*)

Factors	ID	Item	Factor analysis	Cronbach's alfa	Mean (SD)
Intention to Use	IU 1	Assuming I have access to the MRTD, I intend to use it in my daily work	0.884	0.939	5.90 (1.31)
	IU 2	If I had to choose between traditional TD and the MRTD, I would choose the MRTD	0.973		
	IU 3	Assuming I have access to the MRTD, I feel able to consciously interact with MR technology	0.817		

Regarding the task completion time, Fig. 5 shows the comparison between workers and MR experts of the focus group. Except for training and tasks T4 and T6, there are no noticeable differences between completion times.

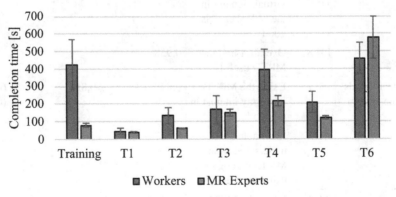

Fig. 5. Comparison of task completion times between workers and MR experts.

5 Discussion

This work is one of the few attempts to investigate the workers' acceptance of a MRTD using a Microsoft HoloLens in a real maintenance context. The obtained results answered our research question supporting a general workers' acceptance towards the MRTD using a HMD for a maintenance task. All the interviewed operators expressed overall high approval for incorporating this new technology into their work routine. According to their feedback, the MRTD allows access to technical documentation information quickly and easily with AR content, making it easier to identify components and understand the task. Users also perceived a significant reduction in errors during task execution to the point that even an inexperienced maintenance worker could perform it with the MRTD. Another added value they identified is the possibility of updating the content with additional information not initially provided in the traditional manual.

All participants emphasized the importance of training for those unfamiliar with HoloLens. In fact, despite the interviewed workers' low familiarity with both MR and HoloLens, there were no indications of negative attitudes regarding the MRTD. Indeed, thanks to the instructions on how the image target works, they were able to figure out how to frame the marker for the "AR scenes" without difficulty. As evidence of this, although the workers' training times are predictably longer than those of the MR experts, the times are comparable for almost all the tasks performed. The highest differences in completion times are found in tasks T4 and T6. Workers accomplished longer times in task T4 because it is the first involving an "AR scene." On task T6, meanwhile, MR experts found it difficult because they lack experience in manually disassembling the machine. An interesting result concerns the standard deviation because while the workers accomplished different times for each task individually, the MR experts all performed at the same speed. This result shows that with practice towards MR technology, every operator can reach high-performance times by overcoming any initial obstacles.

Workers could perform all the tasks even though they showed preferences among the different types of interaction. The users' favorite interaction was the far pointer gesture, while the worst was the voice command. This result shows that although voice command turns out to be an "immediate" interaction as defined by workers, it is unreliable in noisy environments or if the user is wearing a protective system on the face, such as a mask.

From the perspective of the device ergonomics, all users stated the benefits of wearing the HoloLens during maintenance tasks. They also appreciated the opportunity to raise the HoloLens transparent visor if they want to perform a task without seeing the virtual elements that can occlude the real components. However, two users who wore the eyeglasses stated they experienced slight discomfort because the device was pressing on them.

Participants also provided suggestions for improving the MRTD in future developments. Although there was an option to enlarge the interface for greater readability, users suggested a large font for text and wiring diagrams by default. In addition to the PDF provided, illustrative videos might be helpful, even if not essential. Finally, an auxiliary voice can help inexperienced users to find some features in case they have doubts.

Due to the nature of this research on a selective population, the number of participants and the sample assortment provided by the company were limited. Nevertheless, we can extract important insights for the MR adoption in companies from this study. Except for an interaction through HMD to be improved with technological advancement, the MR shows important advantages, so it should be encouraged. User needs analysis was found to be fundamental. Indeed, one example is the decision not to include all "AR scenes" in the manual unless they provided significant added value. Readability with good contrast and the MRTD authoring using the "Minimal AR" approach, thus avoiding the use of attractive visual assets that may provide excessive information, also proved to be successful choices, highlighted by the fact that workers had no difficulties while performing the tasks without negative comments.

6   Conclusion and Future Work

This work aims to focus on the industrial operators' behavior and attitude towards using a MRTD via smart glasses in a real maintenance context. The following research question is investigated: "in an industrial maintenance context, how much is the workers' acceptance towards a MR technology using a HMD in their daily work life?". To answer our research question, we conducted a user study to evaluate the user's attitude towards this emerging technology adopting the TAM model. 7 real workers were asked to perform navigation and disassembly tasks with the developed MRTD of a gas-fired radiant heating system. The feedback obtained allows us to positively evaluate MR technology applied through smart glasses in a real industrial context. Therefore, we can summarize the following lessons learned:

- Even with limited familiarity with MR and smart glasses, workers can successfully incorporate the MR technology into their daily work routine after an initial training.
- Eyeglasses could be a problem for operator ergonomics, so it would also be necessary to design the HMDs considering this aspect.
- Including all the manual content, even that for which AR has no added value, is a valid choice. However, it is recommended to divide the content into smaller sections as presenting it all together could make the text difficult to read.
- "Minimal AR" turns out to be a good authoring approach where the information provided through AR visual assets is the minimum needed to accomplish the task in a real industrial context to avoid excessive information.

In future works, we intend to improve the developed MRTD following the suggestions provided by workers and include a larger group of participants. Their perceptions and attitudes towards the use of the MRTD would be very helpful in enhancing the future design and development of MR-based maintenance instructions.

References

1. Eschen, H., Kötter, T., Rodeck, R., Harnisch, M., Schüppstuhl, T.: Augmented and virtual reality for inspection and maintenance processes in the aviation industry. Procedia Manuf. **19**, 156–163 (2018). https://doi.org/10.1016/j.promfg.2018.01.022
2. Espíndola, D.B., Pereira, C.E., Henriques, R.V.B., Botelho, S.S.: Using mixed reality in the visualization of maintenance processes. IFAC Proc. **1**, 30–35 (2010). https://doi.org/10.3182/20100701-2-pt-4012.00007
3. Speicher, M., Hall, B.D., Nebeling, M.: What is mixed reality? Conf. Hum. Factors Comput. Syst. Proc. 1–15 (2019). https://doi.org/10.1145/3290605.3300767
4. Lang, S., Dastagir Kota, M.S.S., Weigert, D., Behrendt, F.: Mixed reality in production and logistics: Discussing the application potentials of Microsoft HoloLensTM. Procedia Comput. Sci. **149**, 118–129 (2019). https://doi.org/10.1016/j.procs.2019.01.115

5. Kerin, M., Pham, D.T.: A review of emerging industry 4.0 technologies in remanufacturing. J. Clean. Prod. **237**, 117805 (2019). https://doi.org/10.1016/j.jclepro.2019.117805

6. Dede, C.J., Jacobson, J., Richards, J.: Virtual, augmented, and mixed realities in education. 1–16 (2017). https://doi.org/10.1007/978-981-10-5490-7

7. Guo, Q.: Learning in a mixed reality system in the context of industrie 4.0. J. Tech. Educ. **3** (2015). https://doi.org/10.48513/JOTED.V3I2.60

8. Evans, G., Miller, J., Iglesias Pena, M., MacAllister, A., Winer, E.: Evaluating the Microsoft HoloLens through an augmented reality assembly application. Degrad. Environ. Sensing Process. Disp. **10197**, 101970V (2017). https://doi.org/10.1117/12.2262626

9. Siyaev, A., Jo, G.S.: Towards aircraft maintenance metaverse using speech interactions with virtual objects in mixed reality. Sensors. **21**, 1–21 (2021). https://doi.org/10.3390/s21062066

10. Laviola, E., Gattullo, M., Manghisi, V.M., Fiorentino, M., Uva, A.E.: Minimal AR: visual asset optimization for the authoring of augmented reality work instructions in manufacturing. Int. J. Adv. Manuf. Technol. **119**, 1769–1784 (2022). https://doi.org/10.1007/s00170-021-08449-6

11. Radkowski, R., Herrema, J., Oliver, J.: Augmented reality-based manual assembly support with visual features for different degrees of difficulty. Int. J. Hum. Comput. Interact. **31**, 337–349 (2015). https://doi.org/10.1080/10447318.2014.994194

12. Kim, S., Nussbaum, M.A., Gabbard, J.L.: Influences of augmented reality head-worn display type and user interface design on performance and usability in simulated warehouse order picking. Appl. Ergon. **74**, 186–193 (2019). https://doi.org/10.1016/j.apergo.2018.08.026

13. Ariansyah, D., Rosa, F., Colombo, G.: Smart maintenance: a wearable augmented reality application integrated with CMMS to minimize unscheduled downtime. Comput. Aided. Des. Appl. **17**, 740–751 (2020). https://doi.org/10.14733/cadaps.2020.740-751

14. Schlagowski, R., Merkel, L., Meitinger, C.: Design of an assistant system for industrial maintenance tasks and implementation of a prototype using augmented reality. IEEE Int. Conf. Ind. Eng. Eng. Manag. **2017**, 294–298 (2018). https://doi.org/10.1109/IEEM.2017.8289899

15. Piedimonte, P., Ullo, S.L.: Applicability of the mixed reality to maintenance and training processes of C4I systems in Italian Air Force. In: Proceeding of 2018 5th IEEE International Workshop on Metrology for AeroSpace, Metroaerospace, pp. 559–564 (2018). https://doi.org/10.1109/MetroAeroSpace.2018.8453612

16. Pusch, A., Noël, F.: Augmented reality for operator training on industrial workplaces – comparing the Microsoft hololens vs. small and big screen tactile devices. In: Fortin, C., Rivest, L., Bernard, A., Bouras, A. (eds.) Product Lifecycle Management in the Digital Twin Era. PLM 2019. IFIP Advances in Information and Communication Technology, vol. 565. Springer, Cham (2019). https://doi.org/10.1007/978-3-030-42250-9_1

17. Alves, F., et al.: Deployment of a smart and predictive maintenance system in an industrial case study. In: 2020 IEEE 29th International Symposium on Industrial Electronics (ISIE), pp. 493–498. IEEE (2020). https://doi.org/10.1109/ISIE45063.2020.9152441

18. Yusoff, R.C.M., Ibrahim, R., Zaman, H.B., Ahmad, A.: Evaluation of user acceptance of mixed reality technology. Australas. J. Educ. Technol. **27**, 1369–1387 (2011). https://doi.org/10.14742/ajet.899

19. Müller, B.C., et al.: Motion tracking applied in assembly for worker training in different locations. Procedia CIRP. **48**, 460–465 (2016). https://doi.org/10.1016/j.procir.2016.04.117

20. Davis, F.D., Bagozzi, R.P., Warshaw, P.R.: User acceptance of computer technology: a comparison of two theoretical models. Manage. Sci. **35**, 982–1003 (1989). https://doi.org/10.1287/mnsc.35.8.982

21. Gattullo, M., Uva, A.E., Fiorentino, M., Gabbard, J.L., Tech, V.: Visual computing challenges legibility in industrial AR: text style, color coding, and illuminance. IEEE Comput. Graph. Appl. **35**(2), 52–61 (2015).

22. Papakostas, C., Troussas, C., Krouska, A., Sgouropoulou, C.: User acceptance of augmented reality welding simulator in engineering training. Educ. Inf. Technol. **27**, 791–817 (2022). https://doi.org/10.1007/s10639-020-10418-7

23. Iqbal, J., Sidhu, M.S.: Acceptance of dance training system based on augmented reality and technology acceptance model (TAM). Virtual Real. **26**, 33–54 (2022). https://doi.org/10.1007/s10055-021-00529-y

24. Sanna, A., Manuri, F., Piumatti, G., Paravati, G., Lamberti, F., Pezzolla, P.: A flexible AR-based Training system for industrial maintenance. In: De Paolis, L., Mongelli, A. (eds.) Augmented and Virtual Reality. AVR 2015. LNCS, vol. 9254, pp. 314–331. Springer, Cham (2015). https://doi.org/10.1007/978-3-319-22888-4_23

25. Daling, L.M., Abdelrazeq, A., Isenhardt, I.: A comparison of augmented and virtual reality features in industrial trainings. In: Chen, J.Y.C., Fragomeni, G. (eds.) Virtual, Augmented and Mixed Reality. Industrial and Everyday Life Applications. HCII 2020. LNCS, vol. 12191, pp. 47–65 Springer, Cham (2020). https://doi.org/10.1007/978-3-030-49698-2_4

26. Chesney, T.: An interdisciplinary journal on humans in ICT environments an acceptance model for useful and fun information systems. Hum. Technol. Interdiscip. J. Humans ICT Environ. **2**(2), 225–235 (2006)

27. Santos, J.R.A.: Cronbach's alpha: a tool for assessing the reliability of scales. J. Ext. **37**, 1–5 (1999)

Changes in Concentration Performance After Short-Term Virtual Reality Training in E-Athletes

Maciej Lachowicz[1]([✉]), Anna Serweta-Pawlik[1][iD], Dariusz Jamro[2][iD], and Grzegorz Żurek[1][iD]

[1] Wroclaw University of Health and Sport Sciences, 51-12 Wrocław, Poland
maciej.lachowicz@awf.wroc.pl
[2] General Tadeusz Kosciuszko Military University of Land Forces, 51-147 Wrocław, Poland

Abstract. Changes in concentration performance after short-term virtual reality training in e-athletes Abstract. E-sports, or electronic sports, have emerged as a popular form of competition in the digital age. With growing involvement from well-known and established enterprises, e-sports has grown into a thriving industry. Being a professional e-athlete has become a dream for many young people. A crucial aspect of e-athletic performance is the level of cognitive functions, including concentration performance and reaction time. Both conventional and virtual reality trainings have been shown to improve these skills. In this study, 66 amateur e-athletes (45 males, 21 females, mean age 22.7 ± 0.66) who confirmed in a pre- study questionnaire that they were active amateur athletes (with no participation in professional e-sports competitions) were selected to evaluate the effectiveness of training in virtual reality (VR) on concentration performance. Participants were randomly divided into E - experimental group (n = 32) and C - control group (n = 34), with a similar number of men and women in both groups (E = 9 females and 23 males, C = 12 females and 22 males). Differences in daily gaming time and e-sports experience between groups E and C were not statistically significant. The study group underwent 15-min training sessions in the VR game, Beat Saber, for eight consecutive weekdays. The study found that training in VR improved concentration performance, demonstrating the potential of VR as a valuable tool for e-athletes to enhance their cognitive functions.

Keywords: cognitive functions · e-sport · Beat Saber

1 Introduction

Sport has always been an important part of contemporary culture, since the first Olympic Games in 776 BC [37] many disciplines emerged and disappeared. In the modern world football, volleyball and basketball are all well-known and,

G. Zachmann et al. (Eds.): EuroXR 2023, LNCS 14410, pp. 181–191, 2023.
https://doi.org/10.1007/978-3-031-48495-7_12

during most important events, gather millions of viewers [41, 42, 44] importantly, new disciplines and new types of sports are also emerging. One of them is Electronic Sports, more commonly known as an e-sport. In the last decades of the 20th century, as the technological revolution progressed, digital competition also grew and developed [38]. The beginning of the 21st century brought growing popularity and higher numbers of players in the industry [1,2]. Since then, e-sport has developed remarkably, growing involvement from well-known and established enterprises provided support and foundation for the creation of professional teams competing against each other in international tournaments [40]. which now are, similarly to conventional disciplines, attracting millions of viewers [44, 45] and, accordingly, significant financial rewards for the best of competitors [3]. The presence and importance of e-sport has been also noted by educational systems in many countries, both as a separate field of study and as one of the training methods/subjects included in the curriculum [4, 5]. Being a professional e-athlete in one of the major games or leagues became a dream for many young people [6]. The level of gaming performance depends on factors such as motivation [7], sleep time [8], and the level of cognitive functions, e.g. concentration performance [9], although it also depends on the specifications of the computer or the transfer quality of the Internet connection. It has been proven that both conventional [10], and Virtual Reality (VR) [11]. short-term training can cause significant changes in the level of cognitive functions and improve stress tolerance [39]. Such intervention may be beneficial for amateur e-athletes, but it is important to note that the required set of highly developed cognitive functions may vary depending on the type of game. It has been proven that players competing in First Person Shooter (FPS) games develop shorter reaction time and compromised inhibitory control [12]. while players of Multiplayer Online Battle Arena (MOBA) games had more developed cognitive functions such as working memory, focus of attention, and problem-solving abilities. The authors suggest that the complex nature of MOBA games may require players to constantly adapt their strategies and make quick decisions, which can enhance their cognitive abilities over time. These findings suggest that playing MOBA games may not only be a form of entertainment but also a way to improve cognitive function [13]. VR is described is the "use of interactive simulations created with computer hardware and software to present users with opportunities to engage in environments that appear and feel similar to real-world objects and events" [14], due to its immersive environment, it gives the user the unique opportunity to become part of the VR world and not just remain an observer. The technological versatility allows the software to be used for entertainment as well as training or therapy [15, 16]. Originally, virtual reality was used in the military [17], over time, it left aviation simulators and began to be used in the pre-training of other services as well, including nurses, doctors, miners, mechanics, or police officers [18, 19]. To our knowledge, there have been no studies to date of short-term cognitive stimulation in e-sports users and therefore, we have selected a group of amateur e-athletes to measure and evaluate how effective training in VR can be. This study aimed to determine whether short-term training in immersive VR can improve concentration performance.

2   Materials and Methods

2.1   Participants

Participation Criteria. All participants underwent a pre-study questionnaire, which served as the inclusion criterion. They were required to affirm their status as active amateur e-athletes while also confirming their non-participation in professional e-sports competitions. The exclusion criterion for participation was an inability to engage in VR training due to neurological visual, auditory, or motor disorders.

Sample Size. The sample size for this study underwent a meticulous assessment that factored in several critical components. To begin with, an extensive review of prior research in the field was undertaken. While there were no direct precedents for the specific focus of this study, similar studies with comparable methodologies were considered as a base for calculating the appropriate sample size. This process allowed us to contextualize our study within the existing body of knowledge and helped us establish a foundation for determining the sample size. Furthermore, we took into account the time required for participants to undergo the training program of our study. Additionally, practical considerations regarding resource availability and the feasibility of conducting the study within the available timeframe were carefully weighed. Furthermore, it is noteworthy that our determined sample size was not only grounded in the considerations of previous research, time commitments, and practical constraints but was also confirmed to be sufficient for all the statistical tests conducted throughout the study.

Characteristics. Sixty-six participants (45 males, 21 females, mean age 22.7 $\pm$ 0.66 years) were included in the study. A pre-study questionnaire was administered to gather information about the types of games they most frequently played, average daily gaming time, e-sports experience, and age. The distribution of responses was similar across both groups, with MOBA games being the most popular, followed by FPS games. There were no statistically significant differences between the E and C groups in terms of average daily gaming time, e-sports experience, age and initial level of concentration performance. Utilizing simple 1:1 randomization [20] the participants were randomly assigned to E - experimental group (n = 32) and a C - control group (n = 34), with similar numbers of men and women in both groups (E = 9 women and 23 men, C = 12 women and 22 men). Recruitment took place in November and December of 2022. All presented data were collected in December 2022 at the Wrocław University of Health and Sport Sciences. All participants were expected to undergo three tests (pre, post, and follow-up), in the final analysis, only participants who were tested three times were taken into consideration. The study encountered 21.21 percent of dropout.

Ethics. This study's methods and protocol were approved by the Research Ethics Committee of the Wroclaw University of Health and Sport Sciences (no. 19/2022 dated 19 January 2023). All procedures in this study involving human participants were performed in accordance with the Helsinki Declaration of 1964 and its later amendments or comparable ethical standards. A written, informed consent was signed by all participants before their participation in the study (Fig. 1).

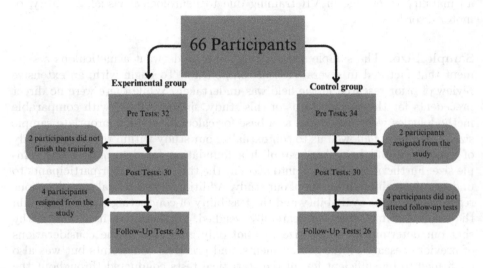

Fig. 1. Participants distribution flowchart

2.2 Intervention

E-athletes selected to the study group participated in 15-min training sessions in the immersive VR game Beat Saber for eight consecutive weekdays (Tuesday to Thursday). To display the training environment Valve Index VR headset was used. Participants selected to the C group did not undergo VR training. The main objective of the game is to cut through colorful blocks, appearing to the rhythm of the song, wielding two virtual lightsabers. Each block must be hit with the lightsaber of the according color and from indicated, by the arrow on it, direction. Every two days the difficulty level of the game was set higher (from normal to expert). The choice of the songs played was randomized.

2.3   Measurements

In the E group tests assessing the level of concentration performance were conducted before the first training and 30 min after the last one. In the C group pre and post tests were performed 8 consecutive weekdays apart. Follow-up tests were, in both groups, conducted 31 days after post tests. To assess the level of concentration performance S4 COGNITRONE (COG) test from Vienna Test System was used [21,22]. In the COG test respondents compare a geometric figure with other geometric figures, then state whether the comparison figure is identical to one of the other four geometric figures. Obtained results consisted of number of correct responses, number of incorrect responses, number of omitted responses, average time of correct response, and average time of correct and incorrect responses.

2.4   Statistical Analysis

All calculations were performed in Statistica v. 13 software from StatSoft Poland in the Department of Biostructure of the Wroclaw University of Health and Sport Sciences, certified by ISO 9001. The statistical significance level was set at $p = 0.05$. The normality of variable distribution was assessed using the Shapiro-Wilk test. Differences in concentration performance between pre, post, and follow-up tests were calculated using the Analysis of Variance for Repeated Measures. Differences between groups were calculated using the Analysis of Variance for Independent Measures.

3   Results

The analysis of concentration performance showed statistically significant differences in both groups. In E group comparison between pre and post tests showed that such difference occurred in amount of correct, incorrect, and omitted reactions, additionally, it was also observed in average time of correct reactions. Comparison between post and follow-up tests failed to show statistically significant difference, however, in comparison between pre and follow-up tests statistically significant difference occurred again. In the C group, statistically significant differences were observed in comparison pre vs post tests in number of incorrect reactions and average time of correct reaction. Comparisons post vs follow-up failed to show any statistically significant difference. In comparison pre vs follow-up, the only difference in average time of correct reactions remained statistically significant. Analysis of Variance proved that there were no statistically significant differences between E and C groups in tests pre, however, in post tests analysis differences in a number of correct and omitted responses were statistically significant. It was also found that differences in the number of correct, incorrect and omitted reactions in follow-up tests were statistically significant (Table 1, 2 and 3).

Table 1. Obtained results as mean values ± standard deviation.

Variable	Group	COG Test Pre	COG Test Post	COG Test Follow-Up
Correct Reactions	E	64.42 ± 5.82	71.42 ± 3.98	71.5 ± 5.30
	C	64.65 ± 6.93	65.53 ± 6.91	64.96 ± 7.27
Incorrect Reactions	E	13.92 ± 6.27	10.69 ± 5.34	9.35 ± 4.04
	C	16.19 ± 6.96	13.38 ± 7.49	14.08 ± 7.51
Omitted Reactions	E	15.15 ± 5.57	8.57 ± 3.98	8.5 ± 5.30
	C	15.35 ± 6.93	14.46 ± 6.91	15.08 ± 7.28
Average time of correct reaction (s)	E	1.08 ± 0.06	1.04 ± 0.08	1.03 ± 0.07
	C	1.07 ± 0.06	1.03 ± 0.09	0.97 ± 0.20
Average time of incorrect reaction (s)	E	1.12 ± 0.14	1.05 ± 0.14	1.07 ± 0.21
	C	1.08 ± 0.13	1.06 ± 0.16	1.01 ± 0.17

Table 2. Results of Analysis of Variance for repeated measures

Variable	Group	ANOVA for repeated measures
Correct Reactions	E	p = 0.0001
	C	p = 0.8710
Incorrect Reactions	E	p = 0.0188
	C	p = 0.6637
Ommited Reactions	E	p = 0.0001
	C	p = 0.8693
Average time of correct reaction	E	p = 0.0103
	C	p = 0.0392
Average time of incorrect reaction	E	p = 0.2783
	C	p = 0.3104

Table 3. Post-hoc HSD Tukey test results

Variable	Group	HSD Tukey Test		
		Pre Test vs Post Test	Post Test vs Follow-Up Test	Pre Test vs Follow-Up Test
Correct Reactions	E	p = 0.0001	p = 0.9977	p = 0.0001
Incorrect Reactions	E	p = 0.0127	p = 0.4382	p = 0.0004
Ommited Reactions	E	p = 0.0001	p = 0.9978	p = 0.0001
Average time of correct reaction	E	p = 0.0414	p = 0.8993	p = 0.0137

4   Discussion

One of the advantages of VR technology is its ability to provide a highly immersive and engaging environment for cognitive training. VR environments can be designed to challenge cognitive processes in a way that is difficult to replicate in traditional cognitive training programs. It has been proved that a VR-based training program was more effective at improving memory performance compared to a traditional computer-based program [26]. The authors suggested that the immersive and interactive nature of the VR environment may have enhanced the learning experience and motivated participants to engage in the training, however, some studies have also reported mixed or inconsistent results in the effectiveness of VR-based cognitive training. One of such studies [27] found that while VR-based training improved cognitive performance in some tasks, it did not have a significant effect on overall cognitive functioning in healthy older adults. These findings suggest that the effectiveness of VR technology in enhancing cognitive abilities may depend on factors such as the type of task, the population being studied, and the specific features of the VR environment. Beat Saber, a VR game used in presented study proved to have an influence on cognitive and physical performance in healthy young adults [28]. Playing Beat Saber improved cognitive flexibility and executive functioning compared to a C group who engaged in a non-VR video game. The authors suggested that the highly engaging and immersive nature of Beat Saber may have contributed to its cognitive benefits. Additionally, the usage of immersive VR games in cognitive training is further supported by a study by Eng et al. (2021) who found that playing Beat Saber resulted in significant improvements in executive functions in healthy adults [29]. Another study by Gustavsson et al. (2022) showed that playing Beat Saber for ten weeks proved to be a useful way of therapy for patients suffering from chronic stroke [30]. These findings suggest that Beat Saber may be a useful tool for concentration training and cognitive enhancement, especially for individuals with cognitive deficits or those looking to improve their overall cognitive abilities. Shown in our study improvement is not isolated to concentration performance. Playing mentioned game can also improve different cognitive functions, in the study by Rutkowski et al. (2021), young musicians received four training sessions using a commercial immersive virtual reality system [11]. Results showed significant improvements in hand-eye coordination and reaction time in the virtual reality training group compared to the C group. The authors suggest that the immersive and interactive nature of the virtual reality system, coupled with its capacity for individualized feedback, may have contributed to the observed improvements in motor skills. VR training provides a highly engaging and interactive environment, additionally, and may provide a more realistic and dynamic training experience compared to traditional training methods, allowing e-athletes to better simulate the challenges of competitive play [31]. Such activity engages multiple sensory modalities, including vision, hearing, and touch. This multisensory stimulation may lead to increased neural activation, in response to new experiences and stimuli [32], which may enhance cognitive processing and improve attentional focus, a study by Kang et al. (2021)

found that immersive virtual reality experiences led to increased activation in brain areas associated with visuospatial processing, such as the parietal cortex [33]. A study by Calabrò et al. (2017) found that VR-based motor training led to an increase in gray matter volume in the primary motor cortex, a brain region important for motor control [34]. Similarly, a study by Liao et al. (2019) showed that VR-based cognitive training improved cognitive function and increased the activity in brain regions related to attention and memory [35]. Another study by Gonçalves et al. (2020) reported that VR exposure therapy resulted in changes in the amygdala, a brain region involved in fear and anxiety, indicating that VR may have therapeutic potential for mental health conditions [36]. These findings suggest that VR training may have positive effects on brain structure and function, which could lead to improvements in various cognitive domains and mental health outcomes. However, further research is needed to better understand the potential of VR training in improving cognitive skills and to find the mechanism explaining them.

5   Conclusions

The aim of this study was to assess the efficacy of immersive VR training in enhancing concentration performance. The findings revealed that the VR music game used in the study resulted in a significant improvement in concentration performance. This finding supports previous research that has demonstrated the potential benefits of VR technology in improving cognitive abilities [23–25]. Immersive 8-days VR training can enhance concentration performance in e-sports athletes. It indicates its potential as a useful tool for early-stage e-sports preparation, however, it is important to acknowledge that the observed changes in our study, which occurred over the course of an eight-days training program, may reflect short-term adaptations. Even considering statistically significant differences in follow-up vs pre test comparisons we recognize, given the relatively brief duration of the intervention, the possibility that these effects may not present long-lasting or enduring changes.

6   Limitations

Despite our diligent efforts to conduct a thorough study, it is imperative to acknowledge certain limitations. One such constraint stemmed from our inability to oversee participants' activities during weekends. Although we provided clear instructions for them to maintain their existing lifestyle, we lacked the means to monitor their adherence to these directives outside the confines of the research environment. Additionally, another limitation pertains to the reliance on self-report questionnaires. Self-report measures are susceptible to various response biases, including social desirability and recall biases, which may lead participants to present themselves in a more favorable light, potentially introducing inaccuracies into the collected data. Furthermore, while our study's findings may indicate positive outcomes in the assessment measures following a one-week training period, we acknowledge the necessity for further investigation. To establish a comprehensive understanding of the long-term effects and the underlying mechanisms associated with these observed changes, future research endeavors should be undertaken.

References

1. Jonasson, K., Thiborg, J.: Electronic sport and its impact on future sport. Sport, Soc. Culture **13**, 287–299 (2010)
2. Hamari, J., Sjöblom, M.: What is eSports and why do people watch it? Internet Res. **27**, 211–232 (2017)
3. Boffard, R.: Esports: to make how money [Sports technology gaming]. Eng. Technol. **11**(4), 66–69 (2016)
4. Gunathilake MM., Ramanayeka N.: Education through e-sport: impact of digital games on cognitive skills of management undergraduates (2016)
5. Ayar, H.: Development of e-sport in Turkey and in the world. Int. J. Sport Cult. Sci. **6**(1), 95–102 (2018)
6. Hou, J., Yang, X., Panek, E.: How about playing games as a career? The evolution of e-sports in the eyes of mainstream media and public relations. Int. J. Sport Commun. **13**(1), 1–21 (2020)
7. Martončik, M.: E-sports: playing just for fun or playing to satisfy life goals? Comput. Hum. Behav. **48**, 290–294 (2015)
8. Lam, A.T.W., Perera, T.P., Quirante, K.B.A., Wilks, A., Ionas, A.J., Baxter, G.D.: E-athletes' lifestyle behaviors, physical activity habits, and overall health and well-being: a systematic review. Phys. Ther. Rev. **25**(5–6), 449–461 (2020)
9. Mackenzie, S., Busemeyer, J.: Enhancing cognitive skills through action video gaming: a brief review of the literature on the effects of action video gaming on cognition, includ- ing attention, concentration, perception, and decision-making. Front. Psychol. **10**, 2982 (2019)
10. Daanen, H.A., Lamberts, R.P., Kallen, V.L., Jin, A., Van Meeteren, N.L.: A systematic review on heart-rate recovery to monitor changes in training status in athletes. Int. J. Sports Phys. Perform. **7**(3), 251–260 (2012)
11. Rutkowski, S., Adamczyk, M., Pastuła, A., Gos, P., Luque-Moreno, C., Rutkowska, J.: Training using a commercial immersive virtual reality system on hand-eye coordination and reaction time in young musicians: A pilot study. Int. J. Environ. Res. Public Health **18**(3), 1297 (2021)
12. Deleuze, J., Christiaens, M., Nuyens, F., Billieux, J.: Shoot at first sight! First person shooter players display reduced reaction time and compromised inhibitory control in com- parison to other video game players. Comput. Hum. Behav. **72**, 570–576 (2017)
13. Riva, G., Wiederhold, B.K., Mantovani, F.: Virtual reality: A new clinical set- ting for the assessment and treatment of mental health disorders. Cyberpsychology, Behav. Soc. Networkingr **24**(3), 131–132 (2021)
14. Liu, S., Li, W., Lin, H., Li, H., Wang, L.: The cognitive function of online game players: a quantitative meta-analysis. Cyberpsychol. Behav. Soc. Netw. **20**(4), 220–226 (2017)
15. Weiss, P.L., Kizony, R., Feintuch, U., Katz, N.: Virtual reality in neurorehabilitation. Textbook Neural Repair Rehabil. **51**(8), 182–197 (2006)

16. Falah, M.A.: Virtual reality medical training system for anatomy education. Sci. Inf. Conf. **51**(8), 182–197 (2006)
17. Lele, S.: Virtual reality and its military utility. J. Ambient. Intell. Humaniz. Comput. **4**(6), 747–756 (2013)
18. Shahrbanian, S., Ma, M.: A systematic review of immersive virtual reality applications for higher education: design elements, lessons learned, and research agenda. Comput. Educ. **147**, 1–20 (2019)
19. Mekacher, L.: Augmented reality (AR) and virtual reality (VR): the future of interactive vocational education and training for people with handicap. Int. J. Teach. Educ. Learn. **3**(1), 118–129 (2019)
20. Kim, J., Shin, W.: How to do random allocation (randomization). Clin. Orthop. Surg. **6**(1), 103–109 (2014)
21. Ong, N.C.H.: The use of the Vienna test system in sport psychology research: a review. Int. Rev. Sport Exerc. Psychol. **8**(1), 204-223, (2015)
22. Scharfen, H.-E., Memmert, D.: The relationship between cognitive functions and sport-specific motor skills in elite youth soccer players. Front. Psychol. **10**, 817 (2019)
23. Yu, D., Li, X., Lai, F.H.: The effect of virtual reality on executive function in older adults with mild cognitive impairment: a systematic review and meta-analysis. Aging Ment. Health **27**(4), 663–673 (2023)
24. Michalski, S.C., Szpak, A., Loetscher, T.: Using virtual environments to improve real-world motor skills in sports: a systematic review. Front. Psychol. **10**, 2159 (2023)
25. Yan, M., et al.: Effects of virtual reality combined cognitive and physical interventions on cognitive function in older adults with mild cognitive impairment: a systematic review and meta-analysis. Ageing Res Rev. **81**, 101708 (2022)
26. Varela-Aldás, J., et al.: The cupboard task: an immersive virtual reality-based system for everyday memory assessment. Int. J. Hum.-Comput. Stud. **167**, 102885 (2022)
27. Anguera, J.A., Boccanfuso, J., Rintoul, J.L., Al-Hashimi, O., Faraji, F., Janowich, J., Gazzaley, A.: Video game training enhances cognitive control in older adults. Nature **501**(7465), 97–101 (2013)
28. Szpak, A., Michalski, S., Loetscher, T.: Exergaming with beat saber: an investigation of virtual reality aftereffects. J. Med. Internet Res. **22**(10), e19840 (2020)
29. Eng, C.M., Calkosz, D.M., Yang, S.Y., Williams, N.C., Thiessen, E.D., Fisher, A.V.: Enhancing brain plasticity and cognition utilizing immersive technology and virtual reality contexts for gameplay, pp. 395–398. IEEE (2020)
30. Gustavsson, M., Kjörk, E.K.: Mattias Erhardsson margit alt murphy virtual reality gaming in rehabilitation after stroke - user experiences and perceptions. Disabil. Rehabil. **44**(22), 6759–6765 (2022)
31. Miah, A., Fenton, A., Chadwick, S.: Virtual reality and sports: the rise of mixed, augmented, immersive, and Esports experiences. In: 21st Century Sports: How Technologies will Change Sports in the Digital Age, pp. 249–262 (2020)
32. Baniqued, P.L., Kranz, M.B., Voss, M.W., Lee, H., Cosman, J.D., Severson, J., Kramer, A.F.: Cognitive training with casual video games: points to consider. Front. Psychol. **4**, 1010 (2014)
33. Kang, J.M., Kim, N., Lee, S.Y., Woo, S.K., Park, G., Yeon, B.K., Park, J.W., Youn, J.H., Ryu, S.H., Lee, J.Y., Cho, S.J.: Effect of cognitive training in fully immersive virtual reality on visuospatial function and frontal-occipital functional connectivity in predementia: randomized controlled trial. J. Med. Internet Res. **23**(5), e24526 (2021)

34. Calabrò, R.S., Naro, A., Russo, M., Leo, A., De Luca, R., Balletta, T., Buda, A., La Rosa, G., Bramanti, A., Bramanti, P.: he role of virtual reality in improving motor performance as revealed by EEG: a randomized clinical trial. J. Neuroeng. Rehabil. **14**(1), 1–16 (2017)
35. Liao, Y.Y., Tseng, H.Y., Lin, Y.J., Wang, C.J., Hsu, W.C.: Using virtual reality-based training to improve cognitive function, instrumental activities of daily living and neural efficiency in older adults with mild cognitive impairment. Eur. J. Phys. Rehabil. Med. **56**(1), 47–57 (2019)
36. Gonçalves, R., Pedrozo, A.L., Coutinho, E.S.F., Figueira, I., Ventura, P.: Efficacy of virtual reality exposure therapy in the treatment of PTSD: a systematic review. PLoS ONE **7**(12), e48469 (2012)
37. Finley, M.I., Pleket, H.W.: The Olympic Games: the First Thousand Years. Couricr Corporation, North Chelmsford (2012)
38. Wolf, M.J.: The Video Game Explosion: a History from PONG to Playstation and Beyond. ABC-CLIO, Santa Barbara (2008)
39. Lachowicz M., Dulnik M., Jamro D., Żurek G. Evaluation of changes in students' stress tolerance under the influence of virtual reality. in Żuchowska-Kotlarz E., Tokarski A. Wirtualna rzeczywistość w perspektywie nauk: spolecznych pedagogiki, psychologii i zarządzania. Akademia Handlowa Nauk Stosowanych w Radomiu **T.1**, 115–129 (2022)
40. Menasce, R.M.: From Casual to Professional: How Brazilians Achieved Esports Success in Counter-Strike: Global Offensive. Ph.D. Thesis, Northeastern University, Boston, MA, USA (2017)
41. beIN Sports https://tinyurl.com/2us5mwk9. Accessed 11 May 2023
42. SportsPro Media https://tinyurl.com/4tmcvh8a. Accessed 11 May 2023
43. ESPN Press Room. https://tinyurl.com/5nr8u88s. Accessed 11 May 2023
44. Statista. https://tinyurl.com/5n7hu5d9. Accessed 11 May 2023
45. AFK Gaming. https://tinyurl.com/5732be5b. Accessed 11 May 2023

XR for First Responders: Concepts, Challenges and Future Potential of Immersive Training

Jakob C. Uhl[1,2](✉) ⓘ, Georg Regal[1,2] ⓘ, Helmut Schrom-Feiertag[1] ⓘ,
Markus Murtinger[1,2] ⓘ, and Manfred Tscheligi[1,2] ⓘ

[1] AIT - Austrian Institute of Technology, Vienna, Austria
jakob.uhl@ait.ac.at
[2] PLUS University of Salzburg, Salzburg, Austria

Abstract. This paper highlights the significance of Extended Reality
(XR) technology as a crucial component of future first responder (FR)
training to address the challenges faced by Europe in maintaining public
safety and peace. XR, which includes virtual reality (VR), augmented
reality (AR), and mixed reality (MR), offers unique opportunities to
enhance FR training. We present a mapping of specific training goals
to different XR solutions, categorizing them based on immersion level
and extent of world knowledge. We discuss the benefits of XR, while
also acknowledging the challenges and ethical considerations. Lastly, we
discuss the main future developments we deem to be crucial for the
field. With this, we hope to foster a common understanding of terminology, needs and future directions between end-users, researchers and
tech-providers.

Keywords: extended reality · simulation training · first response

1 Introduction

Europe faces various challenges to public safety, which seem to have increased in
recent years. Natural disasters have escalated due to climate change, as reported
in a European Environment Agency (EEA) report [8]. Terrorism remains a key
threat to the EU's internal security, according to Europol's TE-SAT 2022 report
[9]. Additionally, various incidents such as industrial accidents and health emer-
gencies call for more efficient and effective responses, as emphasized by the European Commission's Joint Research Centre's report on disaster risk management
for 2022 [7]. This illustrates an ongoing need for highly trained and effective first
responders.

Various approaches exist for training first responders (FR) in challenging
environments. In this position paper, we argue that Extended Reality (XR) is a
key pillar for the future of FR training and safety in Europe. XR is a relatively
new term shaped by both industry and research, making it somewhat elusive.
This work aims to adapt the framework of Skarbez, Smith, and Whitton [34]
to FR training, mapping specific goals to XR solutions. This will help end-users

© The Author(s), under exclusive license to Springer Nature Switzerland AG 2023
G. Zachmann et al. (Eds.): EuroXR 2023, LNCS 14410, pp. 192–200, 2023.
https://doi.org/10.1007/978-3-031-48495-7_13

understand the XR landscape for their training needs and inform developers and researchers about future directions in the context of XR for FR training.

Our conclusions and statements are further informed by existing work in the field and our experience from three Horizon 2020 projects MED1stMR[1], SHOTPROS[2] and VERTIgO[3] concerned with XR training for FRs. In Sect. 2 we define XR and map training goals to the XR space, discussing benefits and challenges in this context as well as ethical considerations. In Sect. 3 we delve into what we consider the main topics for XR FR training in the future, and conclude with Sect. 4.

2   XR for First Responder Training

A first responder is a professional (e.g. a police officer or medical FR), who is among those who go immediately to the scene of an accident or emergency. Though there are different occupations that are considered FRs, they face similar challenges: When arriving at a scene, they need a good situational awareness of the threats and challenges of the environment, have the knowledge of standard processes and rules in that situation and then act accordingly. All these steps are interwoven with communication aspects, both internal and external.

From these common challenges we extracted the main training goals that are frequently mentioned in the literature of FR training: (1) Knowledge of processes and rules [3,40,42], (2) cognitive and emotional skills relating to the environmental threats [31,39], (3) technical skills of the occupation (e.g. handling a weapon, treating patients) [10,18], (4) physical skills [6,36] (e.g. endurance/fatigue during an operation) and (5) communication [14,19] (with the different stakeholders). We see the potential of XR to accommodate these different training goals, though not every variant of XR is suited for every training goal.

2.1   Definition of XR and Mapping of Training Goals

To assess what training goals can be achieved by XR, the application field needs a clear definition and classification of XR. In this work we build on the framework by Skarbez, Smith, and Whitton [34], who propose three dimensions of XR. The first dimension *Immersion* (IM) describes the fidelity of the technical system to provide sensory sensations as reality would, which relates to Slater's *Place Illusion* [35]. The second dimension, *Extent of World Knowledge (EWK)* describes how aware the system is of its surroundings, meaning whether the simulation has a model of its environment or nearby objects. The third dimension–*Coherence*– relates to Slater's *Plausibility Illusion*, as it describes the coherence of events that happen within the simulation.

In the sense of 'strong concepts' [15] we believe it to be important to connect theory with practice. To achieve that on a high level for the context of training

---

[1] medfirstmr.eu.
[2] shotpros.eu.
[3] cbrn-vertigo.eu/.

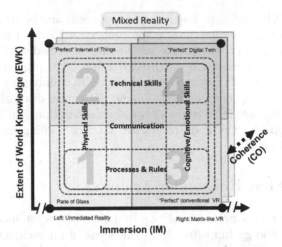

Fig. 1. Model of MR adapted from [34].

FRs, we propose a broad mapping of the main identified training goals onto the XR framework, to support end-users in navigating the different possibilities XR offers. This mapping is presented in Fig. 1 and divides the XR space spanned by *EWK* and *IM* into four quadrants.

Quadrant 1 (bottom left) features low immersion and low extent of world knowledge of the technology. An example would be a mission planning table to train planning missions on an interactive map or screen based situational training. This quadrant is mostly used for training logistics and organisation, as well as communication, as little world knowledge and immersion are needed in that regard. Q1 could be a screen-based training of the procedure when arriving at an accident scene.

Quadrant 2 (top left) features lower immersion but higher world knowledge of the system. Typical example are AR training applications or – with less immersion – motion-tracked real training. As this quadrant is strongly related to the physical environment, this enables real skills training in the sense of handling objects as in reality with some augmentation. Q2 could entail an augmented real-life exercise, e.g. with tracked behaviour.

Quadrant 3 (bottom right) describes technologies with higher immersion but no to low world knowledge. This relates to 'conventional' VR, with purely virtual content in a given space. VR is mostly used for training Decision-Making and Acting, as it allows for a realistically simulated environment and thereby the necessary context for making decisions and choosing the right path of action. Q3 could be a first triage training in a virtual accident scenario.

Quadrant 4 (top right) features high levels of immersion combined with high levels of world knowledge. This would correspond with MR solutions that feature more elaborate haptic feedback from real world objects, or even mix the virtual with video pass-through from reality. This quadrant is useful for training technical skills in an immersive environment (e.g., [2,11,37]), but also decision making and acting, as the immersive environment gives crucial contextual cues for action. Q4 could be a CPR training with a physical manikin in MR.

Communication is a ubiquitous aspect in XR, thereby we did not map it to any specific quadrant. The *Coherence* factor is central for any occupational training: the virtual environment and whats happening in it must be plausible in the respective context. We did not use it for categorization, as it is an inherent necessity of virtual training. The mapping presented in this section is intended as a starting point for discussing the mapping of training goals in the XR space. We believe, that in particular Q4 shows the most promise for the future of training, as it enables the training of all identified skills in one simulation.

2.2   Benefits of XR for Training First Responders

Simulation of Realistic Scenarios. With the increasing sensory fidelity of XR technology, realistic scenarios for FR training can be simulated. VR training technology especially is promising for "realistic and chaotic situations that are difficult to replicate with existing approaches" [14, p. 57]. By adding interactive, occupation-specific *stressors* [25], trainees can be prepared for real-life scenarios (e.g. an aggressive dog threatening police officers). Furthermore, trainers can dynamically add or remove stressors to control the experience of their trainees.

Safe Learning Environment. First responder deployments often happen in challenging environments that are (potentially) dangerous (e.g. mines [1,12], construction sites [30], CBRN environments [22], fires [11], etc.) or hard to access (e.g. a subway station [32], evacuation exercises for buildings [20]). XR enables training in these environments with no physical danger while maintaining the possibility to fail without serious threats. We like to refer to [17] for a literature review on safety training.

Repeated Practise. Real simulation training is often cumbersome and involves many actors, which leads to a decreased frequency of training. XR on the other hand, enables repeatability in exactly the same environment and condition and high experimental control [14,23], which is an advantage for the effectiveness of training, as repetition is at the root of the learning experience [13,21].

AI-Driven Adaptive Virtual Environments. With XR, training can be tracked automatically in multiple ways. This logging of information (e.g., crossing line of fire, assign a triage color, ...) enables a replay of the scenario, where different perspectives can be explored and mistakes can be identified in a transparent and clear manner. This *After Action Review (AAR)* is mentioned frequently by end users as the main advantage of XR training [14,24]. With the use of physiological and positional data of the participants, XR can also enable AI-driven adaptive training based on the users behavior and physiological state [43].

2.3   Challenges of XR for Training First Responders

By increasing the efficiency, repeatability and realism of training, XR can be a powerful enabling technology, that is already in use in various training programs, but simultaneously faces multiple challenge to fulfill it's inherent potential [27].

Logistical and Organizational Aspects. Resistance to new technology can be a major hurdle, as decision-makers might not see the benefits for XR and hold skeptical beliefs about the technology [38]. Therefore it is crucial to find 'champions' within a given organization to help inform and resolve any reservations. Part of this is the logistic aspect: Integrating XR training needs continuous support from technology partners and training of operators and trainers.

Remote Collaboration and Communication. Training collaboration and communication are key both within and between organizations [14, 27]. Joint training involving firefighters, medical teams, and police is scarce due to resource constraints [14, p. 57]. XR offers solutions by facilitating remote and asynchronous training with simulated inter-agency interactions. Despite often standardized communication protocols, the unique nature of incidents makes communication a primary challenge in FR training [14].

Tangible Objects/Tools in VR. Tangible Interaction [16] has been put forward as a way to make virtual training more realistic and even enable motor-skills training next to decision-making in highly immersive virtual environments. With the help of active trackers, fiducial markers or WIFI tracking, physical props can be integrated into the virtual world. For example, Uhl et al. [37] have proposed a MR solution for medical skills training, which enables the use of real tools in XR; Calandra et al. [4] used passive haptics in firefighter training; Baek et al. [2] used tangible, real tools in a VR-based job training system.

2.4   Ethical Considerations

With the use of XR for training FRs and thereby the simulation of distressing and stressful scenarios, certain ethical considerations arise. One central question is that of the needed **amount of realism**. [5] compared different fidelity versions of an airplane evacuation showed that "The more participants were scared by the virtual experience [...], the more new knowledge they acquired through it." However, when simulating stressful scenarios [25] in a highly realistic manner, there is the danger of overwhelming trainees. Thus, the amount of realism needs to be weighed against the benefits, with the opportunity to opt-out. Further, the question of **data security** is of importance, as the training data generated could be possibly harmful in the wrong hands. When speaking of integrating bio-sensors into the training for monitoring the trainees state, **data-privacy and informed consent** need to be considered even more. For a comprehensive discussions of ethics in VR training, see Zechner et al. [44].

3   The Future of XR Training

In this section, we want to highlight key developments that we deem crucial for the future of the field.

Interoperability and Exchangeability of Scenarios: Interoperability in this context means, that the same virtual environment can be used to train the different roles involved in e.g. an accident, and not just for one occupation group. This point is supported by Rozman [29, p. 2] in the context of military training, who states that "programs that are not interoperable and cannot train convergence across all five war-fighting domains are obsolete". We observe many stand-alone developments of institutions and propose a central exchange platform for organisations to share digital assets.

Increasing Immersion and Realism: When training FRs for challenging situations, simulation realism is crucial to avoid training incorrect behaviors due to low fidelity. As stated by Haskins et al., "Poor training can be worse than no training due to negative training effects." [14, p. 57]. This necessitates collaboration between end-users and developers to capture occupation-specific details. This involves simulating various sensory modalities depending on the context. For fire evacuation training, Shaw et al. [33] observed more realistic behaviour when including a heat source in VR. Multi-sensory enhancement, alongside realistic audio-visual content, shows promise in XR training.

AI-controlled Virtual Agents: With the rapidly growing field of natural language processing and AI in general, virtual agents in XR training scenarios (e.g. patients, by-standers, other organisations) can be fully automated in the future, where today often role-players are still needed to convey the appropriate amount of social realism (e.g., [37]). This would include adequate text-to-speech responses, facial expressions and actions, dependent on the behavior of the trainee(s) in the virtual scenario. However, the impact of agent design [28] on the trainee and training outcome needs to be considered.

Interweavement with Existing Training Curriculum: As repeatedly stated in this work, we see XR as *one* pillar of future training of FRs. The consensus among end-users and researchers [26, 41] is that XR training is not intended to replace traditional forms of training, but rather to extended the toolbox of different training methods. As such, it will be detrimental to develop novel training curricula in the institutions that interweave traditional and XR training, so that the two training forms complement each other.

4   Conclusion

In this work, we illustrated the benefits and challenges of XR for training FRs with the goal of positioning XR as a main pillar of future training in this context. The identified future topics of XR FR training and the mapping of training goals to different XR technologies aim to inform end-users and urge researchers and developers to tackle the challenges and visions this highly relevant field.

Acknowledgements. This work was funded by the H2020 project MED1stMR (No 101021775) and by the Austrian research promotion agency (FFG, No FO999887876).

References

1. Andersen, K., Gaab, S.J., Sattarvand, J., Harris, F.C.: METS VR: mining evacuation training simulator in virtual reality for underground mines. In: Latifi, S. (ed.) 17th International Conference on Information Technology–New Generations (ITNG 2020). AISC, vol. 1134, pp. 325–332. Springer, Cham (2020). https://doi.org/10.1007/978-3-030-43020-7_43
2. Baek, S., Gil, Y.H., Kim, Y.: VR-based job training system using tangible interactions. Sensors **21**(20), 6794 (2021)
3. Baetzner, A.S., et al.: Preparing medical first responders for crises: a systematic literature review of disaster training programs and their effectiveness. Scand. J. Trauma Resusc. Emerg. Med. **30**(1), 1–23 (2022)
4. Calandra, D., De Lorenzis, F., Cannavò, A., Lamberti, F.: Immersive virtual reality and passive haptic interfaces to improve procedural learning in a formal training course for first responders. Virtual Reality **27**, 1–28 (2022)
5. Chittaro, L., Buttussi, F., Zangrando, N.: Desktop virtual reality for emergency preparedness: user evaluation of an aircraft ditching experience under different fear arousal conditions. In: Proceedings of the 20th ACM Symposium on Virtual Reality Software and Technology, pp. 141–150 (2014)
6. Corrigan, S.L., Roberts, S., Warmington, S., Drain, J., Main, L.C.: Monitoring stress and allostatic load in first responders and tactical operators using heart rate variability: a systematic review. BMC Public Health **21**, 1–16 (2021)
7. European Commission & Joint Research Centre Publications Office, Poljanšek, K., Clark, I., Casajus Valles, A., Marín Ferrer, M.: Science for disaster risk management 2020: acting today, protecting tomorrow. European Commission & Joint Research Centre Publications Office (2021). https://dx.doi.org/10.2760/438998
8. European Environment Agency: Climate change, impacts and vulnerability in Europe 2016: an indicator-based report. Technical report, European Environment Agency, Copenhagen (2016). https://www.eea.europa.eu/publications/climate-change-impacts-and-vulnerability-2016
9. Europol: European union terrorism situation and trend report. Technical report, Publications Office of the European Union, Luxembourg (2022)
10. Ford, J.K., Schmidt, A.M.: Emergency response training: strategies for enhancing real-world performance. J. Hazard. Mater. **75**(2–3), 195–215 (2000)
11. Grabowski, A.: Practical skills training in enclosure fires: an experimental study with cadets and firefighters using cave and HMD-based virtual training simulators. Fire Saf. J. **125**, 103440 (2021)
12. Grabowski, A., Jankowski, J.: Virtual reality-based pilot training for underground coal miners. Saf. Sci. **72**, 310–314 (2015)
13. Grantcharov, T.P., Bardram, L., Funch-Jensen, P., Rosenberg, J.: Learning curves and impact of previous operative experience on performance on a virtual reality simulator to test laparoscopic surgical skills. Am. J. Surg. **185**(2), 146–149 (2003)
14. Haskins, J., et al.: Exploring VR training for first responders. In: 2020 IEEE Conference on Virtual Reality and 3D User Interfaces Abstracts and Workshops (VRW), pp. 57–62. IEEE (2020)

15. Höök, K., Löwgren, J.: Strong concepts: intermediate-level knowledge in interaction design research. ACM Trans. Comput.-Hum. Interact. (TOCHI) **19**(3), 1–18 (2012)

16. Ishii, H., Ullmer, B.: Tangible bits: towards seamless interfaces between people, bits and atoms. In: Proceedings of the ACM SIGCHI Conference on Human Factors in Computing Systems, pp. 234–241 (1997)

17. Kanade, S.G., Duffy, V.G.: Use of virtual reality for safety training: a systematic review. In: Duffy, V.G. (ed.) HCII 2022, Part II. LNCS, vol. 13320, pp. 364–375. Springer, Cham (2022). https://doi.org/10.1007/978-3-031-06018-2_25

18. Koutitas, G., Smith, S., Lawrence, G.: Performance evaluation of AR/VR training technologies for ems first responders. Virtual Reality **25**, 83–94 (2021)

19. Manoj, B.S., Baker, A.H.: Communication challenges in emergency response. Commun. ACM **50**(3), 51–53 (2007)

20. Menzemer, L.W., Ronchi, E., Karsten, M.M.V., Gwynne, S., Frederiksen, J.: A scoping review and bibliometric analysis of methods for fire evacuation training in buildings. Fire Safety J., 103742 (2023)

21. Miller, J.L., Rambeck, J.H., Snyder, A.: Improving emergency preparedness system readiness through simulation and interprofessional education. Public Health Rep. **129**(6_suppl4), 129–135 (2014)

22. Mossel, A., Peer, A., Göllner, J., Kaufmann, H.: Towards an immersive virtual reality training system for CBRN disaster preparedness. In: The 12th International Multidisciplinary Modeling & Simulation Multiconference. DIMF University of Genoa, DIMEH University of Calabria (2015)

23. Murtinger, M., Jaspaert, E., Schrom-Feiertag, H., Egger-Lampl, S.: CBRNe training in virtual environments: SWOT analysis & practical guidelines. Int. J. Saf. Secur. Eng. **11**(4), 295–303 (2021)

24. Murtinger, M., Uhl, J., Schrom-Feiertag, H., Nguyen, Q., Harthum, B., Tscheligi, M.: Assist the VR trainer – real-time dashboard and after-action review for police VR training. In: 2022 IEEE International Conference on Metrology for Extended Reality, Artificial Intelligence and Neural Engineering (MetroXRAINE), pp. 69–74 (2022). https://doi.org/10.1109/MetroXRAINE54828.2022.9967532

25. Nguyen, Q., Jaspaert, E., Murtinger, M., Schrom-Feiertag, H., Egger-Lampl, S., Tscheligi, M.: Stress out: translating real-world stressors into audio-visual stress cues in VR for police training. In: Ardito, C., et al. (eds.) INTERACT 2021. LNCS, vol. 12933, pp. 551–561. Springer, Cham (2021). https://doi.org/10.1007/978-3-030-85616-8_32

26. Pottle, J.: Virtual reality and the transformation of medical education. Future Healthc. J. **6**(3), 181 (2019)

27. Regal, G., et al.: Challenges in virtual reality training for CRBN events. In: De Paolis, L.T., Arpaia, P., Sacco, M. (eds.) Extended Reality: XR Salento 2022, Part II. LNCS, vol. 13446, pp. 79–88. Springer, Cham (2022). https://doi.org/10.1007/978-3-031-15553-6_6

28. Regal, G., et al.: Marcus or Mira-investigating the perception of virtual agent gender in virtual reality role play-training. In: Proceedings of the 28th ACM Symposium on Virtual Reality Software and Technology, pp. 1–11 (2022)

29. Rozman, J.: The synthetic training environment. Spotlight SL, pp. 20–6 (2020)

30. Sacks, R., Perlman, A., Barak, R.: Construction safety training using immersive virtual reality. Constr. Manag. Econ. **31**(9), 1005–1017 (2013)

31. Sanquist, T., Brisbois, B., Baucum, M.: Attention and Situational Awareness in First Responder Operations. Pacific Northwest National Laboratory, Alexandria (2016)

32. Sharma, S., Jerripothula, S., Mackey, S., Soumare, O.: Immersive virtual reality environment of a subway evacuation on a cloud for disaster preparedness and response training. In: 2014 IEEE Symposium on Computational Intelligence for Human-Like Intelligence (CIHLI), pp. 1–6. IEEE (2014)

33. Shaw, E., Roper, T., Nilsson, T., Lawson, G., Cobb, S.V., Miller, D.: The heat is on: exploring user behaviour in a multisensory virtual environment for fire evacuation. In: Proceedings of the 2019 CHI Conference on Human Factors in Computing Systems, pp. 1–13 (2019)

34. Skarbez, R., Smith, M., Whitton, M.C.: Revisiting milgram and Kishino's reality-virtuality continuum. Front. Virtual Real. **2**, 647997 (2021)

35. Slater, M.: Place illusion and plausibility can lead to realistic behaviour in immersive virtual environments. Philos. Trans. Royal Soc. B Biol. Sci. **364**(1535), 3549–3557 (2009)

36. Sweeney, P., Matthews, M.D., Lester, P.D., Hannah, S., Reed, B.: Leadership in Dangerous Situations: A Handbook for the Armed Forces, Emergency Services and First Responders. Naval Institute Press, Annapolis (2022)

37. Uhl, J.C., Schrom-Feiertag, H., Regal, G., Gallhuber, K., Manfred, T.: Tangible immersive trauma simulation: is mixed reality the next level of medical skills training? In: Proceedings of the 2023 CHI Conference on Human Factors in Computing Systems (2023). (in press)

38. Widagdo, P., Susanto, T., Setyadi, H., Wardhana, R., Taruk, M., Pakpahan, H.: The influence of user generation differences on individual performance in using information technology. J. Phys. Conf. Ser. **1803**, 012031 (2021)

39. Wild, J., et al.: Pre-incident training to build resilience in first responders: recommendations on what to and what not to do. Psychiatry **83**(2), 128–142 (2020)

40. Wilkerson, W., Avstreih, D., Gruppen, L., Beier, K.P., Woolliscroft, J.: Using immersive simulation for training first responders for mass casualty incidents. Acad. Emerg. Med. **15**(11), 1152–1159 (2008)

41. Wismer, P., Lopez Cordoba, A., Baceviciute, S., Clauson-Kaas, F., Sommer, M.O.A.: Immersive virtual reality as a competitive training strategy for the biopharma industry. Nature Biotechnol. **39**(1), 116–119 (2021)

42. Yang, L., Prasanna, R., King, M.: On-site information systems design for emergency first responders. J. Inf. Technol. Theory Appl. (JITTA) **10**(1), 2 (2009)

43. Zahabi, M., Abdul Razak, A.M.: Adaptive virtual reality-based training: a systematic literature review and framework. Virtual Real. **24**, 725–752 (2020)

44. Zechner, O., Kleygrewe, L., Jaspaert, E., Schrom-Feiertag, H., Hutter, R.V., Tscheligi, M.: Enhancing operational police training in high stress situations with virtual reality: experiences, tools and guidelines. Multimodal Technol. Interact. **7**(2), 14 (2023)

Biophilic Design of Virtual Workplaces: Effect of Animations on User Attention

Sara Romano(iD), Enricoandrea Laviola(iD), Antonio Emmanuele Uva(iD), and Michele Gattullo(✉)(iD)

Department of Mechanics, Mathematics, and Management, Polytechnic University of Bari, Via Orabona, 4, 70125 Bari, Italy
s.romano3@phd.poliba.it, michele.gattullo@poliba.it

Abstract. The biophilic design of virtual workplaces consists of introducing additional natural elements in the virtual environment (VE) with respect to those needed for the main task. It has received increasing attention in recent years, and an increasing number of studies are showing that exposure to biophilic elements in an immersive VE produces positive effects on human well-being. However, in the literature, there are no guidelines about the setting of the different variables of biophilic design in a VE. In this work, we investigated one of these variables, i.e., the effect of the animations of biophilic elements, formulating the following research question: how do animations of biophilic virtual elements affect user attention while performing a working task? We carried out an experiment in which users performed two levels of difficulty of the n-Back cognitive test in three VEs: two identical biophilic VE, one with all static elements and another one in which some of these elements were animated, and an additional empty VE used as a baseline. Performance measurements, eye-tracking measurements, and subjective measurements were collected from 24 users. We found that introducing animations of biophilic elements does not affect user performance in the cognitive task. Furthermore, we found that users' gaze remains fixed on the main task for more than 94% of the time. However, the use of animations does not bring added value to users in terms of user experience, whereas it causes an increase in perceived distraction and mental effort.

Keywords: Virtual Reality · Biophilic Design · Animations · Positive Computing

1 Introduction

Extended Reality (XR) technologies have reached a maturity that allows the study of novel design variables beyond the basic human needs (e.g., efficiency, accuracy) towards higher-level needs. For example, these technologies could contribute to the enhancement of happiness and psychological well-being [1]. Sander defined this approach as Positive Computing, which is "the study and development of information and communication technologies that are consciously designed to support people's psychological well-being in a way that honors the diverse ideas of the good life of individuals and communities." A

G. Zachmann et al. (Eds.): EuroXR 2023, LNCS 14410, pp. 201–214, 2023.
https://doi.org/10.1007/978-3-031-48495-7_14

consequence of applying positive computing principles is the improvement of working conditions, which directly affects productivity, health, and well-being [2]. In this way, it is possible to place the well-being of industrial workers at the center of the production process, as requested by the novel paradigm of Industry 5.0 [3].

A proven way to increase human well-being is exposure to natural features and environments [4]. In fact, as described by Wilson [5] in his biophilia hypothesis, humans have "an innate tendency to focus on life and lifelike processes". Ryan et al. presented various biophilic design patterns to inform, guide and assist in the design process, such as the "visual connection with nature" [6]. In real working environments, introducing plants, water, and natural materials are examples of the biophilic design [7–9] application. From the literature, it is evident that there is stress reduction in both experiencing real nature and seeing images of nature [10–13]. Then, showing virtual representations of biophilic elements in XR applications may improve human well-being as done by the real nature in physical workplaces. Various fields can benefit from applying biophilic design in XR, considering that many working activities are already performed in XR environments. For example, in the manufacturing field, Virtual Reality (VR) industrial environments are used for the training of operators [14, 15] and Augmented Reality (AR) instructions support assembly and maintenance processes [16]. XR is producing new forms of education [17, 18]. The limitation to physical interactions due to the SARS-CoV-2 pandemic induced to the application of contactless methods of rehabilitation, exploiting XR systems [19]. Moreover, an increasing number of companies are adopting virtual offices for telework [20]. In addition, retailing is shifting from traditional shopping channels to VR shops [21]. These are only some examples of XR working environments, but it is reasonable to think that many others will come due to the extensive use of Metaverse [22].

The application of the biophilic design was investigated in XR applications only recently [23–25], confirming that exposure to virtual biophilic elements positively affects human well-being. Emamjomeh et al. found that natural element exposure in immersive Virtual Environments (VEs) reduced negative mood like natural element exposure in situ [24]. Yin et al. showed that people experiencing virtual work environments that mimic office spaces with biophilic elements had consistently lower levels of physiological stress indicators and higher creativity scores than those experiencing the same spaces without biophilic elements [26]. Wang et al. demonstrated that forest resting VR environments could produce stress relief effects to some extent [23].

However, in previous works, no design guidelines exist for placing biophilic virtual elements in the XR environment. Such guidelines are important because introducing additional virtual elements (i.e., unrelated to the main task) may also distract users from the main task. In our previous work [27], we compared a VR training environment with and without biophilic design and found that introducing biophilic virtual elements does not distract users during the training task. Though this preliminary study was fundamental to exclude an overall detrimental effect of biophilic enrichment, we did not evaluate the effect of the single design variables of biophilic virtual elements, such as type, location, quantity, animation, and sound. Therefore, further studies addressing the effect of these design variables are needed to understand how to reach the best compromise between positive effects on well-being and (possible) negative effects on performance.

The main contribution of this work is a study about the use of animations for the design of biophilic elements in a VR workplace, considering only the visual aspect and excluding the auditory one. As far as the authors know, in the literature, no studies are addressing whether the biophilic enrichment of VEs should be performed using only static elements or animated, too. In fact, animated biophilic elements could provide a user experience similar to what happens in real environments. On the other hand, however, they could be a source of distraction with a consequent detriment to performance in the main task. Therefore, we formulated the following research question: *how do animations of biophilic virtual elements affect user attention while performing a working task?*

To answer our research question, we conducted a user study during which users accomplished a cognitive test in a VR workplace, simulating a working task. We evaluated user attention in three different VEs, for each of which we collected performance, eye-tracking, and subjective measurements. We developed an empty scenario used as a baseline and two identical biophilic VEs, one with all static elements and another in which some of these biophilic elements were animated. All the elements were the same in static and animated biophilic VEs and positioned in the same location. In this preliminary study, we deliberately incorporated a comprehensive range of biophilic elements within the biophilic virtual environment to push the boundaries of Virtual Reality technology and explore the potential effects, although we acknowledge that an exaggerated inclusion of biophilic elements might appear unusual from a practical standpoint. This allows us to assess user attention under extremely unnatural conditions. The three scenarios (Fig. 1; a video, showing the three VEs from the participant's point of view, is available at https://youtu.be/Q7BynTec3pE) were:

- *Minimal Environment* (MIN), a 3D empty scenario populated only by a table and a monitor on which the test was displayed.
- *Static Biophilic Environment* (STAT), the same scenario as MIN enriched with static biophilic elements (e.g., trees, paintings reproducing naturalistic landscapes, green walls, and animals).
- *Animated Biophilic Environment* (ANIM), the same scenario as STAT with the addition of animations of some biophilic elements already present (e.g., birds flying, fish swimming in the aquarium, fountain water movement).

The paper is organized into five sections. Section 2 reports the experiment's design and the VEs' implementation. In Sect. 3, the results of the user study are presented. Section 4 discusses the overall results obtained as well as the limitations of the study and offers future research directions. Finally, in Sect. 5, a conclusion is provided.

2   Materials and Method

We used a within-subjects design for the experiment. We administered the N-Back test as a cognitive task [28, 29]. In this work, we relied only on industrial tasks in which the operator must focus on a specific working area without necessarily moving around. We took inspiration from a real case study presented in our previous work [27] on assembling a truck engine in a workstation, whereby in this study we simulated a similar condition, in which the worker is required to be focused on the task (the N-Back test) he/she must

Fig. 1. The three evaluated scenarios: Minimal Environment (above), which represents our baseline; Static Biophilic Environment (middle) with all static elements; Animated Biophilic Environment (bottom), where some biophilic elements are animated (picture modified to show the simulated effect of some animation examples; for better visualization of the animations a video is provided at https://youtu.be/Q7BynTec3pE).

perform in a dedicated working area (the monitor). The N-Back test allows the operator to remain still, not walking freely, and focus only on a narrow area like in a real work scenario. Moreover, unlike other cognitive tests (e.g., the Stroop Test) in which users must continually look at the task without taking their eyes off the task due to the mode of the test, in the N-Back test users can turn their gaze elsewhere in their surroundings.

In this work, each user performed two levels of difficulty of the N-Back test [30, 31] in each VE for a total of six experimental conditions. A balanced Latin Square design was used to establish both the order of the VE scenarios and the order of the N-Back test levels for each user, to minimize the order effect and the carry-over effect on the collected data.

2.1 Experiment Procedure

At the beginning of each session, the experimenter collected general information about users, informed them about the experiment procedure, and instructed them on how to use the VR equipment. During the experiment, users had to perform the test sitting on a chair and using two controllers. First, an eye calibration procedure was conducted to ensure the accuracy of eye-tracking data. Then, users performed a few practice trials of the N-Back test in a scenario consisting of a black skybox populated only by a table and a monitor on which the test was displayed. When users became familiar with the controller commands and understood how the test worked, the experimenter allowed them to start the experiment. When users entered each VE, they could explore it before starting the N-back test. Then, when users claimed to be ready, the experimenter told them to start the test by pressing a "start" button on the virtual monitor. Finally, users pressed the "finish" button at the end of the test. After the six experimental conditions, users answered the subjective questionnaires. The entire experiment procedure lasted, on average, 30 min and is summarized in Fig. 2.

During the N-Back test, participants observed a sequence of phonologically distinct letters [B, F, K, H, M, Q, R, X] [32], randomly appearing on the center of the virtual monitor in each VE. They were instructed to respond as quickly and accurately as possible, pressing the trigger of the right controller whenever the current stimulus was the same (match) as the one presented N positions back in the sequence or pressing the trigger of the left controller if the stimulus did not match. N depended on the load level (e.g., N = 1 for level 1, N = 2 for level 2, N = 3 for level 3). Our work used two levels of task difficulty, respectively, level 1 and level 2 (1-back and 2-back). The virtual monitor was placed orthogonally at about 600 mm from the user in the VE, and the font size of the letters was 40 mm with a consequent visual angle of $3.8°$. Each letter was presented for 500 ms and followed by a 2500 ms inter-stimulus interval (a hyphen) [33]. The N-back task in each VE took 2 min, for a total of 40 trials [32].

2.2 VR Implementation

Our VR application was displayed on a Head-Mounted Display (HMD), the HTC Vive Pro Eye. It was implemented with Unity 3D Engine 2019.4.12 version with the integration of Steam VR, running on a PC Windows 11 Home, having a 64-bit operating

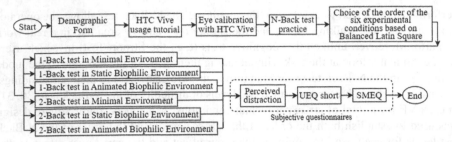

Fig. 2. Experiment procedure.

system, an Intel Core i7-12700H, 2.30 GHz, 16 GB RAM, and an NVIDIA GeForce RTX 3070 Ti graphics card.

The experiment was carried out in our laboratory, exploiting the room-scale wide area tracking with two SteamVR Base Stations appropriately positioned to track the exact locations of the HTC Vive headset and controllers. In the middle of the room-scale area, we placed a chair on which users had to sit during the experiment.

The VR application recorded eye-tracking data collected from the HTC Vive HMD with TOBII Pro eye-tracking integration and SRanipal Unity SDK. In this way, the binocular dark pupil tracking technique has been used to detect the object fixation time, which is when the gaze is relatively fixed or focused on acquiring and processing information [34].

2.3 Measurements

To evaluate user attention, we measured both objective and subjective data. Objective data derived from the N-Back test performance and eye-tracking measurements. Subjective data were collected through questionnaires submitted to users after each experiment.

Performance Measurements (N-Back Test). Performance was assessed in terms of *reaction times* (time from when the letter appears to when the user pressed the controller trigger; hits only) and *accuracy* (misses and errors in the hits) [35].

Eye-Tracking Measurements. We used eye-tracking technology to monitor users' eye movement to collect the fixation time of all virtual elements in the scenario that users could observe during the execution of the task. The object fixation time was measured from when users pressed the "start" button to begin the task to when they pressed the "finish" button. The application automatically acquired all the time data and stored them in an Excel spreadsheet at the end of each session. Then, for each user, we calculated the *distraction rate* as the percentage of the total task time (i.e., 120 s), spent by users in fixing virtual elements different from the virtual monitor (main task). This objective ocular measurement allowed us to evaluate if participants were distracted by pointing their eyes in a different direction from the working area.

Subjective Measurements. After the entire session, users were asked to fill out three questionnaires for each scenario regardless of the difficulty level of the N-Back test. We administered the short version of the User Experience Questionnaire (*UEQ*) [36] to assess the user experience in each VE in terms of *pragmatic and hedonic quality*. The Subjective Mental Effort Question (*SMEQ*) [37] was used to evaluate the *cognitive load* perceived during the task and generated by the elements in each scenario. Moreover, although we measured the users' distraction rate from eye-tracking data, to be sure to assess all variables for the evaluation of user distraction, we also investigated the *perceived distraction* caused by the virtual elements in the surroundings through a specific question. In fact, due to the peripheral view of humans, they can perceive the presence of elements, that could cause distraction, within their field of view even if their gaze does not stare directly at them. Therefore, we formulated a specific question on a 7-point Likert Scale (1 = "Never" to 7 = "Every time"): "Evaluate how much the virtual elements in the scenario deconcentrated you during the execution of the test."

2.4 Participants

A total of 24 participants (8 females, 21 to 37 years old, mean = 24.13, SD = 3.35) took part in the experiment. They were recruited from our university, and they received no payment. They were 5 bachelor's and 13 master's students, 5 Ph.D. students, and 1 post-doc research fellow in mechanical engineering. The mean familiarity level with VR was 3.29 (SD = 1.67, Min = 1, Max = 7).

3 Results

All data recorded from each participant were classified as matched continuous variables because data were obtained for each user under all the experimental conditions.

The Shapiro-Wilk normality test, AS R94 algorithm, was used for statistical analysis to verify if the data followed a normal distribution. In case the data did not follow it, if applicable, a Box-Cox transformation was performed to obtain normal samples, and, on these data, the Repeated measures ANOVA was performed to compare the three samples (Minimal Environment, Static Biophilic Environment, Animated Biophilic Environment). If the Box-Cox transformation was unsuccessful, a nonparametric test, Friedman 2-way ANOVA, was performed to compare the three samples.

3.1 Performance measurements

Accuracy. There was no statistically significant difference in the Error rate (Fig. 3) committed by participants among the three VEs during the execution of the 1-Back test ($\chi 2(2) = 3.129$, p $= 0.209$) and 2-Back test ($\chi 2(2) = 2.074$, p $= 0.355$). In the box plot of 1-Back test, the median of distribution MIN is 0.0, while STAT and ANIM distributions have the same median value of 2.5. In the box plot of 2-Back test, the median of MIN distribution is 8.7, while STAT and ANIM distributions have the same median equal to 10.0.

Reaction Time. In both analysis of 1-Back ($F(1.830, 42.079) = 0.545$, P $= 0.568$) and 2-Back test ($\chi 2(2) = 4.750$, p $= 0.093$), there was no statistically significant difference in the reaction times among the three VEs (Fig. 4). In the box plot of 1-Back test, the medians of MIN, STAT, and ANIM distributions are respectively 618, 717, and 684. In the box plot of 2-Back test, the medians are respectively 1009, 1111, 1104.

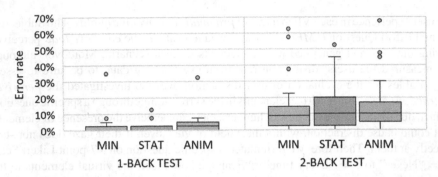

Fig. 3. Box plots of error rate committed during the execution of 1-Back and 2-Back test. Horizontal line indicates the median, box the interquartile range (IQR), whiskers extend to upper adjacent value (largest value = 75th percentile + 1.5 × IQR) and lower adjacent value (smallest value = 25th percentile – 1.5 × IQR), and dots represent outliers.

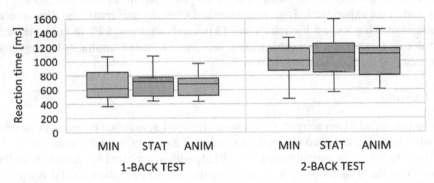

Fig. 4. Box plots of reaction time during the execution of 1-Back and 2-Back test. For an explanation of the box plot refer to Fig. 3 caption.

3.2 Eye-Tracking Measurements

Distraction Rate. As shown in Fig. 5, the 1-Back test showed a statistically significant difference in the distraction rate among the three VEs ($\chi 2(2) = 11.627$, p = 0.003). In particular, the Wilcoxon signed-rank test showed a statistically significant difference between MIN and STAT (Z = −3.516, p < 0.001). In the 2-Back test, there was not a statistically significant difference ($\chi 2(2) = 1.000$, p = 0.607). In the box plot of the 1-Back test, the medians of the three distributions in order are equal to 0.00, 0.14, and 0.00; in the box plot of the 2-Back test, the medians are equal to 1.52, 0.59, and 1.33. The MIN distribution of 2-BT shows that, even if there is no statistically significant difference with the other VEs, there were some users who watched the surrounding in search of visual stimuli, maybe when they missed the task.

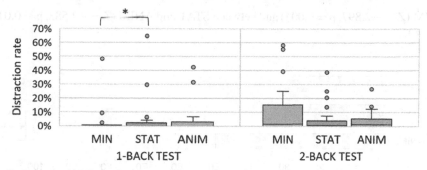

Fig. 5. Box plots of distraction rate in the three VEs for 1-Back test and 2-Back test. The asterisk indicates a statistically significant difference. For an explanation of the box plot refer to Fig. 3 caption.

3.3 Subjective Measurements

UEQ. Analyzing the Pragmatic Quality scores (Fig. 6), there was no statistically significant difference among the three VEs. On the contrary, analyzing the Hedonic Quality scores, the test revealed a statistically significant difference among the three VEs. In particular, the Wilcoxon signed-rank test showed that there was a statistically significant difference between MIN and STAT ($Z = -4.204$, $p < 0.001$) and between MIN and ANIM ($Z = -4.288$, $p < 0.001$).

SMEQ. Analyzing the average SMEQ scores (Fig. 7), it was found that there was a statistically significant difference among the three VEs. In particular, the Wilcoxon signed-rank test showed that there was a statistically significant difference between MIN and ANIM ($Z = -2.661$, $p = 0.008$) and between STAT and ANIM ($Z = -2.670$, $p = 0.010$).

Perceived Distraction. There was a statistically significant difference among the three VEs on the perceived distraction caused by each VE. In particular, the Wilcoxon signed-rank test showed that there was a statistically significant difference between MIN and

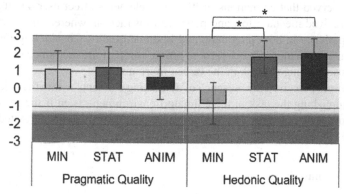

Fig. 6. Mean UEQ scores for the Pragmatic and Hedonic Quality in the three VEs. The asterisks indicate statistically significant different conditions.

ANIM (Z = −2.897, p = 0.004) and between STAT and ANIM (Z = −2.582, p = 0.010) (Fig. 8).

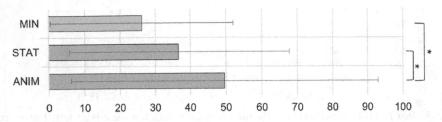

Fig. 7. Mean SMEQ scores for the three VEs. The asterisks indicate statistically significant different conditions.

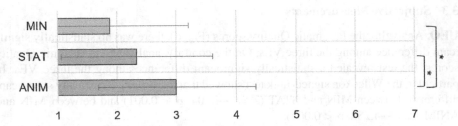

Fig. 8. Mean scores on the perceived distraction. The asterisks indicate statistically significant different conditions.

4 Discussion

The results of the experiment allowed us to answer our research question: *how do animations of biophilic virtual elements affect user attention while performing a working task?* We observed that animations of biophilic elements affect user attention only in terms of perceived mental effort and perceived distraction, whereas they do not affect the user experience in both pragmatic and hedonic quality. Considering the objective measurements, animations do not seem to affect user performance since users remained equally focused during the task in the three environments.

Hence, users perceived the presence of disturbing elements within their field of view, while accomplishing the task in the animated environment, even if the results of eye-tracking showed that the gaze of users does not stare directly at the animated elements, as well as their presence did not worsen users' task performance.

4.1 Results Analysis

We did not find a statistically significant worsening of error rate and reaction time in both level 1 and level 2 of the N-back test among all the scenarios. This result shows that users are not influenced by the presence of biophilic elements in the surroundings while doing their task, even if they are animated. This result is further confirmed by the eye-tracking data, which shows that users keep their gaze on the virtual monitor, even when animations are present. The overall time spent observing other elements in the surroundings is less than 6% of the total task time during the execution of both test difficulty levels.

From the analysis of user performance and eye-tracking, we could conclude that animation does not distract users from the main task. However, users reported that animated virtual elements were distracting for them, since we found statistically significant differences among the three scenarios for both the perceived mental effort and the perceived distraction. Both subjective measurements in the animated environment are higher compared with the minimal environment and become further higher with the use of static biophilic elements. Other studies found that potential distractions, such as noise [38], affected only perception rather than performance. In fact, by assessing all variables for the evaluation of user distraction, we observed that, due to the peripheral view of humans, they could perceive the presence of disturbing animated elements within their field of view, even if eye-tracking data showed that they did not look at them as many times. Analyzing the results of UEQ scores, we found that, as regards the pragmatic quality, there are no statistically significant differences among the three VEs. This result confirms that users judged biophilic elements, either static or animated, as not relevant to the main task. However, they improve the user experience in terms of hedonic quality compared to an empty VE. In fact, from eye-tracking analysis, we observed that during the execution of the 2-Back test, which required more concentration than the 1-Back test due to the increased difficulty of the test, users seemed to be more distracted in the minimal environment than in the others populated with biophilic elements. This is explained by the hedonic quality perceived by users in the Minimal environment that was significantly lower than that of other scenarios. Users expressed discomfort due to the perceived emptiness of the surrounding, leading them to constantly look around in search of visual stimuli.

This result confirms what was found in previous studies in the literature [26, 27, 39] and supports the use of a biophilic design to promote human well-being in VR. However, we found no statistically significant differences between the scenario with all static elements and the scenario enriched with animated elements. This result allows us to say that, on the one hand, the use of animations does not lead to a worsening of performance but, on the other hand, it does not contribute to improving the user experience.

4.2 Limitations and Directions for Future Research

In this work, we limited to evaluating the effect of animations of biophilic virtual elements, while we kept fixed other design variables such as the quantity, the location, and the type. Then, the results of this work derive from a combined effect of all these variables. As regards the perceived distraction, we found that the main source of distraction were the animals (bird and butterfly) placed near the main task (reported by 54% of users) and the fox (33% of users), while all the other elements were marked by less than 10% of users. Therefore, we can hypothesize that placing animated elements far from the main task could distract less than placing them closer, as well as using animals that do not frighten users, like the fox, could be a better choice. However, further studies are needed to test these hypotheses.

We did not find a statistically significant reduction in performance using animations, even if users perceived a higher distraction. A possible reason for this result is that we evaluated the effect on user attention in a cognitive task that lasted 120 s. In this reduced time, it is not difficult for users to focus on the main task, even with distracting elements. Further studies are needed to evaluate if, in longer tasks, the perceived distraction caused by animations reflects on user performance, too. In longer tasks (more than 4 min), it will also be possible to evaluate the effect of animated biophilic elements on human well-being through physiological measures [39].

5 Conclusion

In this study, we evaluated the effect of animations of biophilic virtual elements through performance measurements, eye-tracking, and subjective measurements while doing a cognitive task. This study aims to understand if animated biophilic virtual elements are a source of distraction for users working in a virtual environment. We developed and compared three VEs (Minimal Environment, Static Biophilic Environment, and Animated Biophilic Environment). From the results of this work, it is possible to say that the introduction of animations of biophilic elements in a VE does not bring added value to users. In fact, we did not find an improvement in user experience, but an increase in perceived mental effort and distraction. However, we found that the user gaze was very little attracted by animated virtual elements during the cognitive task, and this led to no worsening user performance with respect to the static scenario.

References

1. Amichai-Hamburger, Y.: Technology and Psychological Well-being (2009)
2. Samet, J.M., Spengler, J.D.: Indoor environments, and health: moving into the 21st century. Am. J. Public Health 93, 1489–1493 (2003). https://doi.org/10.2105/AJPH.93.9.1489
3. Fraga-Lamas, P., Varela-Barbeito, J., Fernandez-Carames, T.M.: Next generation auto-identification and traceability technologies for Industry 5.0: a methodology and practical use case for the shipbuilding industry. IEEE Access. 9, 140700–140730 (2021). https://doi.org/10.1109/ACCESS.2021.3119775
4. Gullone, E.: The biophilia hypothesis and life in the 21st century: increasing mental health or increasing pathology? J. Happiness Stud. 1, 293–322 (2002). https://doi.org/10.1023/a:1010043827986
5. Wilson, E.O.: Biophilia and the conservation ethic. In: Evolutionary Perspectives on Environmental Problems, pp. 250–258. Routledge (2017). https://doi.org/10.4324/9780203792650-18
6. Ryan, C.O., Browning, W.D., Clancy, J.O., Andrews, S.L., Kallianpurkar, N.B.: Biophilic design patterns: emerging nature-based parameters for health and well-being in the built environment. Archnet-IJAR 8, 62–76 (2014). https://doi.org/10.26687/archnet-ijar.v8i2.436
7. Gray, T., Birrell, C.: Are biophilic-designed site office buildings linked to health benefits and high performing occupants? Int. J. Environ. Res. Public Health 11, 12204–12222 (2014). https://doi.org/10.3390/ijerph111212204

8. Kellert, S.R.: Building for Life: Designing and Understanding the Human-Nature Connection (2006)
9. Kaplan, S.: The restorative benefits of nature: toward an integrative framework. J. Environ. Psychol. **15**, 169–182 (1995). https://doi.org/10.1016/0272-4944(95)90001-2
10. Grahn, P., Stigsdotter, U.K.: The relation between perceived sensory dimensions of urban green space and stress restoration. Landsc. Urban Plan. **94**, 264–275 (2010). https://doi.org/10.1016/j.landurbplan.2009.10.012
11. Kellert, S.R., Heerwagen, J.H., Mador, M.L.: The picture window: the problem of viewing nature through glass. In: Biophilic Design: The Theory, Science and Practice of Bringing Buildings to Life (2008)
12. Kahn, P.H., et al.: A plasma display window?-The shifting baseline problem in a technologically mediated natural world. J. Environ. Psychol. **28**, 192–199 (2008). https://doi.org/10.1016/j.jenvp.2007.10.008
13. Hartig, T., Evans, G.W., Jamner, L.D., Davis, D.S., Gärling, T.: Tracking restoration in natural and urban field settings. J. Environ. Psychol. **23**, 109–123 (2003). https://doi.org/10.1016/S0272-4944(02)00109-3
14. Abidi, M.H., Al-Ahmari, A., Ahmad, A., Ameen, W., Alkhalefah, H.: Assessment of virtual reality-based manufacturing assembly training system. Int. J. Adv. Manuf. Technol. **105**, 3743–3759 (2019). https://doi.org/10.1007/s00170-019-03801-3
15. Numfu, M., Riel, A., Noel, F.: Virtual reality based digital chain for maintenance training. Procedia CIRP **84**, 1069–1074 (2019). https://doi.org/10.1016/j.procir.2019.04.268
16. Gattullo, M., Scurati, G.W., Evangelista, A., Ferrise, F., Fiorentino, M., Uva, A.E.: Informing the use of visual assets in industrial augmented reality. In: Rizzi, C., Andrisano, A.O., Leali, F., Gherardini, F., Pini, F., Vergnano, A. (eds.) ADM 2019. LNME, pp. 106–117. Springer, Cham (2019). https://doi.org/10.1007/978-3-030-31154-4_10
17. Mystakidis, S.: Metaverse. Encyclopedia **2**, 486–497 (2022). https://doi.org/10.3390/encyclopedia2010031
18. Gattullo, M., et al.: Design of a mixed reality application for STEM distance education laboratories. Computers **11**, 50 (2022). https://doi.org/10.3390/computers11040050
19. Wang, S.S.Y., Teo, W.Z.W., Teo, W.Z.Y., Chai, Y.W.: Virtual reality as a bridge in palliative care during COVID-19 (2020). https://doi.org/10.1089/jpm.2020.0212
20. Choi, H.-Y.: Working in the metaverse: does telework in a metaverse office have the potential to reduce population pressure in megacities? Evidence from young adults in Seoul, South Korea. Sustainability **14**, 3629 (2022). https://doi.org/10.3390/su14063629
21. Grewal, D., Motyka, S., Levy, M.: The evolution and future of retailing and retailing education. J. Mark. Educ. **40**, 85–93 (2018). https://doi.org/10.1177/0273475318755838
22. Lee, J.Y.: A study on metaverse hype for sustainable growth. Int. J. Adv. Smart Converg. **10**, 72–80 (2021). https://doi.org/10.7236/IJASC.2021.10.3.72
23. Wang, X., Shi, Y., Zhang, B., Chiang, Y.: The influence of forest resting environments on stress using virtual reality. Int. J. Environ. Res. Public Heal. **2019** (2019). https://doi.org/10.3390/ijerph16183263
24. Emamjomeh, A., Zhu, Y., Beck, M.: The potential of applying immersive virtual environment to biophilic building design: a pilot study. J. Build. Eng. **32**, 101481 (2020). https://doi.org/10.1016/j.jobe.2020.101481
25. Yin, J., Zhu, S., MacNaughton, P., Allen, J.G., Spengler, J.D.: Physiological and cognitive performance of exposure to biophilic indoor environment. Build. Environ. **132**, 255–262 (2018). https://doi.org/10.1016/j.buildenv.2018.01.006
26. Yin, J., Arfaei, N., MacNaughton, P., Catalano, P.J., Allen, J.G., Spengler, J.D.: Effects of biophilic interventions in office on stress reaction and cognitive function: a randomized crossover study in virtual reality. Indoor Air **29**, 1028–1039 (2019). https://doi.org/10.1111/ina.12593

27. Gattullo, M., et al.: Biophilic enriched virtual environments for industrial training: a user study. In: Proceedings - 2022 IEEE International Symposium Mixed Augmented Reality, ISMAR 2022, pp. 206–214 (2022). https://doi.org/10.1109/ISMAR55827.2022.00035
28. Cohen, J.D., Forman, S.D., Braver, T.S., Casey, B.J., Servan-Schreiber, D., Noll, D.C.: Activation of the prefrontal cortex in a nonspatial working memory task with functional MRI. Hum. Brain Mapp. **1**, 293–304 (1994). https://doi.org/10.1002/hbm.460010407
29. Rich, D.L.: Effects of Exposure to Nature and Plants on Cognition and Mood: A Cognitive Psychology Perspective (2007)
30. Kirchner, W.K.: Age differences in short-term retention of rapidly changing information. J. Exp. Psychol. **55**, 352–358 (1958). https://doi.org/10.1037/h0043688
31. Mackworth, J.F.: Paced memorizing in a continuous task. J. Exp. Psychol. **58**, 206–211 (1959). https://doi.org/10.1037/h0049090
32. Kane, M.J., Conway, A.R.A., Miura, T.K., Colflesh, G.J.H., Kirchner, W.K., Mackworth, J.F.: Working memory, attention control, and the N-back task: a question of construct validity. J. Exp. Psychol. Learn. Mem. Cogn. **33**, 615–622 (2019). https://doi.org/10.1037/0278-7393.33.3.615
33. Thayer, E.R., Stevens, J.R.: Effects of human-animal interactions on affect and cognition. Hum.-Animal Interact. Bull. **2022** (2022). https://doi.org/10.1079/hai.2022.0015
34. Granka, L.A., Joachims, T., Gay, G.: Eye-tracking analysis of user behavior in WWW search. In: Proceedings of Sheffield SIGIR - Twenty-Seventh Annual International ACM SIGIR Conference on Research and Development in Information Retrieval, pp. 478–479. Association for Computing Machinery (2004). https://doi.org/10.1145/1008992.1009079
35. Jaeggi, S.M., Buschkuehl, M., Perrig, W.J., Meier, B.: The concurrent validity of the N-back task as a working memory measure. Memory **18**, 394–412 (2010). https://doi.org/10.1080/09658211003702171
36. Schrepp, M., Hinderks, A., Thomaschewski, J.: Design and evaluation of a short version of the user experience questionnaire (UEQ-S). Int. J. Interact. Multimed. Artif. Intell. **4**, 103 (2017). https://doi.org/10.9781/ijimai.2017.09.001
37. Zijlstra, F.R.H., Van Doorn, L.: The Construction of a Scale to Measure Perceived Effort (1985)
38. Manghisi, V.M., et al.: Investigating the effects on user performance and perceived workload of environmental noise in immersive virtual reality. In: 2022 IEEE International Conference on Metrology for Extended Reality, Artificial Intelligence and Neural Engineering (MetroXRAINE), pp. 46–51, October 2022
39. Yin, J., Yuan, J., Arfaei, N., Catalano, P.J., Allen, J.G., Spengler, J.D.: Effects of biophilic indoor environment on stress and anxiety recovery: a between-subjects experiment in virtual reality. Environ. Int. **136**, 105427 (2020)

Author Index

G. Zachmann et al. (Eds.): EuroXR 2023, LNCS 14410, pp. 215–216, 2023.
https://doi.org/10.1007/978-3-031-48495-7

Printed in the United States
by Baker & Taylor Publisher Services

Printed in the United States
by Baker & Taylor Publisher Services